High-Tech Tots

Childhood in a Digital World

A volume in
Research in Global Child Advocacy

Series Editors:
Ilene R. Berson
Michael J. Berson
University of South Florida

Research in Global Child Advocacy

Ilene R. Berson and Michael J. Berson, Series Editors

High-Tech Tots: Childhood in a Digital World (2010)
edited by Ilene R. Berson and Michael J. Berson

Overcoming AIDS: Lessons Learned from Uganda (2006)
edited by Donald E. Morisky, W. James Jacob,
Yusuf K. Nsubuga, and Steven J. Hite

Childhood in South Asia (2004)
edited by Jyotsna Pattnaik

Advocating for Children and Families in an Emerging Democracy (2003)
edited by Judy W. Kugelmass and Dennis J. Ritchie

Cross Cultural Perspectives in Child Advocacy (2001)
edited by Ilene R. Berson, Michael J. Berson, and Bárbara C. Cruz

High-Tech Tots

Childhood in a Digital World

edited by

Ilene R. Berson and Michael J. Berson
University of South Florida

GOVERNORS STATE UNIVERSITY
UNIVERSITY PARK, IL

Information Age Publishing, Inc.
Charlotte, North Carolina • www.infoagepub.com

Library of Congress Cataloging-in-Publication Data

High-tech tots : childhood in a digital world / edited by Ilene R. Berson
and Michael J. Berson.
    p. cm. -- (Research in global child advocacy)
Includes bibliographical references.
ISBN 978-1-61735-009-2 (pbk.) -- ISBN 978-1-61735-010-8 (hardcover) --
ISBN 978-1-61735-011-5 (e-book)
  1. Computers and children. 2. Children--Effect of technological
innovations on. 3. Mass media and children. 4. Mass media and
globalization. 5. Digital communications. I. Berson, Ilene R. II. Berson,
Michael J.
  QA76.9.C659H54 2010
  302.23083--dc22

              2010006706

Sponsored by the Research in Global Child Advocacy SIG of the American Educational Research Association

Copyright © 2010 IAP–Information Age Publishing, Inc.

Printed in the United States of America

CONTENTS

ACKNOWLEDGMENTS

Working on this book has been a gift that brought us together with insightful and creative colleagues from around the world. Each contributor is devoted to understanding young children in digital spaces and has shared meaningful and thought-provoking perspectives with us. We gratefully acknowledge their collaboration and collegiality throughout this endeavor.

The editors have many people to thank for their assistance in developing this book series and promoting learning and research in global child advocacy. George Johnson, our publisher, has provided support and guidance to this project. We are very appreciative of his vision and assistance in highlighting this important work. Members from the American Educational Research Association Special Interest Group on Research in Global Child Advocacy have assisted us in the identification of topics of focus and have provided opportunities to begin a dialogue about children's rights and well-being in digital spaces. We also are thankful for our colleagues and doctoral students who assisted in the editing and revision of the book to ensure that the words and innovative insight of the scholars, educators, and policy makers whose work we have collected can speak with clarity and capture the essence of the topic. We especially want to recognize the contributions of Dr. Jolyn Blank, Ken Carano, Mike Dotson, Natalie Keefer, and Mark Pearcy from the University of South Florida; Dr. Suzanne Quinn, Roehampton University; and Dr. Caroline Sheffield, University of Louisville.

Our children are always close to our hearts and provide us with the richness and depth of understanding through the lived experience of their own growth and development in this digital age. They inspire and challenge us with their sense of agency and of endless possibilities to explore the expansiveness of the world around them. It is therefore with great warmth, love and joy that we thank Elisa and Marc. Their inquisitive presence constantly engages us in reflecting on our research as we continue our exploration of new horizons.

CHAPTER 1

INTRODUCTION

High-Tech Tots: Childhood in a Digital World

Ilene R. Berson and Michael J. Berson

To be surprised, to wonder, is to begin to understand.

—Jose Ortega y Gasset

Young children are coming of age surrounded by information and communication technology (ICT). ICT is a prominent force in their lives, and working with ICT can stimulate students intellectually, incite their creativity, and challenge them to apply developmentally appropriate inquiry approaches that enhance their learning experiences. Digital technologies also allow children to expand their physical space and access many online social environments that transcend time and space. However, any focus on the efficiency and effectiveness of technology applications in the early childhood years cannot overlook the potential consequences of technological development on children with regard to their social functioning, interpersonal interactions, and global understanding. In addition to evaluating technology as a tool of instruction, we must focus on educational implications and ethical issues associated with their use.

This book is the fifth in the Research in Global Child Advocacy Series. The volume examines theoretical assumptions as well as the application

High-Tech Tots: Childhood in a Digital World, pp. 1–4
Copyright © 2010 by Information Age Publishing
All rights of reproduction in any form reserved.

of innovative strategies that optimize the interface between young children and ICT from a global perspective. Despite divergent perspectives, the chapter authors share a commitment to explore the immersion of ICT into the lives of young children and consider the educational value of these tools as well as the developmental appropriateness of technological affordances. This volume brings together scholars and policymakers whose rich discourse delves into questions such as: How do communication technologies benefit young children's social and cognitive development? What standards and technical specifications are needed to effectively safeguard young children engaged with ICT? How are young children introduced to ICT? What are the challenges and risks for young children online? What programs are effective in mediating risk? What are the educational applications for ICT in early childhood? Is social networking the new "online playground" for young children? How can young children become competent users of digital technology and media? How can early childhood educators and families encourage positive usage and discourage negative social consequences associated with today's technology? How can ICT enhance teaching and learning for young children? What ICT activities are developmentally appropriate for young children?

In the book there are three primary areas of emphasis: (a) ICT as a teaching and learning tool across cultures and countries to promote the social and cognitive development of young children; (b) research on developmentally appropriate education on cybersafety and cybercitizenship; and (c) studies on the influence of digital technologies on young children, including exposure to inappropriate content and participation in online social networks. This resource offers readers a glimpse into the experience of children and the expertise of researchers and professionals who diligently work toward crafting a framework for action that reflects intercultural and cross-national initiatives. Given the role that electronic media plays in the lives of children as both an educational and entertainment tool, understanding the physical and social contexts, as well as the developmental issues, is critical to programs aiming to optimize the full potential of digital tools that support and enhance the experiences of young children.

Technology is now such an important part of children's everyday lives that a learning environment without it would be completely out of touch with their own realities. Several chapter authors consider how to appropriately use technology to build on children's creativity and develop independent learning skills. ICT offers new forms of social interaction and participation that mobilize children's imagination and potential for growth and learning. They extend the opportunity for children to go beyond the role of consumers of technology resources, and provide the tools to allow them to foster social interaction, pursue inquiry and problem solving skills, and engage young children as creators of new technology-infused applications and products. In an increasingly interconnected world, children are exposed to diverse people and cultures at an early age. Young children need new skills and perspectives to constructively participate in these global settings. Early childhood teachers have a wonderful opportunity to prepare a new generation of children for democratic participation in civic processes that take place online.

Other authors discuss young children's cognitive and emotional abilities to participate in immersive worlds and explore the influence of virtual experiences on children's learning and development. ICT can provide opportunities for children to play with friends, imagine and create. It provides new ways of engaging children; new shared resources for representing things differently. There are a growing number of virtual worlds that are geared toward young children. These sites tend to integrate immersive worlds with games and social networking elements. Some sites are specifically designed to provide young learners with experiences that scaffold skills needed for community building and civic engagement. Learning becomes situated within the social processes that take place in virtual worlds. Engagement in these types of learning experiences highlights the advantages of technology to join together communities of learners in exploring new pathways of exploring concepts and expressing ideas.

Several cybersafety initiatives are described in this work that have evolved to develop relevant and meaningful prevention strategies that connect with the experiences of young children online. Just as children are taught to be good citizens of their communities, these resources incorporate instructional strategies to teach young children to be responsible citizens of cyberspace. Electronic media has become a prevalent tool for integrating key ideas associated with cybersafety into the school curriculum and fostering responsible citizenship on the Internet.

In an increasingly interactive and participatory educational environment, ICT enables young children to more actively engage in interpreting, personalizing, reshaping, and creating learning experiences. Enhanced learning does not automatically occur through the introduction of technology into the classroom, but ICT expands the capacity of children to learn through play-based experiences and investigations. In order to optimize the potential of digital technologies teachers need to explore how to situate these tools into the classroom for learning to take place within a constructivist framework that embraces children's creativity, exploration, and connectivity with others in digitally-mediated contexts. This situated form of learning necessitates a focus in the classroom on digital literacy to hone the skill sets young children need to become active producers and participants in diverse digitally-enhanced environments.

The goals are to foster technological fluency, support multimodal literacies, while preparing competent, responsible, and critical learners and
participants in an increasing open and globalized world. Not only does
ICT assist in achieving these goals, but also they serve as instructional
enhancements that facilitate engagement, active learning, creativity, and
social experiences in a learner-centered environment.

ICT enhances and extends the future possibilities of learning across
the curriculum, and the purposeful use of ICT can help unlock children's
imaginations and develop their creativity. In order to use ICT effectively
practitioners need to ensure that it is applied in dynamic and stimulating
ways. This resource can help ensure that children experience quality, technologically creative environments so that they can thrive and become successful and competent thinkers and global collaborators in the twenty-first
century.

CHAPTER 2

NEW TECHNOLOGIES, PLAYFUL EXPERIENCES, AND MULTIMODAL LEARNING

Nicola J. Yelland

This chapter begins with a discussion of the research and literature that supports the contention that young children learn best through play. The work of those such as Piaget and Vygotsky has informed the basis of early childhood curriculum and pedagogies and provided a *raison d'etre* for child-centered learning via play as an essential component of developmentally appropriate practice. The chapter calls for a reconceptualization of play that the author began in 1999 in an article published in *Early Childhood Education Journal* called "Technology as Play," which argued that with the advent of new technologies we need to rethink the notion of play to incorporate activities using new media as playful experiences that are supported by adults. Piagetian theory had posited the centrality of concrete or "real" world experiences as fundamental to young children's learning. During the 1980s and beyond, this contention was used to justify denying young children access to computers since they were regarded as being "too abstract" for them. It will be argued here that what constitutes "concrete" has changed considerably over the past 20 years and further that exploration in virtual worlds as well as being able to cre-

High-Tech Tots: Childhood in a Digital World, pp. 5–22
Copyright © 2010 by Information Age Publishing
All rights of reproduction in any form reserved.

ate new representations with technologies requires us to rethink the nature of play and our interactions with children. The contemporary view of play presented here incorporates new technologies that afford opportunities for young children to play in multiple modes so they are able to acquire deeper understandings about how things work, connect, and are relevant to their lives. It also suggests that teachers and other carers of young children need to scaffold this new learning rather than adopt a passive observation role which has tended to predominate in the traditional literature.

Playful experiences in the early years reflect a new view of play that is located in contemporary learning contexts. Examples will be drawn from new media contexts that young children encounter as part of their everyday lives. These will include dolls that can be played with in the "real world," viewed in books, and manipulated on screens. This is the case with characters from *Sesame Street* that can be viewed on TV and in the movies and then played with as digital and (3D) dolls as well as via a new online environment called *Panwapa*. Finally, the impact of new social media contexts such as *Zula World* and *Club Penguin* will be considered with regard to their potential as being constituted as an online playground for young children. Such playful explorations provide the framework for understanding the critical role that new technologies can play in multimodal learning and suggest ways in which teachers can support this learning with a wider pedagogical repertoire.

PLAY AND LEARNING IN EARLY CHILDHOOD

Pick up any text on the foundations of early childhood or curriculum for young children and the notions that "Play is a rich and varied medium for learning" (Gonzales-Mena, 2008) or "Play develops the cognitive, social, emotional and physical domains" (Justus Suss, 2005) are prevalent. Yet in many of the same texts, actual definitions of play are not abounding. Typically play is viewed as *not* work and characterized with specific qualities that distinguish it from work. For example, Gonzales-Mena suggests that there are five characteristics that separate play and work. They are:

Active engagement
Intrinsic motivation
Attention to the means rather than the ends
Non-literal behavior
Freedom from external rules (p. 99)

However, such characteristics may also be attributed to (teacher) planned learning activities that are commonly regarded as *work* in some classrooms, if they are authentic, relevant to the lives of the children, and thus engaging. In this way the distinction between play and work in school contexts may be superfluous. Indeed, the Qualifications and Curriculum Authority (QCA, 2000) in the United Kingdom have suggested that learning at the Foundation Stage (3 to 5 years of age) should be characterized by:

> opportunities for children to engage in activities planned by adults and also those that they plan or initiate themselves. Children do not make a distinction between "play" and "work" and neither should practitioners. Children need time to become engrossed, work in depth and complete activities. (p. 11)

There is no doubt that the connection of play and learning in early childhood has been acknowledged as fundamental. Forty years ago, this was officially recognized in the comprehensive report of primary schooling in the United Kingdom called the Plowden Report. In paragraph 523 (Central Advisory Council for Education, 1967) the committee stated:

> Play is the central activity in all nursery schools and in many infant schools. This sometimes leads to accusations that children are wasting their time in school: they should be "working." But this distinction between work and play is false, possibly throughout life, certainly in the primary school. Its essence lies in past notions of what is done in school hours (work) and what is done out of school (play). We know now that play—in the sense of "messing about" either with material objects or with other children, and of creating fantasies—is vital to children's learning and therefore vital in school.

In the United Kingdom, the Curriculum Guidance for the Foundation Stage of schooling exemplifies the traditional belief that young children learn best through play and recommends that planning a curriculum rich in play opportunities is fundamental to quality early years programs. The QCA (2000) contends that with play as the main form of learning, effective early education provides a context in which children are able to:

Explore, develop and represent learning experiences that help them make sense of the world

Practice, and build up ideas, concepts and skills

Learn how to control impulses and understand the need for rules

Be alone, alongside others or cooperate as they talk or rehearse their feelings

Take risks and make mistakes

Think creatively and imaginatively

Communicate with others as they investigate and solve problems

Express fears or relive anxious experiences in controlled and safe situations

Thus essentially, play has been viewed, as Klugman (1995) noted as:

a major interactive process through which children learn about themselves, their environment, the other people in that environment, and the interrelationships among all of these. Play is intrinsic, self-selected, active, mind involving, and a focus for personal powers. It is intriguing and captivating and frequently involves practice of needed mental and / or physical skills. Play engages and fulfills the player. Authentic play involves choice on the part of the player and can be self-perpetuating. Play takes a variety of forms. Some of these are exploratory, functional, constructive, symbolic, and games with rules. (p. 196)

Sutton-Smith (1997) actually asked children what they thought play was and found that they thought it should include "having fun, being outdoors, being with friends, choosing freely, not working, pretending, enacting fantasy, drama and playing games" (p. 49). Such views led early childhood educators to create play opportunities for young children by providing a variety of materials (e.g., puzzles, construction blocks [Duplo/ Lego]), activities, (e.g., outdoor climbing frames, sand pits), and centers (e.g., dress up, home corner). Play in these centers might have allocated times in order to manage access and use, but generally the children choose what they do in them, and the teacher intervenes minimally.

However, it is apparent that to simply state that "young children learn through play" is problematic and misleading. Young children might have fun while participating in free play sessions and should have them as part of a quality program, but it is relevant to ask what type and kind of learning is taking place in these contexts. What connections are being made to the child's lived experiences and knowledge building, and how are these articulated and extended in supporting activities? Quality learning environments support children's learning with a rich variety of materials that enable them to explore and make discoveries. The effective teacher is able to identify children's needs via careful observation of their actions and in discussion with parents, who bring vital funds of knowledge from home and community contexts. Sh/e will intervene in children's explorations to pose interesting and relevant questions and will often make suggestions about extending the activity in various ways. In this way, the role of the early childhood teacher can be regarded as centering on facilitation or enabling. This will occur not only with resources but also with ideas and questions. Drake (2005) has suggested that such support might include:

Stimulating children's interest in the activity

Providing high-quality resources

Listening and responding to children's talk

Questioning children in order to extend learning

Working alongside children, modeling skills and the use of key vocabulary

Encouraging, reassuring and praising children

Valuing and celebrating children's achievements. (pp. 60–61)

Playful Explorations

In becoming a facilitator/enabler the teacher is encouraging the child to be playful and participating in playful explorations when relevant. There are indeed pedagogical challenges to reflect on in order to support such playful explorations. The fact that teachers can and should design playful explorations in the first instance or intervene to suggest new directions might not align with the views of those who regard play as being initiated by the child, self-selected and voluntary, but the change in nomenclature from *play* to *playful explorations* is a deliberate one. It suggests a shift in emphasis with regard to being able to articulate learning outcomes as the result of creating these types of learning scenarios and incorporating adult participation and scaffolding.

Bennett, Wood, and Rogers (1977) noted that we should be wary of stating that:

> A direct relationship between play and learning is assumed. Play is considered to be such an educationally powerful process that learning will occur spontaneously, even if an adult is not present. However, this central belief in the value of play to young children's learning is not borne out by empirical evidence. (p. 1)

Thus, rethinking play as playful experiences in which exploration and meaning making is scaffolded and extended by a teacher has the potential to be a much richer learning environment for young children. The use of new technologies and the opportunities they create is a vital new resource for such explorations.

This view provides opportunities for the use of ICT (information and communication technology) as resources and ways in which young children might share their experiences in new and dynamic ways. Such new technologies can extend what young learners are able to do with traditional materials such as blocks. They can be described as learning scenarios or stories (Carr, 2001) so that the type and range of learning that occurs can be clearly stated and documented. For example, in traditional early childhood texts and programs the use of block play has been justified in terms of the capacity of block building as an open ended play activity in which the children learn (see Hendrick & Weissman, 2006). Such play is said to include learning about physical properties of objects, eye hand coordination, lessons of gravity, cause and effect, object permanence, problem solving, communication skills, planning skills, and more specifically, the early mathematical concepts of matching, sorting, grouping and classification as well as those related to number and understanding spatial relations.

As a result, block play is regarded as central to learning in most early childhood centers. Yet tangible evidence of these stated learning outcomes is rarely provided, and is difficult to document. There is no doubt that creating and designing constructions with blocks have the *potential* to provide a context for rich learning scenarios. Yelland (2007) described a young boy called George who had a propensity to design buildings with blocks as well as other construction materials (Figure 2.1). He created elaborate plans both in drawings and on the computer when supported by adults. George also used a digital camera in order to create a permanent record of his exquisite building adventures. The learning story of George and his block building, later followed by his creation of a short animation with different materials (Duplo) (Yelland, 2007) illustrates the ways in which we need to specify the types of evidence for learning in the early years. It might also been regarded as being too structured and organized by traditional play advocates. However, when teachers interact with the children and focus on their capacity to demonstrate or articulate such skills and knowledge during block play, the case for *playful explorations* and links to specific learnings can be made. The subsequent learning scenarios are rich case studies of both the children's responses and the catalyst that the teacher used to elicit the learning evident in the scene.

CHANGING CONTEXTS FOR LEARNING

In direct contrast to traditional play based programs, we have in recent times witnessed the opposite end of the continuum where increasing pressure has been placed on early childhood educators to become much more prescriptive in their teaching in an era where accountability and learning outcomes are viewed as being measurable commodities. The rhetoric of *No Child Left Behind* (U.S. Department of Education, 2000) suggests that we need to make sure early in a child's life that they have the requisite skills for reading, writing, and mathematics that will ensure later success in school as well as prepare them for a life of employment. The messages

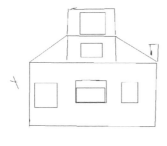

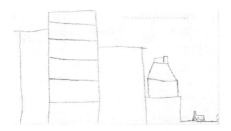

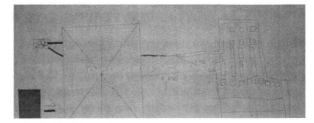

Figure 2.1.   Building Blocks, plans, and drawings in preschool.

seem to be the same globally, from both conservative and liberal governments. Political leaders are in government for 3 to 5 years and want to show their impact in overt ways that can be measured both on national and international scales. They need and want to keep education quantifiable and accountable. This avoids complex discussions and consideration of the long-term goals for an education system that exists in new times that are radically different from those many politicians have experienced. Consequently, play based early childhood curriculum are under stress as academic tasks and prescribed basic tasks activities become commonplace in kindergartens and earlier.

Paradoxically, the use of new technologies is discouraged by both those who advocate traditional play-based curricula, and those who want standardization and the practice of defined (industrial) basic skills via clearly constructed and limited tasks. The former group contends that children need to play in the real world, with actual objects and in materials that are tactile and tangible, with minimum intervention by the teacher. The belief is that with these artifacts the children can embark on make believe and free play in a variety of contexts and thus learn. Adherents contrast this to the abstract, symbolic and supposedly, addictive range of new technologies that they contend take children away from "real life" and inhibit the development of positive social skills. Similarly, the second group defines "basic skills" as being from a pretechnological era and maintain that such heritage skills are fundamental and not to be replaced by equivalent or new skills derived from the technological era. So handwriting lessons are perpetuated, books are privileged in preference to digital texts for sourcing information, and calculators are banned from mathematics classes.

In playful explorations not only are new technologies part of a repertoire of experiences for young children's learning but the teacher is able to scaffold this learning so that it is articulated and represented by the children in a variety of modes. In this way playful explorations provide evidence of children's learning and encourage the use of a variety of media and resources that are part of this learning as well as being artifacts of the learning process.

MULTIMODAL PLAYFUL EXPERIENCES

Multimodal experiences combine the written, visual, gestural, aural, linguistic, and tactile. Multimodal texts mix these components to varying degrees depending on the message that the author wants to convey or leave open to interpretation. Children experience such texts on a daily basis in their lives and enjoy designing and creating their own.

Young children come to early childhood settings with a range of experiences with new media. Yelland, Lee, O'Rourke, and Harrison (2008) have noted that "Their lives are digital and they communicate in a variety of modes with myriad materials that are made of bits and bytes" (p. 1). Parents of these young children report that 48% had a video game and 63% lived in homes that had access to the Internet (Rideout, Roberts, & Foehr, 2005). They also spent about two hours a day using screen media. Interestingly they spent about the same amount of time playing outside, and this was three times more than they spend reading books or being read to. The children are not, however, passive consumers of media. They self-select media content (e.g., favorite TV shows, DVDs, and music) and mostly initiate the activity. They are truly new millennial kids and live in a multimodal world where the impact of new technologies is significant and ubiquitous.

Digital television will have a major influence on the ways in which children watch, interact, and experience new media. For example, *Actimates Barney* is a "plush" toy that takes instructions from the TV program *Barney and Friends*. This toy enables the child to sing and dance with Barney in his show. The toy has the capacity to suggest that the child performs actions and songs and can signal her to "Watch this!" or ask questions like "What do you think will happen next?" during the course of the program. One study (Strommen & Alexander, 1999) revealed that children with such interactive toys are more active in watching the programs than those who do not have the toy. They also reported that the presence of the Interactive *Barney* or *Teletubbies* encouraged more dancing and both verbal and nonverbal actions from the children in their study.

For young children the linking of three-dimensional objects that they play with, with characters from TV shows or movies and then with computer software provides a valuable context for learning that should not be underestimated. For example, Fisher Price has also released CDROMs such as *Discovery Airport, My Very First Farm* and *Ready for School Toddler* which build on their three dimensional dolls or figures that have been popular for some time. The activities that the digital dolls can participate in on the CDROM can be selected by the child playing with them, but what is often missing is the support of adults in extending the concept building or language of the context. In a similar way, linking the characters (e.g., Elmo) from *Sesame Street* with books, dolls, and computer software provides opportunities for adults to scaffold children's learning and help them to make connections between the media and create new meanings from each. There are excellent opportunities for links to be made between the three-dimensional medium of the real world dolls who can be played with in specific ways as compared to those in the virtual world of the computer. Understanding the different properties of both types of dolls will assist children to understand the nature of each medium and how they can interact with the characters.

The challenge for toy makers today would seem to be related to designing objects and environments so that children are able to explore their own ideas and make meaning in their play based activities. The use of commercial toys and "props" have been criticized because they are related to promotional materials that suggest limited forms of interactions and story scenarios that are narrow and connected to particular commercial scripts. This is often viewed as stifling creativity and imagination and detrimental to learning. The manufacture of stand-alone, interactive toys, that is those with computer chips embedded in them, have increased rapidly. In 2000 they represented 60% of the new toy market compared to 10.3% in 1997, and the figure would have increased since that time. However, it would seem that one key to success of these new toys might be related to the same reasons as to why toys have always been successful; that is, the attachment phenomenon that seems to have been associated with the teddy bear for a long period of time. Having toys that respond as your mood changes would seem to have a powerful potential to be long lasting. Imagine a doll or bear that you could tell stories to and have them recorded. You would then be able to play them back any time which would appeal in terms of nostalgia and memory narratives. There is now the potential to extend the capacity of such toys so that they build on children's vivid imagination and allow them to explore the world in ways that were not previously possible. Certainly, it has become evident that such toys need to support diverse opportunities for creating new scenarios rather than limit them to specific opportunities to re-enact already designed and created story scripts.

Some toys are frequently marketed as being interactive, when in fact they simply have a pre-recorded voice that is not able to respond to the nuances required for meaningful interactions with young children. This is where parents and other adults can add value to the play of young children. In doing so they participate in playful experiences, and their interactions encourage dialog and the use of language (e.g., by questioning), help them to make connections to ideas and concepts, and stimulate inquiries. So toys become artifacts of learning that can promote meaning making and also contribute to increasing the social and intellectual capacity of the child in a positive way. Digital toys have the potential to extend such interactions in ways that were not possible and may also be linked to computers to expand this capacity. However Luckin, Connolly, Plowman, and Airey (2003), concluded that "The toys as they stand are not impressive learning partners.... However, the technology has potential ... when the toy is present, children interact with their peer companion in the dyads and with the researcher in both dyad and individual situations" (p. 14).

CREATIVITY AND IMAGINATIVE PLAYFUL EXPERIENCES

Creativity has been regarded as being synonymous with play (Moyles, 2007). As early as 1976 Bruner (1977) demonstrated the ways in which children's play provided contexts for them to pose problems, negotiate several paths to solution, and create scenarios of possibilities. Such playful experiences were characterized by experimentation and engagement with materials and ideas.

In recent times there has also been an increased focus on promoting the creativity and imagination of young children. Social and economic imperatives underpin the international push for educators to teach students to be creative thinkers. Increasingly, a competitive edge is based on knowledge, creativity, and innovation rather than land, labor, and capital (e.g., Amabile, 1988; Florida, 2003; National Advisory Committee on Creative and Cultural Education [NACCCE], 1999). There is a growing recognition that creative individuals will be able to adapt more readily to a world that is increasingly complex, lacks job security, and requires life-long learning to keep up with rapid workplace and technological changes (NACCCE, 1999). Creativity enables individuals to be more effective citizens and workers who can cope with change (Craft, Jeffrey, & Leibling, 2001). Importantly, creativity enhances the educational process by actively engaging students in the learning process so that they view school as a place for discovery, openness to new ideas, independent learning, and exploration with others (Jourbert, 2001; Loveless, 2003; Woods, 2001).

If all the conditions for learning mentioned in the previous sections are experienced by the children, they would be experiencing learning in an environment that enables them to think creatively and act imaginatively. Such activities can be considered alongside those that are traditionally enjoyed, such as constructing with blocks and Lego, painting and creating collages, dressing up, playing in the home corner, creating a bank, garden or zoo and outdoor play, and form a well balanced program that encourages engagement with multimodal learning and ideas. With scaffolding from teachers they will also enable the children to extend their understandings across modalities and communicate their ideas in person or via the use of the new technologies.

BECOMING MULTILITERATE ... PLAYFULLY

Traditionally, literacy in schools has focused on reading, writing, listening and speaking. However, it is now apparent that we need to rethink literacy as a "malleable repertoire of practices" (Luke, 2006, p. xi). In this new century, information and communications technologies have extended our capacity to be literate in many more ways and modalities. The inter-play between visual, aural, spatial, gestural, and linguistic modes of com-munications needs to be understood and practiced. The pedagogy of multiliteracies (New London Group, 1996) heralded this new view and encouraged engagement with the different modalities. This is important since as Kress (1997) has noted, our major forms of public communica-tion are becoming more dominated by the visual than the linguistic. This means that we need to recognize the funds of knowledge (Moll, Amanti, Neff, & Gonzalez, 1992) that young children bring to educational con-texts since the use of new technologies is an integral part of this.

Living in a multimodal world enables us to link the use of new technol-ogies with our experiences in the "real" world. Thinking in this way facili-tates playful explorations and enables the young child to build representations and form new understandings. Traditionally, (three dimensional) play has been viewed as laying the foundation for later abstract or symbolic thought. Research on multimodal learning (e.g. Kress, 1997; Pahl & Rowsell, 2006; Yelland et al., 2008) has given us new insights into the complex ways in which children are able to link modes and how they can do this simultaneously in contexts that involve the use of new technologies.

In the United Kingdom, the Early Years Foundation Stage (The National Strategies, 2008) documentation states that children should engage in experiences that enable them to "Express and communicate their ideas, thoughts and feelings using a widening range of materials" (p. 16). Kress (1997) has also noted that we need to understand the ways in which young children make meanings in a variety of contexts as they are playing as a basis for supporting their literacy development which becomes essential in the early years of schooling.

The use of new technologies is an integral part of becoming multiliter-ate in the twenty-first century. Children can use digital movie cameras to have playful experiences which enable them to create multimodal texts that represent their ideas and understandings. They can use the photo-graphs to make digital stories or podcasts, or they may opt to embed them in PowerPoint slides to make a digital book. Their use can also pro-vide opportunities to document and create a narrative of their own playful explorations in the center.

In initial explorations with digital cameras young children love to take photos of their friends and environments (Figure 2.2), and these can act as a catalyst for extending language opportunities. The logistics of using a digital camera can be unstructured, and the children can take them on excursions to document the visit. Using a movie camera is harder for young children since they are generally not designed to be carried by one small hand. A good place to start is to make a visual diary of the center,

Figure 2.2.   Preschool photographers.

identifying key locations and showing the viewer to classmates. Again taking a video recording of an excursion is a useful second step. Additionally, it might also be possible for the children and their parent to take the camera home so that a link can be established between home and school in a tangible way and might focus on a topic like the garden, the street, the style and structure of the building, pets or indeed any topic that the young child might choose.

By the time preschoolers who are fluent in the use of digital cameras and computers come to school they are able to create multimodal texts for a variety of purposes. One of the most popular is podcasting. The advantage of using new technologies for story writing in the early years of school is that the children are able to create extended narratives that are not hindered by their capacity to write a story with a pencil. This is very exciting for them and means that they are able to explore topics and share their findings in appropriate ways with their peer group, using a variety of modalities.

SOCIAL MEDIA AS A PLAYFUL CONTEXT

Into this mix of events and playful exploration comes the new social media that are available to the very young. They are a totally new learning environment that we have not seen before. Social media sites enable young children to embark on playful experiences that are virtual and in doing so create contexts in which they are able to explore two dimensional worlds in character forms of their own creation. This somewhat turns Piaget's ideas about egocentricity on their head, and how young children relate to their various characterizations warrants further study. Social networking sites for young children include *Panwapa, Zula World,* and *Club Penguin.* Of these the first two are designed for the very young while *Club Penguin* is aimed at those children already in school, that is from 6 to 14 years of age. These virtual worlds present yet another context for playful experiences. They involve playing games, doing activities and interacting with other virtual characters. They vary in their levels of interaction. The older children in *Club Penguin,* after being signed in by parents, are able to meet and greet each other, have conversations, or play soccer with their virtual penguins as their alter ego. Some of the games mimic those traditionally played in early childhood centers. They include memory games which require players to find matching pairs of creatures. In *Panwapa,* which is sponsored by the Children's Television Workshop, characters are created from a bank of items and then used as a sort of data base for problem based questions. For example, each character can choose their favorite animals, food, activities, crafts, music, sports, and state their location. Then, there is a game where questions are asked for the player to search the collection of virtual friends who have particular attributes. So they might be asked—find someone who likes to play the guitar and eat fish.

Such explorations can be supported by adults and extended in new investigations depending on what the children showed interest in. These new play-worlds afford contexts in which young children can not only gain conceptual understandings but also think more deeply about identities and how to interact with each other. This type of learning complements and extends three-dimensional playful explorations. Teachers enable and support their meaning making with interactions and resources that encourage them to make connections between the different modes of representations. It is interesting to note that in *Panwapa* 27,188 members chose computers as their favorite activity. Next, came art (6,514), origami (4,794), and then fishing (4,743).

SUMMARY

This chapter has suggested that reconceptualization of play is needed. Traditionally, play has been inextricably linked to learning. However, it has become apparent that this is too simplistic, and a view of playful experiences that are supported by new media and interactions with adults/ teachers is needed. One important consideration regarding the learning of young children has become apparent. We need to provide contexts so that young children are exposed to different modes of representations which in turn afford them the opportunity to formulate new understandings about their world and make meanings about ideas and concepts on the basis of their experiences.

I have previously stated (e.g., Yelland, 2007) that the challenge for parents and educators is to maintain a balance between the real world (3D) toys, which may have an electronic component, and the newer digital ones, which are screen based. Both are relevant to the lives of young children and will help them to learn if supported by the adults in their lives as well as having individual time for explorations that might have no other motive than just being able to "mess about."

Parents have often expressed the concern that if they let their children play with computers and other new technologies this will take away from their "real" world experiences. It is up to them to ensure that this does not occur. Children should be given opportunities to self select, but parents and other adults should be able to encourage diverse contexts for playful explorations that give children a range of learning opportunities with a variety of materials. Often it would seem that parents think that because they have purchased a toy or software their child will spontaneously want to play with it without adult intervention. This may be the case, but it is also evident that these are learning opportunities in which parents or other adults can interact with the child with a variety of positive outcomes emanating from the conversations. For example, an adult can provide the context to broaden the language base of the child as well as ask probing questions which will facilitate the learning of specific concepts and hopefully enable them to make the appropriate abstractions which lead to higher levels of thinking and knowing.

The focus here has been on new contexts for playful experiences, and it is evident that screen based activities with digital dolls and the new interactive toys are an integral part of young children's lives today. They are very appealing to children and have the potential to broaden the range of play experiences by acting as a catalyst for interactions either with another child or with adults. If the potential of interactive toys is optimized, children may establish connections between diverse representations and thereby achieve greater understandings during their explorations.

Children's use of new technologies, including computers, cameras, iPods, MP3 players and the range of electronic toys, will continue to be extended, and they will bring these experiences to preschools and schools. This will impact the ways in which they will want to explore and use what is available in the center or classroom, and educators should take this into consideration when planning learning activities. The resources and play-things that children have prior to coming to school and in after school activities are becoming increasingly influential in shaping what they are able to do. As these become more sophisticated, the gap between what is available in school and out of it is widening, and schools are in danger of being viewed as irrelevant if they do not contain the experiences and materials that are available to children in their daily lives

REFERENCES

Amabile, T. M. (1988). A model of creativity and innovation in organizations. *Research in Organizational Behavior, 10*, 123-167

Bennett, N., Wood, E., & Rogers, S. (1977). *Teaching through play: Teachers' thinking and classroom practice*. Buckingham, England: OUP.

Bruner, J. (1977). *The process of education*. Cambridge, MA: Harvard University Press.

Carr, M. (2001). *Assessment in early childhood settings*. London: Paul Chapman.

Central Advisory Council for Education. (1967). *Children and their primary schools* (The Plowden Report). London: HMSO. Retrieved from http://www.dg.dial.pipex.com/documents/plowden16.shtml

Craft, A., Jeffrey, B., & Leibling, M. (2001). *Creativity in education.* London: Continuum.

The National Strategies. Department for Children, Schools and Families. (2008). *Statutory Framework for the early years.* Retrieved February 16 2010, from http://nationalstrategies .standards.dcsf.gov.uk/node/151379

Drake, J. (2005). *Planning children's play and learning in the foundation stage.* London: David Fulton.

Florida, R. (2003). *The rise of the creative class.* Melbourne, Australia: Pluto Press.

Gonzales-Mena, J. (2008). *Foundations of early childhood education.* Boston, MA: McGraw Hill.

Hendrick, J., & Weissman, P. (2006). *The whole child.* Saddle River, NJ: Pearson.

Jourbert, M. M. (2001). The art of creative teaching: NACCCE and beyond. In A. Craft, B. Jeffrey, & M. Leibling (Eds.), *Creativity in education* (pp. 17-34). London: Continuum.

Justus Suss, D. (2005). *Supporting play: Birth through eight.* Clifton Park, NY: Delmar.

Klugman, E. (1995). *Play, policy and practice.* St. Paul, MN: Redleaf.

Kress, G. (1997). *Before writing: Rethinking paths to literacy.* London: Routledge.

Loveless, A. (2003). Creating spaces in the primary curriculum: ICT in creative subjects. *The Curriculum Journal, 14*(1), 5-21.

Luckin, R., Connolly, D., Plowman, L., & Airey, S. (2003). With a little help from my friends: Children's interactions with interactive toy technology. *Journal of Computer Assisted Learning* [Special issue on children and technology], *19*(2), 165-176.

Luke, A. (2006). Foreword. In K. Pahl & J. Rowsell (Eds.), *Literacy and education: Understanding the new literacy studies in the classroom* (pp. x-xiv). London: Paul Chapman.

Moll, L. C., Amanti, C., Neff, D., & Gonzalez, N. (1992). Funds of knowledge for teaching: Using a qualitative approach to connect homes and classrooms. *Theory into Practice, 31*(2), 132-141.

Moyles, J. (Ed.). (2007). *Early years foundations: Meeting the challenges.* Maidenhead, England: OUP.

National Advisory Committee on Creative and Cultural Education. (1999). *All our futures: Creativity, culture and education.* Retrieved from http://www.cypni.org.uk/downloads/alloutfutures.pdf

New London Group. (1996). A pedagogy of multiliteracies. *Harvard Educational Review, 60*(1), 66-92.

Pahl, K., & Rowsell, J. (Eds.). (2006). *Travel notes from the new literacy studies: Instances of Practice.* Clevedon, England: Multilingual Matters.

Qualifications and Curriculum Authority. (2000). *Curriculum guidelines for the foundation stage.* London: Author.

Rideout, V., Roberts, D. F., & Foehr, M. A. (2005). *Generation M: Media in the lives of 8-18 year olds.* Menlo Park, CA: Kaiser Family Foundation.

Strommen, E., & Alexander, K. (1999, April). *Learning from television with interactive toy characters as viewing companions.* Paper presented at the biennial meeting of the Society for Research in Child Development, Albuquerque, NM.

Sutton Smith, B. (1997). *The ambiguity of play.* Cambridge, MA: Harvard University Press.

U.S. Department of Education. (2000). *No child left behind.* Jessup, MD: Educational Publications Center.

Woods, P. (2001). Creative literacy. In A. Craft, B. Jeffrey, & M. Leibling (Eds.), *Creativity in education* (pp. 62-79). London: Continuum.

Yelland, N. J. (2007). *Shift to the future: Rethinking learning with new technologies in education.* New York, NY: Routledge.

Yelland, N. J., Lee, L., O'Rourke, M., & Harrison, C. (2008). *Rethinking learning in early childhood education.* Buckingham, England: OUP.

CHAPTER 3

YOUNG CHILDREN'S TECHNOLOGY EXPERIENCES IN MULTIPLE CONTEXTS

Bronfenbrenner's Ecological Theory Reconsidered

X. Christine Wang, Ilene R. Berson,
Candace Jaruszewicz, Lynn Hartle, and Dina Rosen

Information and communication technology (ICT) has an increasing influence in young children's lives and is changing how they interact with their peers, parents, and teachers (Tapscott, 1997), with subsequent consequences for children's learning and development (Calvert, Rideout, Woolard, Barr, & Strouse, 2005; Wang & Hoot, 2006). To help us understand the evolving ecology of children's learning and development in the twenty-first century, in this chapter we reinterpret the ecological theory (Bronfenbrenner, 1979; Bronfenbrenner & Evans, 2000) and apply it to make sense of children's emerging practices with technology in multiple contexts, including virtual worlds. We first discuss four principles of the ecological theory that are most relevant to children's ICT experiences: (1)

High-Tech Tots: Childhood in a Digital World, pp. 23–47
Copyright © 2010 by Information Age Publishing
All rights of reproduction in any form reserved.

the child as an active agent engaging in meaning making of their worlds, (2) importance of understanding children's experiences in multiple contexts, (3) dynamic and fluid interactions among the systems and Contexts, and (4) temporal considerations of the ecology. We then apply these four principles to examine three important issues related to young children's ICT experiences: (1) developmentally appropriate ICT practices; (2) skills needed for students, teachers, and parents in the changing environments; and (3) provision of positive support and guidance in multiple contexts.

JESSICA'S WORLD:
A CHANGING ECOLOGY IN 21ST CENTURY

To illustrate the changing ecology of young children, we start with vignettes featuring Jessica, a kindergartner, navigating technologies in a variety of social contexts, including school, home, the community, and virtual worlds. These vignettes are constructed based on our personal and research experiences with young children.

Jessica in School

On an early spring morning, Jessica's kindergarten class is taking a walking field trip. Several children notice a large bird nesting atop the steeple of a neighborhood church. The group stops, and using binoculars, they take time to draw sketches on the clipboards they always take on excursions. The teacher records their questions and observations using a digital audio recorder and camera that she carries at all times. Back at school, the teacher uploads the audio and photos to her laptop and scans their drawings and clipboard sketches. The children listen to their words and look at the pictures again. Using the interactive electronic whiteboard, the teacher creates a Know, Want to Know, Learned (KWL) chart to organize ideas the children offer about what they know and observed, what they want to learn more about, and how they might proceed.

Subsequently, Jessica asks if her teacher can search online to help them identify the birds, which they learn are red-tailed hawks. They locate many facts about their habitats and migratory patterns, predatory and nesting habits, and differences between males and females. The children decide to construct a scale model of the nest and birds, so over the next several weeks, the class records observations of the hawks found atop the steeple of the church. Jessica is delighted when they find a live-streaming *Red-tailed hawk vs. the Rattler* video on the *National Geographic* website. The children also locate an article from the local paper about the birds, prompting an e-mail from the class to the church pastor to request an interview that they post on their class blog.

The children's interest expands to include a general curiosity about birds of prey. The teacher assists them in searching online for images, and they explore the local library catalog for books that have pictures of red-tail hawks. The students dictate another e-mail to a professor in the zoology department of the local university, inviting him to visit with them to discuss red-tail hawks. Over the next several days, the teacher prints various images chosen by the children. Using a document camera, Jessica and her classmates work to enlarge the pictures, tracing over them on mural paper to make patterns. The children then cut out the patterns, staple them together, stuff them with paper, and paint them to accurately represent the birds. They collect materials similar to those used by the birds to build a nest for their paper creatures. Jessica also works with two other children to create display labels about red-tailed hawks and other birds of prey. Jessica contributes ideas for a group book with audio comments that the teacher records and combines with charts and graphs to make a voice-thread project that is posted on voicethread.com for parents to view. For the duration of the study, Jessica's teacher collects, scans, and saves artifacts from each child's efforts on the project to provide documentation for assessment purposes that will later be shared with their respective families.

Jessica at Home

Coming home from school, Jessica excitedly tells her mother, Sarah, about her "bird project" at school and vividly imitates the very long and high sound made by the hawks. When Sarah tells her daughter she has never heard a red-tailed hawk call, she suggests they search together for the sound on the Internet. Sarah asks about possible search terms, and Jessica suggests, "red-tail hawk bird call." Sarah types the words including the quotation marks since she knows that narrows the search, and when the list displays, she reads the results aloud. She clicks on Whatbird.com, and they listen to the call of the red-tailed hawk. Sarah remarks to her daughter, "What a very strong call. Is it a strong bird?" Jessica answers using facts she learned at school:

> It is. It attacks other animals. Samantha talked about its beak. She noticed it is very sharp, and it is not straight. See look at the beak in the picture. Our teacher said it needs to be that way to eat. We saw photographs online of the hawks eating squirrels. Remember the Chickadee we saw the other day eating seeds from the birdfeeder? Our teacher said hawks do not eat from birdfeeders.

Jessica's mother remarks on her good memory and says, "let's look up Chickadees too, so I can learn some more." Using a similar process, they find this information as well, and continue to discuss differences between the two birds.

Later that evening, Jessica's older brother Eduardo takes out his smart phone and downloads video of his science fair project and presentation he captured earlier in the day. Having learned about safe and ethical practices for digital technology use, Eduardo discusses with Sarah how to safely share the video with his grandparents who live in Florida. They decide that it is best to send a link of the video that has been password protected on a video sharing site. Eduardo edits the video, posts it to Vimeo.com, and e-mails the link to his grandparents.

Eduardo and Jessica's grandparents live far away from their hometown, so they visit only a few times a year. Yet Jessica and Eduardo see their grandparents weekly via Skype. Jessica especially enjoys hearing her grandmother read aloud a new book that Sarah mails ahead of time to Jessica's grandparents. While Jessica's grandmother or grandfather reads aloud to Jessica, she follows along in her copy of the book at home, tracking the words, turning the pages, and enjoying the illustrations.

Jessica at the Museum

Jessica has become good friends with her new neighbor, Abigail, a child of her age who recently moved from Brazil. After helping Jessica with her bird project, Jessica's mother and Abigail's mother decide to take their daughters to see the rainforest exhibit together at the science museum. Jessica and Abigail are fascinated by the different kinds of rainforest birds from around the world. Jessica tells Abigail what she has learned about birds at school and with her mother on the Internet. Using child-friendly digital cameras, they take many pictures of the birds on display, as well as other things they find interesting in the exhibits. Jessica and Abigail record sounds of rainforest birds and animals, Jessica using a digital camera and Abigail using her mother's cell phone.

The children especially enjoy the 3D virtual tour of the rainforest. Each of them puts on the 3D glasses and starts their "wild journey" through the rainforest. Their virtual experience includes "walking" through different layers of the rainforest, encountering indigenous creatures, and immersing themselves in the sights and sounds of the multisensory tour. They also walk through a destroyed rainforest and learn how the birds have lost their homes and some animals have died. Afterwards, both of them ask their mothers a lot of questions, as they wonder why people cut down trees in the rainforest. Their mothers then take them to see rainforest preservation videos in another part of the museum so that they can learn different ways to participate in protecting these habitats.

Returning home, Jessica and Abigail download the pictures and audio recordings of the birds and other animals. With the help of Jessica's mother, they also use their media to create a YouTube video about deforestation and the harmful consequences for birds and other animals. Jessica's mother e-mails the YouTube link of the presentation to her teacher, who then plays it in class for the children to view and discuss and upload it to the class website. Jessica's mother also volunteers to assist the classroom teacher in enrolling the class in a rainforest preservation network. Abigail and her mother make a Portuguese version of the video and e-mail it to Abigail's friends in Brazil.

Jessica in Cyberspace

To complement their real-world investigation of birds, Jessica and Abigail have joined Panwapa, a PBS website where they can meet other children around the world who share their interests (Berson & Berson, 2009). Both girls have created personal flags that include bird symbols to represent their favorite creatures, so other children can connect with them and celebrate their similarities and differences.

The girls decide to virtually "visit" a girl from Mexico with a bird symbol on her flag and a cool red house, so they click on her house to hear her introduce herself. All user names are coded by country and a number, so the identities of Jessica, Abigail, and the girl from Mexico are protected. Abigail and Jessica send the girl a Panwapa Card—"I see we both like the same animal." The site reads all message choices so the girls can also learn a few new greeting words as they build their global awareness.

Jessica's online activity is limited by her parents to 15-30 minutes per session. Jessica's ability to handle the virtual world often amazes them. They find fascinating her ability to transition so easily between virtual and real worlds, and often discuss how her understandings have evolved over time. In particular, they remember when she was 3-years-old, and during one of Jessica's regular Skype video conferences with her grandparents, she was drawing a picture on a piece of paper for them. Jessica's mom adjusted the camera to capture Jessica at work. Jessica described aloud her drawing as she worked and frequently looked at the monitor for feedback from her grandparents. After a few minutes, her pen stopped working. Knowing grandpa's skill for repairing broken items, Jessica tried to push the pen through the camera to ask her grandfather to fix it!

Making Sense of Jessica's Experiences

The preceding vignettes show great breadth and depth of Jessica and her peers' experiences with technology. Through a range of different technologies from low (paper/pencil) to high (virtual tour), and from common and widely available (e.g., cell phone, digital camera) to emerging and more advanced forms (e.g., Panwapa), their learning about birds is greatly enhanced. They are learning through direct observational experience, searching the Internet, communicating with experts, experiencing a virtual rainforest, and connecting with other children in the world who are also interested in birds. They are also interacting with a wide range of people: siblings, parents, relatives in different cities, teachers, classmates, neighbors, experts, scientists in the museum, friends in different countries, as well as others in the online world.

Jessica's experiences clearly represent children with a high level of access to technologies, and her experience is certainly not universal at this point in time. However, the technology landscape is continually changing, and the scenarios we discuss here may well become increasingly prevalent in the near future. To make sense of children's learning and development in this environment requires a framework such as the ecological systems theory to help us understand and study the relationships between children and the digital world (Kaiser Family Foundation, 2003, 2005; Rosen, Lee, & Hicks, in press; Shuler, 2007).

RECONSIDERING BRONFENBRENNER'S ECOLOGICAL THEORY

The ecological theory was first introduced by Bronfenbrenner (1979), and it emphasizes understanding children's development in a variety of social contexts and the interrelation among the various settings in which the child functions. According to Bronfenbrenner, an ecological perspective can be a helpful conceptual tool to understand and study differentiated but integrated levels of the context in which human development occurs. The levels are described as a series of nested spheres that comprise the microsystem, mesosystem, exosystem, and macrosystem.

Subsequent development of the theory by Bronfenbrenner (Bronfenbrenner & Evans, 2000) and others (e.g., Barab & Roth, 2006, Crowley & Jacobs, 2002; Gutierrez & Rogoff, 2003; Lemke, 2000) have particular relevance to conceptualizations of ICT in the early years. For example, Rosen and Jaruszewicz (2009) have suggested that an ecological perspective provides a practical framework for contextualization of developmentally appropriate technology use. For the purpose of this chapter, we focus on four major principles drawn from these materials due to their salience to our theoretical conception of technological engagement and competence: (1) the child as an active agent, (2) understanding experiences in multiple contexts, (3) dynamic and fluid interactions, and (4) temporal considerations. We specifically discuss how these four principles help us understand the changing ecology of young children's learning and development, with special attention paid to the role of technology. To illustrate the updated interpretation of the ecological theory, we envisioned and crafted the following diagram (Figure 3.1).

Child as an Active Agent

At the center of the ecological system (see Figure 3.1) are the child and his or her unique personal characteristics, which shape and are shaped by

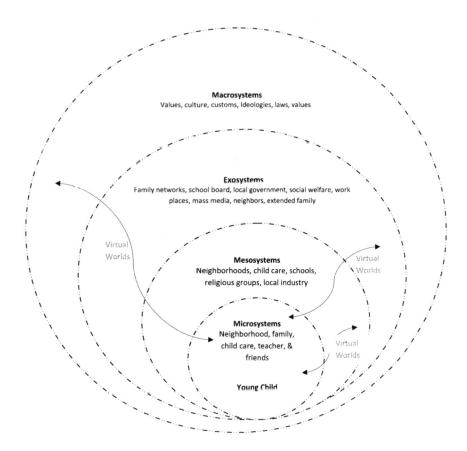

Figure 3.1.   Beyond Bronfenbrenner's ecological theory.

experiences and interactions in multiple contexts and systems. Children vary in the extent to which they are predisposed to explore particular technologies. Some of this variety in use reflects diversity in access and familiarity with the tools. Experience is also impacted by variations in cultural and social norms. This view has been highlighted and emphasized by scholars who have applied sociocultural theory to the interpretation of the ecological system (Gutierrez & Rogoff, 2003). They emphasize the prominent role that cultural practices play and how children interpret the meaning of their experiences and internalize them while involved in culturally relevant activities with parents, adults, and peers.

Viewing young children as active agents in their development and learning has important consequences for studying children's interactions with technology, via technology, and around technology. Children in the 21st century do not and should not take the stance of a passive receiver of technology and its influence. Instead, children like Jessica can actively appropriate and use technology to serve their social, learning, and emotional needs (e.g., Berson & Berson, 2004; Wang & Ching, 2003). Young children's engagement with ICT as active agents is influenced by their personal characteristics as well as the dispositions of parents, teachers, caregivers, peers, and other individuals with whom the child interacts. Jessica's family embraced and provided technologies for their children. Physical and cognitive ability to interact with ICT, knowledge of the technology, access to the tools, and skill to apply this knowledge are idiosyncratic to each child and may be enhanced or discouraged by the social environment and context in which the child functions.

Understanding Children's Experiences in Multiple Contexts

The most important contribution of the ecological theory focuses on children's development in the systems of multiple contexts rather than in one narrowly defined context. According the Bronfenbrenner (1979) the child is involved in a series of complex interacting contexts (micro-, meso-, exo-, and macrosystems) that directly and indirectly impact the child's development. The microsystem includes the home and family environment, child-care and school settings, community, and neighborhoods. These are the intimate, primary contexts that directly influence young children's development. Children's interactions with parents, siblings, and other adults at home, and their interactions with peers and teachers in schools or child care settings are of primary importance to young children's development and learning. At the same time, they are also influenced by other more diffuse contexts, including their neighborhoods and communities, and by broad societal, cultural, economic, and environmental factors.

When Brofenbrenner and his colleague Evans (1979, 2000) theorized the ecology of children's development, technology was less significant in children's lives than it is today. As illustrated in our vignettes, technology is becoming ubiquitous in children's lives. Rosen, Lee and Hicks (in press) suggest that current and emerging digital tools and virtual environments stretch the boundary of Bronfenbrenner's model by providing new microsystems in which children interact and learn. Online communities, such as Panwapa, complicate Bronfenbrenner's nested model because while most children access Panwapa from their homes, a typically intimate context, they can connect online with children from geographically remote systems. For example, in our vignettes, Jessica expands her intimate classroom world with e-mail communication with experts, and she expands her home environment as she interacts with the global community from the comfort of her home in the online world of Panwapa. As such, digital spaces, which are more diffuse contexts, may be accessed while physically located within the home, a more intimate context, thereby presenting a paradox for Bronfenbrenner's model (Rosen, Lee, & Hicks, in press). Our new diagram (Figure 3.1) reflects the added contexts with seamless transitions facilitated via virtual connections.

Technology as an important cultural artifact (Wang & Ching, 2003) has rapidly changed how children's learning and lives are organized and transformed, as well as how children interact with others and learn content in different subject areas. Bronfenbrenner and Evans' (2000) concept of "exposure" —the extent of contact maintained between the developing person and the proximal processes in which that person engages—is key to understanding developmental changes. They suggest five dimensions of exposure: frequency, duration, interruption, timing, and intensity. These five dimensions provide a useful framework to examine how technology has been integrated into home, neighborhoods and communities, and schools with specific focus on the duration, frequency, continuity, timing, and intensity of exposure to technology.

In the vignettes, Jessica has frequent exposure to technology, many times during the day, within a variety of settings. As is typical for young children, home and school serve as the settings where Jessica is introduced to various forms of ICT. Despite this extensive exposure, the adults in her life guide Jessica by setting limits on the time she spends online, thereby providing a balanced learning experience that is appropriate for a young child her age.

In our technology-driven society, digital environments have connected to and expanded upon children's experiences within the immediacy of home, school, and neighborhood settings. Figure 3.1 depicts how children as Internet users simultaneously become members of global communities while maintaining continuous links to real-life contexts. The Internet affords them the opportunity to share ideas and communicate with family and established friends as well as interact with new acquaintances around the world (Berson & Berson, 2004). In our vignette, websites, such as National Geographic, allow Jessica to transcend time and place and explore far away locations. Similarly, the growing number of virtual worlds geared toward young children (e.g., Panwapa, Whyville world) "provide young learners with experiences that scaffold skills needed for community building and civic engagement" (Berson & Berson, 2009, p. 28) while interconnecting with people and issues they confront in real life. As a phenomenon, we need to explore how immersive digital experiences and online social networks figure into the changing ecology of children's learning and development.

Dynamic and Fluid Relations Among the Systems and Contexts

Besides the systematic view of children's development in multiple contexts, ecological theory also emphasizes the importance of investigating interrelations among the various contexts. Bronfrenbrenner's (1979) conceptualization of diverse environments as nested spheres might connotate static relationships among different systems and contexts; however, the ecology in its entirety is interconnected, dynamic, and fluid. This interplay manifests in different forms for different children and groups. For example, in religious communities, the church's teachings have a significant influence on children's development and learning. Similarly, children's relatives and extended family play a central role in a community where child rearing is a communal experience.

For each child, different components of the ecological system are shifting and changing all the time, compensating and complementing, or perhaps conflicting and undermining one another. If a positive synergy is fostered between different contexts, they can function as parts of a congruous network, and the developmental potential of a specific environment is enhanced. For example, a child who lacks strong family connections might be helped by resources and supports in the neighborhood and community. Thus, as depicted in Figure 3.1, it is important to understand children's development beyond isolated physical contexts, and instead explore interconnected virtual and real systems and their aggregated effects.

In the same vein, interaction between children's technology experiences in different settings can lead to complementary or conflicting effects on their learning and development. The technology activities in which children engage can be unique to an environment, or they can be shared, with similar exposure occurring in each setting. It is useful to ask questions such as what or how specific technologically-enhanced activities occurring in one environment may interact with the way activities occur in another context. Development is enhanced by the degree to which environments are well coordinated in terms of practices, activities, and systems of learning and development. For example, our vignettes illustrated synergy of technology uses in multiple contexts. The school uses technology for inquiry-based learning, which is also supported and empowered by Jessica's parents as Jessica constructs learning through active exploration. The community provides further opportunities for her to explore at the museum so she can bring additional questions back to the classroom, subsequently linked to extended learning in a virtual world.

On the other hand, we believe that conflicting views, activities, and practices involving technology in different contexts can lead to adverse consequences. For instance, in the classroom, if teachers limit use of technology to drill and practice activities with fill in or click electronic worksheets or restrict technology to an extra activity once the "real" work is completed, children may view technology for learning as meaningless and distinct from their technology experiences outside of class. At home, if children engage in excessive use of video games, this reinforces a dichotomy of technology: boring learning versus exciting gaming. When adverse technology experiences in selected contexts or as Bronfenbrenner terms "spheres," evoke negative connotations, those adverse experiences detract from potential rich opportunities to promote transformative learning, knowledge building, and sharing.

Temporal Dimension of Development and Ecology

Time and timing are important to understand children's development in multiple contexts (Lemke, 2000; Mercer, 2008). Bronfenbrenner and Evans (2000) specify that

> a developmental outcome at a later point in time is a joint function of a process; characteristics of the developing person; the nature of the immediate, "face-to-face" environmental context in which the person lives; and of the length and frequency of the time interval during which the developing person has been exposed to the particular process and to the environmental setting under consideration. (p. 119)

From a developmental perspective, each child's ecology system evolves and changes over time, and their growth in competency and skill also affects the shape and nature of their ecology of development. According to Sameroff's transactional approach to development (Sameroff, 2009), new microsystem child-context interactions and transactions between family, teachers, peers, and those in the broader spheres (i.e., neighbors or others through the Internet) contribute to each child's development at various points. These child-context interactions are contingent on existing psychological capacities that evolved from interactions at earlier points in the child's development (Sameroff, 2009). As a result, the sphere of the different systems is no longer static, depending on the child's action. As children transition from early childhood to primary and middle childhood, their interactions shift from a focus on family members to an emphasis on peers and friends. Thus, the child's contact and interaction with networks of systems expands, and the spheres of influence identified in Figure 3.1 become increasingly fluid. It is important to consider how children's interaction with technology (experience, length, intensity, etc.) across multiple contexts within a specified timeframe may affect their subsequent developmental outcomes. Societal as well as immediate family attitudes toward ICT, and children's exposure and direct experience with technology are constantly changing. Therefore, a static view of these factors would be counterproductive; any change in one domain can potentially lead to other changes in the entire ecological environment. In short, we recommend rethinking how different settings or spheres of influence can adjust to these changes and be responsive to young children's evolving needs in learning and development.

UNDERSTANDING AND
FACILITATING YOUNG CHILDREN'S TECHNOLOGY EXPERIENCE

Technology has increasingly changed the world of young children today, as illustrated in the opening vignettes. To understand and facilitate young children's technology experience, we need to address three important yet interrelated issues: (1) developmentally appropriate ICT practices; (2) skills needed for students, teachers, and parents in the changing environments; and (3) provision of positive support and guidance in multiple contexts. Our updated interpretation of the ecology theory and the four principles discussed above lend useful lenses for our examination of these three issues in the following sections.

Developmentally Appropriate Practices With ICT

Although the appropriateness of technology for young children has been debated in early childhood education (Clements & Sarama, 2003; Cordes & Miller, 2000), focus has shifted away from the deficits of ICT and instead emphasizes the identification of developmentally appropriate practices with ICT in the early years (e.g., Wang & Hoot, 2006). The ecology theory brings some interesting insights to this issue, as well as questions to consider, including: What affordances does ICT provide?; What are desirable features?; How does ICT support inquiry-based learning?; and How will ICT affect home-school-community interactions?

Affordance of ICT. While researchers and teachers of young children recognize the importance of concrete objects for providing children hands-on experience exploring and transforming ideas, Wilensky and Resnick (1999) suggest the notion of *concreteness* does not rest in the property of the object, but rather the child's relationship to the object. For example, Clements (1999) demonstrated the mere use of certain math manipulatives does not guarantee abstract or new ideas will become concrete to a child. However, with extended relationships, representations, interactions, and connections, previously abstract concepts or materials may become more real and meaningful to the child.

Compared with traditional play materials, in fact, ICT may provide more affordances for children's imaginative and meaningful activities than physical objects under certain conditions. For example, through digital manipulation the child can potentially see a virtual triangle from many more perspectives than a physical triangle (Sarama & Clements, 2002). As in Jessica's case, new technologies, such as virtual social networks and video conferencing, break down physical or real boundaries and connect her to a broad world that transcends here and now, as well as support a wider network of human contact. By bridging the real home, school, and community worlds, ICT helps young children become active participants in multiple contexts (Bergen, 2008; Buckleitner, 2008; Haugland, 2000; Nir-Gal & Klein, 2004; Yan & Fischer, 2004).

Child-friendly ICT also provides a means for children to manipulate and view an object from multiple perspectives, which is a valuable experience to help children evolve beyond egocentric thinking. For example, digital cameras and recorders afford a glimpse into the way they see, hear, and represent their surroundings, rather than the ways in which adults think they do. These digital photos also afford children opportunities to revisit and reflect upon details within and across their own and others' ideas and products (Ching, Wang, & Kedem, 2006). For example, the interactive whiteboard in Jessica's class facilitates collaborative discussion and learning, resolving the practical needs of young children to be involved directly with the screen. Many of ICT tools are portable, accessible from multiple locations across children's ecological sphere, and can be used indoors, outdoors, on field trips, in the car, or at a community festival, as seen in Jessica's case. Thus, they support children's agency and control, as well as help sustain children's investigation and reflection over time and across multiple contexts.

Desirable features of ICT. Recent studies have investigated desirable features of ICT for young children and suggest four important qualities (Bergen, 2008; Carr, 2000; Kafai, 2006; Yelland, 2005). First, ICT for young children should be transparent in purpose and function. For example, technology-enhanced toys require visible buttons that are easy to press to reduce frustration and increase the enjoyment of children's experimentation. Second, the technology should help sustain and extend young children's natural curiosity. Upgraded and emerging technologies provide opportunities for children to conduct investigations indefinitely, as long as their curiosity and questions are nurtured. It is relevant here to point out the important role of adults—the parent who helps with internet search terms, the teacher who records children's questions and ideas and then helps children revisit and revise their ideas and tentative theories with access to additional information, or the virtual world product developers who incorporate decision-making options that the users can manipulate.

Third, desirable technology also should provide multiple ways of challenging young children's thinking. Technologies that can be used in more than one way or require increasing skill over time offer opportunities for developing problem-solving skills and critical thinking. These challenges can also support and extend children's natural curiosity, as well as empower children as they master those challenges. Finally, technology should be ergonomically designed to meet young children's developmental needs. It is important to consider young children's small hands and developing motor skills when designing technology hardware.

Inquiry-based, child-initiated learning with ICT. The ecological theory views children's development as a progressively more complex interplay of a child's inherited factors and environmental influences, as well as the broader cultural influences of school, community, and governmental policies. This view strongly endorses inquiry-based and child-initiated experiences supported by ICT for children's meaning making.

Meaning making is an interaction of the process *within* the child and *between* people in the child's contexts (Wells, 1986). Through such interaction, higher mental functions such as attention, memory, reflection, self-regulation, and thinking are developed (Bodrova & Leong, 2005). Children's play is a natural medium for their meaning making (Isenberg & Quisenberry, 2002). Through dramatic and sociodramatic play and imitation, young children suspend reality and transform objects, people, and symbols into other symbols relevant to children's immediate systems as well as extend them into greater spheres beyond home and school.

As an important part of the new development and learning contexts, ICT should not be imposed in children's activities; instead it should be seamlessly woven into the fabric of their everyday existence, including their play, which is the dominant activity for young children. In Jessica's classroom, the project-based, technology-infused curriculum represents such an effort. It also shifts from teacher-directed to a more child-initiated early childhood curriculum. It is consistent with the view that children are active agents in their own learning.

Home-school-community interactions. The ecological theory also strongly supports the interactions and synergy among homes, schools, and communities. The way in which technologies are being used in Jessica's classroom appropriately exemplify integration of her micro- and mesosystems and respect for her own idiosyncratic developmental timeline.

Technology makes it easier for familiar and trusted adults to virtually share time in the classroom and commit their own intellectual resources to a project. Publishing interactive blogs, stories, video, and audio recordings that link school and home can now be accomplished online in a variety of ways, all of which can be controlled for privacy access that can be adapted as needed or warranted. As a result, children's images of themselves as learners are reinforced and their excitement and engagement in the learning process extended. When, for example, the zoology professor answered the children's e-mail, the intellectual authenticity of Jessica's questions was validated, and she was encouraged to continue including experts as supportive adults in her environment. When the pastor from the church made a visit to the school to share the congregation's experience with the hawks and the decisions made to safeguard them during the nesting period, Jessica's world was expanded to include elements of the immediate neighborhood with which she was previously unfamiliar.

Skills Needed for Children, Parents, and Teachers

An increasingly global, technological economy driven by innovation and constant renewal requires comprehensive knowledge and skills for children, as well as for parents and teachers.

New skills for children. Diverse workplaces of the future require schools and informal learning settings to develop renewed and more comprehensive expectations and outcomes for the whole child which "weave together the threads that connect not only math, science, the arts, and humanities, but also mind, heart, body, and spirit" (Association for the Society of Child Development, 2007, p. 2). Children will need to develop critical and creative thinking to problem-solve and develop information literacy skills to evaluate knowledge gained from a variety of sources; print as well as ICT (i.e., online libraries, search engines, wiki's, books, periodicals, podcasts). Children will need to be able to work harmoniously with people from many cultures and develop social skills to work in collaborative, rather than solitary environments (Gewertz, 2007).

We have adapted the skill set advocated by the *Partnership for 21st Century Skills* (see Table 3.1). This skill set requires concerted efforts from all spheres of the ecological model—business, schools, state policy makers, and families to ensure children acquire skills for the future (Partnership for 21st Century Skills, 2001).

Parent education and training. As parents acquire new devices, they encounter a learning curve and new skills that must be mastered before they can make decisions about how and when their child will be included in applications. For example, access to e-mail, voice, or videoconferencing applications is very attractive to families, as it bridges distances in new ways. But parents have to set up those applications to make sure they work properly and be prepared to deal with those occasions when they don't. At Jessica's developmental level, she might not understand why a Skype call does not work or cuts out in the middle of the call when she is expecting to see and hear Grandma on her birthday.

Similarly, Jessica illustrates in the vignettes that a young child can easily master taking photos with a cell phone or digital camera, but parents often bear the responsibility for teaching a child to use these tools. They must also decide on a comfort level with the potential for accidents, the probability of some damage cost/control, the additional time Jessica will

Table 3.1.   21st Century Skills

1.   Core Subjects, such as reading, math, and science

2.   21st Century Themes, such as

   a. Global awareness
   b. Financial, economic, business and entrepreneurial literacy
   c. Civic literacy
   d. Health literacy

3.   Learning and Innovation Skills

   a. Creativity and Innovation
   b. Critical Thinking and Problem Solving
   c. Communication and Collaboration

4.   Information, Media, and Technology Skills

   a. Information Literacy
   b. Media Literacy
   c. ICT Literacy

5.   Life and Career Skills

need to set up and take photos, and the choices she makes about what she wants to photograph.

Teacher education and professional development. Equally important is for teachers to acquire expertise in the following four areas to achieve developmentally appropriate technology use in classrooms (Rosen & Jaruszewicz, 2009).

First, teachers need to become technologically literate themselves. Acquisition of technological literacy is an ongoing effort informed by the teacher's appreciation for and knowledge of the variety of available products and accessibility options and awareness of how they can be used effectively for a variety of purposes. This knowledge will aid teachers in making responsible choices about access to technology, equipment, and media. It is important to know the possibilities and limitations of equipment and applications for the specific goals teachers wish to accomplish in order to make responsible, practical, and ethical decisions about technology.

Second, teachers need to understand the developmental and cultural characteristics and particular needs and interests of their students as related to technology. While some developmental generalizations can be made about preschoolers (Bredekamp & Copple, 2008), each child in the classroom presents at school from a particular ecological microsystem already in place and influenced at a mesosystemic level in diverse ways (Bronfenbrenner, 1979, 2004). Therefore, effective teaching practices should be adapted to include assessment of attitudes towards, and prior experiences with technology. The use of technology should not compete with or interfere, but enhance and support natural development and expansion of the child's ecological framework.

Clearly, from a Vygotskian (1934/1978) perspective, a great deal of scaffolding is required in a technology-infused classroom, as there are limits to the kind of equipment and programs a young child can operate independently or with help, and activities that need teacher direction and/or control. For example, a kindergarten child can easily learn to responsibly operate a digital camera, but may need to dictate an e-mail to the teacher; a teacher can easily sit next to one or two children to search her laptop online for information, but the interactive white board is a much more practical choice when the entire class is collaborating on a story to be published and printed. Further, it is the teacher's responsibility to make ethical decisions on children's behalf about access to appropriate content and privacy protection of products generated by children when sharing their work electronically via online resources such as blogs, wikispaces, or classroom websites.

Third, teachers need to know how to scaffold children's technology exposure and experiences with appropriate expectations and strategies. A technology-infused classroom, especially one that is project-oriented as depicted in the classroom vignette presented in this chapter, can be an exciting and busy place, but must be managed well and responsibly. Traditional practices focusing on whole group, teacher-directed instruction, worksheet skill-and-drill activities, and desk-based work are generally incompatible with the opportunities for the active and individualized instruction and investigation that new technologies present. It is much more desirable that teachers be able to orchestrate and manage a classroom that emphasizes individual and small-group work, movement and mostly hands-on activities, and varying levels of prior experience with technology. While classroom rules and management procedures do not need to be completely reinvented, they certainly need to be revisited to accommodate for and respect use and care of equipment, consideration for community needs and interests versus those of individuals, and allocation of the time needed for interaction with hardware and interactive electronic resources.

Finally, teachers need to engage in regular documentation and assessment of, and reflection about children's emerging technological competencies and literacy. Although many of the current generation of teachers did not grow up with technology, we are fast approaching a generation of teachers who did. We are in a transition period that can be challenging to teachers for whom use of technology does not come naturally, but correspondingly presents unique and exciting opportunities to create an ecological environment that integrates the classroom with the real world in engaging and intellectually authentic ways. In many respects, the technology learning curves of teacher and child represent parallel processes. The teacher who acknowledges, considers reflectively, and appreciates technology from a personal ecological perspective can apply those insights to decisions made on behalf of students.

Support and Guidance for Children

To take advantage of the tremendous potential of technology to support an ecological view of learning and development, young children require support and guidance across multiple contexts. Adults play a crucial role in children's meaningful interaction with ICT (Bowman, Donovan, & Burns, 2001; Clements & Sarama, 2003; Haugland, 2000; Thouvenelle & Berwick, 2003; Van Scoter & Boss, 2002). For example, Siraj-Blatchford and Siraj-Blatchford (2002) identified scaffolding provided by an adult or more experienced peer critical to young children's use of video conferencing to expand learning. Similarly, Nir-Gal and Klein (2004) found adult-mediation during technology-supported activities improved kindergartners' level of cognitive performance on measures of abstract thinking, planning ability, vocabulary, visual-motor coordination, and reflective responses. Our discussion focuses on the three major contexts in which adults can have a significant impact—school, home, and community.

Support and guidance in school. Teaching practices supportive of an ecological approach to technology integration include hands-on, discussion-oriented instruction where adults model collaborative knowledge construction by engaging in learning with the learners and others in face-to-face and virtual environments. As stated in the International Society for Technology in Education (ISTE) National Educational Technology Standards (NETS*T) (2008), teachers should "engage students in exploring real-world issues and solving authentic problems using digital tools and resources" (section 1.b). From an ecological perspective, when working with digital tools, it is very important for young children to have clear motivation for using the tools across settings as well as clear understanding of ways to apply newly discovered information once it is encountered. Such application of knowledge should be open-ended, creative, and happen across multiple settings.

Teachers must treat children as active agents. Allowing for free exploration is a key instructional support enabling students to pursue their individual curiosities using digital tools. For example, rather than leading children in information searches, the teachers and parents in our vignettes involved children by encouraging inquiry, reminding children of the query they are forming and encouraging them to expand ideas and shared-reading of information found in their searches. Teachers and parents can learn much from giving up the keyboard and mouse to children and observing how the children search and the strategies they employ to create increasing complex queries.

Schools should offer professional development programs that help teachers understand NETS*T standards and current literature on benefits and challenges of using technology with young children. Schools should engage teachers, parents, and caregivers in discussions that explore the ubiquitous nature of technology in young children's worlds, the current technology practices common to their own specific community, and what can/should be done to plan for educationally sound development of technology skills.

To help teachers encourage family involvement in their classroom, different strategies should be implemented to reach out to all parents/guardians. According to NETS*T, teachers should "communicate relevant information and ideas effectively to students, parents, and peers using a variety of digital-age media and formats" (ISTE, 2008, section 3.c). In our example, the digital camera was an essential tool for observation, assessment, and developing children's learning journeys. Photographs were shared via e-mail, on the class blog, and in a class book.

Support and guidance in the home. Although not universal, using technology to communicate is becoming a more common practice within today's families. For example, modern families often engage children in the real-world challenge of communicating with extended family and friends. As in our vignettes, teachers and parents can support children's involvement by encouraging their participation in digital communication, providing/scheduling time for such communication, and providing oversight so that children learn skills and knowledge needed for safe communication.

Jessica's experiences with technology at home are clearly dependent on what resources her parents have available and use, and the extent to which she is included in or encouraged to initiate activities on her own. It is clear that even preschool children can handle such equipment as a digital or cell phone camera, an iPod and headset, and a mouse-driven or touchscreen computer. The two issues relevant in this particular context are availability and controlled access. Socioeconomic factors will determine to a large degree how much technology is available to the child, and parents' values will govern what exactly children will be allowed or prohibited from doing.

Most importantly, computer time and access to Internet resources present a host of challenges to parents that are well documented, not the least of which is adequate supervision for Jessica's cyber-protection (Berson & Berson, 2004). Parents bear responsibility for what a young child can see, hear, and do online and must be willing to invest the time and thought needed to preview and establish limits appropriate to her age, developmental readiness, and amount of online time that is reasonable and appropriate (Haugland, 2000).

Community access and support. Access to technologies in the community can compensate in many ways for families whose economic resources are limited. Excursions and experiences at the public libraries or Internet café can provide opportunities not otherwise available at home, but parents must still assume responsibility and accountability for all of these activities. It may be advisable for Jessica's parents to seek instruction or guidance prior to introducing her to virtual resources in the community so that they can make the same kinds of decisions on her behalf that they would make at home.

Revised community investment models are needed in many early childhood settings, as traditionally technology has not been a resource included in early childhood budgets. Many early childhood settings currently have policies that do not reflect appreciation for the potential contributions of technology to the education of young children. At a policy level, early childhood teaching professionals who have traditionally taken a passive stance will need to revisit this position, as teacher advocacy is heretofore assumed. While, some school districts and programs will adopt new policies that support an ecological approach to technology integration, others may need to be persuaded to anticipate and invest in the equipment, supplemental resources, and professional development needed to explore and implement technology-immersed classrooms, assessment, and curriculum that support an ecological approach. Persuasion will be needed in schools where technology initiatives are typically a top-down driven process, not necessarily informed by the very individuals expected to implement them at the classroom level. Persuasion efforts can emerge from within the school system itself or from other stakeholders, such as parents and the community.

To affect policy change, teachers will need to access, understand, analyze, and interpret the technology literature so their recommendations and requests are made from an informed perspective grounded in developmental theory and research. They will need to develop dispositions towards collaboration for collective action and identifying resources and individuals in their communities that can assist in efforts to change the way we teach with technology. Parents and the community can affect policy change by encouraging hands-on use of child-friendly technology at home to communicate, explore, and document. It is important to encourage children to share their technology-rich home explorations and communication with others in the school setting, thereby accentuating an ecological approach to technology use among young children. Schools and programs should extend children's experiences by using both technology commonly found outside of schools (in the home and the community) and technology most appropriate for school use (such as electronic whiteboards and other expensive digital tools).

CONCLUSIONS

We set out to apply the ecological perspective and provide a more comprehensive framework to help us understand children's experience in a changing technological landscape, as well as the subsequent impact on their development and learning. As an initial attempt to reframe a conceptual framework, this work inevitably has a number of limitations. First, limited existing research prevents us from generalizing the framework to a broad context. Second, the technologies are evolving rapidly, and new forms of cultural practices are emerging accordingly. We need to test the framework by applying it to the changing cultural and technological world.

Nevertheless, the four principles of the ecological perspective—active role of children, understanding children's development in multiple contexts, dynamic and fluid relations among the systems and contexts, and importance of temporal dimension of the ecology—provide a useful lens to understand the intricate ecology of children's ICT experiences and development. First, the framework helps us better understand the role of ICT in early development and education. Jessica's experience supports our assertion that ICT can be used to enrich children's learning. Second, putting children at the center as active agents of their learning and development helps shift the discussion away from concerns about whether ICT should be used with young children and refocuses on the kinds of technologies and their affordance criteria that are best suited to early childhood. Third, the framework helps identify new sets of skills as well as support and guidance needed for young children in a systematic way. Finally, the framework helps us identify areas in need of ongoing research. By studying the dynamic and fluid relations among the systems and contexts, complementary and contradictory experiences of children with ICT may be identified. Subsequently, evidence based practice can assist teachers and families in scaffolding young children's learning with ICT and optimize children's learning and development in a technology-rich world.

REFERENCES

Association for the Society of Child Development. (2007). *Learning compact redefined: A call to action. A Report of the Commission on the Whole Child.* Retrieved from http://www.wholechildeducation.org/resources.dyn/ Learningcompact7-07.pdf

Barab, S. A., & Roth, W. (2006). Curriculum-based ecosystems: Supporting knowing from an ecological perspective. *Educational Researcher, 35*(5), 3-13.

Bergen, D. (2008). New technologies in early childhood: Partners in play? In O. Saracho & B. Spodek (Eds.), *Contemporary perspectives on science and technology in early childhood education* (pp. 87-104). Charlotte, NC: Information Age.

Berson, M. J., & Berson, I. R. (2004). Developing thoughtful "cybercitizens." *Social Studies and the Young Learner, 16*(4), 5-8.

Berson, I. R., & Berson, M. J. (2009). Panwapa: Global kids, global connections. *Social Studies and the Young Learner, 21*(4), 28-31.

Bodrova, E., & Leong, D. J. (2005). High quality preschool programs: What would Vygotsky say? *Early Education and Development, 16*(4), 437-446.

Bowman, B., Donovan, S. M., & Burns, S. (Eds.). (2001). *Eager to learn: Educating our preschoolers.* Washington, DC: National Research Council.

Bredekamp, S., & Copple, C. (2008). *Developmentally appropriate practice for programs serving children birth-eight.* Washington, DC: National Association for the Education of Young Children.

Bronfenbrenner, U. (1979). *The ecology of human development: Experiments by nature and design.* Cambridge, MA: Harvard University Press.

Bronfenbrenner, U. (2004). *Making human beings human: Bioecological perspectives on human development.* Thousand Oaks, CA: SAGE.

Bronfenbrenner, U., & Evans, G. (2000). Developmental science in the 21st century: Emerging questions, theoretical models, research design and empirical findings. *Social Development, 9*(1), 115-125.

Buckleitner, W. (May, 2008). *Like taking candy from a baby: How young children interact with online environments.* Yonkers, NY: Consumer Reports WebWatch. Retrieved from http://www.consumerwebwatch.org

Calvert, S. L., Rideout, V., Woolard, J. L., Barr, R. F., & Strouse, G. A. (2005). Age, ethnicity and socioeconomic patterns in early computer use: A national survey. *American Behavioral Scientist, 48*(5), 590-607.

Carr, M. (2000). Technological affordance, social practice and learning narratives in an early childhood setting. *International Journal of Technology and Design Education, 10*(1), 61-79.

Ching, C. C., Wang, X. C., & Kedem, Y. (2006). Digital photo journals in a K-1 classroom: A novel approach to addressing early childhood technology standards and recommendations. In S. Tettegah & R. Hunter (Eds.), *Technology: Issues in administration, policy, and applications in K-12 classrooms* (pp. 253-269). Oxford, England: Elsevier.

Clements, D. H. (1999). Young children and technology. In G. D. Nelson (Ed.), *Dialogue on early childhood science, mathematics, and technology education* (pp. 92-105). Washington, DC: AAAS.

Clements, D., & Sarama, J. (2003). Strip mining for gold: Research and policy in educational technology: A response to "Fool's Gold." *AACE Journal, 11*(1), 7-69.

Cordes, C., & Miller, E. (2000). *Fool's gold: A critical look at computers in childhood.* College Park, MD: Alliance for Childhood.

Crowley, K., & Jacobs, M. (2002). Building islands of expertise in everyday family activities. In G. Leinhardt, K. Crowley, & K. Knutson (Eds.), *Learning conversations in museums* (pp. 401–423). Mahwah, NJ: Erlbaum.

Gewertz, C. (2007). "Soft Skills" in big demand: Interest in teaching students habits of mind for success in life is on the rise. *Education Week, 26* (40). Retrieved from http://www.edweek.org/ew/articles/2007/06/12/40soft.h26.html

Gutierrez, K., & Rogoff, B. (2003). Cultural ways of learning: Individual traits or repertoires of practice. *Educational Researcher, 32*(5), 19-25.

Haugland, S. W. (2000). Early childhood classrooms in the 21st century: Using computers to maximize learning. *Young Children, 55*(1), 12-18.

Isenberg, J. P., & Quisenberry, N. (2002). *Play: essential for all children.* A position paper of the Association for Childhood Education International. Retrieved from http://www.acei.org/playpaper.htm

International Society for Technology in Education. (2008). *National Educational Technology Standards (NETS) for Teachers.* Retrieved from http://www.iste.org/Content/NavigationMenu/NETS/ForTeachers/2008Standards/NETS_for_Teachers_2008.htm

Kafai, Y. B. (2006). Playing and making games for learning: Instructionist and constructionist perspectives for game studies. *Games and Culture, 1*(1), 36-40.

Kaiser Family Foundation. (2003). *The effects of electronic media on children ages zero to six: A history of research.* Retrieved from http://www.kff.org/entmedia/7239.cfm

Kaiser Family Foundation. (2005). *Zero to six: Electronic media in the lives of infants, toddlers and preschoolers.* Retrieved from http://www.kff.org/entmedia/3378.cfm

Lemke, J. (2000). The long and the short of it: Comments on multiple timescale studies of human activity. *Journal of the Learning Sciences, 10*(1-2), 193-202.

Mercer, N. (2008). The seeds of time: Why classroom dialogue needs a temporal analysis. *Journal of the Learning Sciences, 17*(1), 33-59.

Nir-Gal, O., & Klein, P. S. (2004). Computers for cognitive development in early childhood: The teachers' role in the computer learning environment. *Information Technology in Childhood Education Annual, 1,* 97-119.

Partnership for 21st Century Skills. (2008). *21st century skills, education, and competitiveness: A resource and policy guide.* Retrieved from http://www.21stcenturyskills.org/

Rosen, D., Lee, J., & Hicks, D. (in press). Play within traditional and virtual microsystems: A study of young children's WebKinz play. *Early Childhood Development and Care.*

Rosen, D., & Jaruszewicz, C. (2009). Developmentally appropriate technology use and early childhood teacher education. *Journal of Early Childhood Teacher Education, 30*(2), 162-171.

Sameroff, A. (Ed.). (2009). *The transactional model of development: How children and contexts shape each other.* Washington, DC: American Psychological Association.

Sarama, J., & Clements, D. H. (2002). Learning and teaching with computers in early childhood education. In O. N. Saracho & B. Spodek (Eds.), *Contemporary Perspectives in Early Childhood Education* (pp. 171-219). Greenwich, CT: Information Age.

Shuler, C. (2007). *D is for digital: An analysis of the children's interactive media environment with a focus on mass marketed products that promote learning.* New York: The Joan Ganz Cooney Center at Sesame Workshop. Retrieved from http://www.joanganzcooneycenter.org/pdf/DisforDigital.pdf

Siraj-Blatchford, J., & Siraj-Blatchford, I. (2002). Developmentally appropriate technology in early childhood: "Video conferencing." *Contemporary Issues in Early Childhood, 3*(2), 216-225.

Tapscott, D. (1997). *Growing up digital: The raise of net generation.* New York: McGraw-Hill.

Thouvenelle, S., & Bewick. C. J. (2003). *Completing the computer puzzle: A guide for early childhood educators.* Boston, MA: Allyn & Bacon.

Van Scoter, J., & Boss, S. (2002, March). *Learners, language, and technology: Making connections that support literacy.* Northwest Regional Educational Laboratory, Child & Family. Retrieved from http://www.netc.org/earlyconnections/pub/llt.pdf

Vygotsky, L. S. (1978). *Mind in society.* Cambridge, MA: Harvard University Press (Original work published in 1934).

Wang, X. C., & Ching, C. C. (2003). Social construction of computer experience in a first-grade classroom: Social processes and mediating artifacts. *Early Education and Development, 14*(3), 335-361.

Wang, X. C., & Hoot, J. (2006). Technology in early childhood education: An introduction. *Early Education and Development, 17*(3), 317-322.

Wells, G. (1986). *The meaning makers: Children learning language and using language to learn.* Portsmouth, NH: Heinemann.

Wilensky, U., & Resnick, M. (1999). Thinking in levels: A dynamic systems perspective to making sense of the world. *Journal of Science Education and Technology, 8*(1), 3-19.

Yan, Z., & Fischer, K. W. (2004). How children and adults learn to use computers: A developmental approach. *New Directions for Child and Adolescent Development, 105*, 41-61.

Yelland, N. (2005). The future is now: A review of the literature on the use of computers in early childhood education (1994-2004). *AACE Journal, 13*(3), 201-232.

CHAPTER 4

TANGIBLE PROGRAMMING IN EARLY CHILDHOOD

Revisiting Developmental Assumptions Through New Technologies

Marina Umaschi Bers and Michael S. Horn

We are surrounded by technology. From pens and pencils to cell phones and digital cameras, technology permeates our existence. Yet, in the early grades, children learn very little about this. For decades early childhood curriculum has focused on literacy and numeracy, with some attention paid to science, in particular to the natural world—insects, volcanoes, plants, and the Arctic. And, while understanding the natural world is important, developing children's knowledge of the surrounding man-made world is also important (Bers, 2008). This is the realm of technology and engineering, which focus on the development and application of tools, machines, materials, and processes to help solve human problems.

Early childhood education has not ignored this; it is common to see young children using cardboard or recycled materials to build cities and bridges. However, what is unique to our man-made world today is the fusion of electronics with mechanical structures. We go to the bathroom to

High-Tech Tots: Childhood in a Digital World, pp. 49–69
Copyright © 2010 by Information Age Publishing
All rights of reproduction in any form reserved.

wash our hands, and the faucets "know" when to start dispensing water. The elevator "knows" when someone's little hands are in between the doors and shouldn't close. Our cell phones "know" how to take pictures, send e-mails, and behave as alarm clocks. Even our cars "know" where we want to go and can take us there without getting lost. We live in a world in which bits and atoms are increasingly integrated (Gershenfeld, 2000); however, we do not teach our young children about this. In the early schooling experiences, we teach children about polar bears and cacti, which are probably more remote from their everyday experience than smart faucets and cellular phones. There are several reasons for the lack of focus on technologies in early childhood, but two of the most common claims are that young children are not developmentally ready to understand such complex and abstract phenomena, and that there is a lack of technology with age-appropriate interfaces that allow children to develop their own technologically-rich projects. In this chapter we address both of these claims by presenting research to evaluate young children's ability to build, program, and understand their own robotic creations through the use of a novel programming interface designed specifically for young children

BACKGROUND

Our work is rooted in notions of developmentally appropriate practice (DAP), a perspective within early childhood education concerned with creating learning environments sensitive to children's social, emotional, physical, and cognitive development. DAP is a framework produced by the National Association for the Education of Young Children (Copple & Bredekamp, 2009) that outlines practice that promotes young children's optimal learning and development. DAP is based on theories of child development, the strengths and weaknesses of individual children uncovered through authentic assessment, and individual children's cultural background as defined by community and family (Copple & Bredekamp, 2009).

DAP is built upon the theory of developmental stages introduced by Jean Piaget, which suggests that children enter the *concrete operational* stage at age 6 or 7. According to Piaget, at this age, a child gains the ability to perform mental operations in his/her head and also to reverse those operations. As a result, a concrete operational child has a more sophisticated understanding of number, can imagine the world from different perspectives, can systematically compare, sort, and classify objects, and can understand notions of time and causality (Richardson, 1998). Based on this developmental model, one might make the argument that a child's ability to program a computer might be predicted by his or her general developmental level, and, that by extension, a preoperational kindergartner (typically 5-years-old) may be too young to benefit from or understand computer programming. However, since its introduction, various problems and inconsistencies have been identified with Piaget's stage model. For example, studies have shown that when a task and its context are made clear to children, they exhibit logical thought and understanding well before the ages that Piaget suggested as a lower limit (Richardson, 1998).

In the early days of personal computing, there was lively debate over the developmental appropriateness of computer technology use in early elementary classrooms (Clements & Sarama, 2003). Today, however, the pressing question in no longer *whether* but *how* we should introduce computer technology in early elementary school (Clements & Sarama, 2002). For example, a 1992 study found that elementary school children exposed to exploratory software showed gains in self-esteem, nonverbal skills, long-term memory, manual dexterity, and structural knowledge. When combined with other noncomputer activities, these students also showed improvements in verbal skills, abstraction, problem-solving, and conceptual skills (Haugland, 1992). Other studies have demonstrated that computer use can serve as a catalyst for positive social interaction and collaboration (Clements & Sarama, 2002; Wang & Ching, 2003). Of course, the developmental appropriateness of the technology used by young children depends on the context. *What software is being used? And how is it integrated with and supported by the broader classroom curriculum?* Fortunately, we live in an advantageous time for introducing technology in early childhood. Given the increasing mandate to make early childhood programs more academically challenging,[1] technology can provide a playful bridge to integrate academic demands with personally meaningful projects (Bers, 2008).

Robotics and Computer Programming in Early Childhood Education

"Computer technology" is a broad term that can mean many things, especially in the context of a classroom. We believe that robotics is one type of educational technology that holds special potential for early childhood classrooms where children engage in cognitive as well as motor and social skills development. Furthermore, in early childhood content areas tend not to be isolated, but integrated more broadly into classroom curriculum that encompasses different content and skills; learning can be project-driven and open-ended; and student work does not have to fit into an hour-long class period. Thus, robotics can be a good integrator of curricular content (Bers, Ponte, Juelich, Viera, & Schenker, 2002).

Robotics provides opportunities for young children to learn about sensors, motors, and the digital domain in a playful way by building their own projects, such as cars that follow a light, elevators that work with touch sensors, and puppets that can play music. Young children can become engineers by playing with gears, levers, motors, sensors, and programming loops, as well as storytellers by creating their own meaningful projects that move in response to their environment (Bers, 2008; Wang & Ching, 2003). Robotics can also be a gateway for children to learn about applied mathematical concepts, the scientific method of inquiry, and problem solving (Rogers & Portsmore, 2004). Moreover, robotic manipulatives invite children to participate in social interactions and negotiations while playing to learn and learning to play (Resnick, 2003).

Robotics, however, is about more than just creating physical artifacts. In order to bring robots to "life" children must also create computer programs—digital artifacts that allow robots to move, blink, sing, and respond to their environment. Previous research has shown that children as young as four years old can understand the basic concepts of computer programming and can build and program simple robotics projects (Bers, 2008; Cejka, Rogers, & Portsmore, 2006; Bers et al., 2006). Furthermore, early studies with the text-based language, Logo, have shown that computer programming, when introduced in a structured way, can help young children with variety of cognitive skills, including basic number sense, language skills, and visual memory (Clements, 1999).

Nonetheless, computer programming is difficult for novices of any age. Kelleher and Pausch (2005) offer a taxonomy containing well over 50 novice programming systems, a great number of which aim to ease or eliminate the process of learning language syntax, perhaps the most often cited source of novice frustration. Beyond syntax, there are many specific conceptual hurdles faced by novice programmers as well as fundamental misconceptions about the nature of computers and computer programming. Ben-Ari (1998) points out that unlike the beginning physics student who at least has a naïve understanding of the physical world, beginning programmers have no effective model of a computer upon which to build new knowledge. Worse, rarely is an effort made to help students develop a working model. According to Norman (1986), the primary problem facing novice programmers is the gap between the representation the brain uses when thinking about a problem and the representation a computer will accept.

In addition to the above challenges faced by novice programmers, we must also consider the developmental needs and capabilities of young children. McKeithen, Reitman, Rueter, and Hirtle (1981) conducted a study that explored the differences in the ability of expert and novice computer programmers to recall details of computer programs. In their analysis, they theorize that because novice programmers lack adequate mental models for programming tasks, they rely on rich common language associations for these concepts. For example, computer words like LOOP, FOR, STRING, and CASE have very different common language meanings. Reflecting on this result, it seems reasonable to expect that young children will have an especially difficult time building conceptual models for programming concepts because they have fewer mental schemas on which to build.

Likewise Rader, Brand, and Lewis (1997) conducted a study with the Apple's KidSim programming system in which second/third graders and fourth/fifth graders used the system for 1 year with minimal structured instruction. At the end of the year, the younger children had significantly more difficulty with programming concepts such as individual actions, rule order, and subroutine. However, the authors suggest that with structured instruction of programming concepts, the young children would have developed a much better understanding of the system.

However, regardless of the way in which the content is presented, most current programming environments are not well-suited for very young children. One problem is that the syntax of text-based computer languages, such as Logo, can be unintuitive and frustrating for novice programmers. This is exacerbated for young children who are still learning how to read. Modern visual programming languages such as ROBOLAB[2] allow children to program by dragging and connecting icons on the computer screen. And, while this approach simplifies language syntax, the interfaces require young children to use a mouse to navigate hierarchical menus, click on icons, and drag lines to very small target areas on a computer screen. All of this requires fine motor skills that make it difficult for young children to participate (Hourcade, Bederson, Druin, & Guimbretière, 2004). As a result, adults often have to sit with young children and give *click-by-click* instructions to make programming possible, which poses challenges for children's learning (Beals & Bers, 2006). It also makes it difficult to implement computer programming in average schools, where there are often only 1 or 2 adults per 25 children. Attempts have been made to create simpler versions of these languages. However, the resulting interfaces often obscure some of the most important aspects of programming, such as the notion of creating a sequence of commands to form a program's flow-of-control. In the next section we will present work on tangible computer programming that explores new interfaces to address some of the challenges presented here.

TANGIBLE COMPUTER PROGRAMMING

With the emergence of tangible user interface technology (TUI), we have a new means to separate the intellectual act of computer programming from the confounding factor of modern graphical user interfaces. And, with this, we have an opportunity to build a much better understanding of developmental capabilities of young children with respect to computer programming. Just as young children can read books that are appropriate for their age-level, we propose that young children can write simple but interesting computer programs, provided they have access to a developmentally-appropriate programming language. Indeed, in our own extensive previous work with robotics and young children, we observed that when presented with new technologies that make use of well-established sensori-motor skills, young children are able to display complex mental operations.

We believe that we can overcome the inherent limitations of modern desktop and laptop computers by doing nothing short of removing them from children's learning experiences. Thus, rather than write computer programs with a keyboard or mouse, we have created a system that allows children to instead *construct* physical computer programs by connecting interlocking wooden blocks (see Figure 4.1). This technique is called *tangible programming*.

Figure 4.1.   A tangible programming language for robotics developed at Tufts University. With this language, children construct programs using interlocking wooden blocks.

A tangible programming language, like any other type of computer language, is simply a tool for telling a computer what to do. With a text-based language, a programmer uses words such as BEGIN, IF, and REPEAT to instruct a computer. This code must be written according to strict, and often frustrating, syntactic rules. With a visual language, words are replaced by pictures, and programs are expressed by arranging and connecting icons on the computer screen with the mouse. There are still syntax rules to follow, but they can be conveyed to the programmer through a set of visual cues.

Instead of relying on pictures and words on a computer screen, tangible languages use physical objects to represent the various aspects of computer programming. Users arrange and connect these physical elements to construct programs. Rather than falling back on implied rules and conventions, tangible languages can exploit the physical properties of objects, such as size, shape, and material to express and enforce syntax. For example, the interlocking wooden blocks shown in Figure 4.1 describe the language syntax (i.e., a sequential connection of blocks). In fact, with this language, while it is possible to make mistakes in program logic, it is impossible to produce a syntax error.

In moving away from the mouse-based interface, our pilot studies, conducted in public schools in the Boston area, have suggested that tangible languages might have the added benefit of improving both the style and amount of collaboration occurring between students. And, since the process of constructing programs is now situated in the classroom at large—on children's desks or on the floor—children's programming work can be more open and visible and can become more a part of presentations and discussions of technology projects. Likewise, physical programming elements can be incorporated into whole class instruction activities without the need for a shared computer display or an LCD projector.

The idea of tangible programming was first introduced in the mid-1970s by Radia Perlman, then a researcher at the MIT Logo Lab. Perlman believed that the syntax rules of text-based computer languages represented a serious barrier to learning for young children. To address this issue she developed an interface called *Slot Machines* (Perlman, 1976) that allowed young children to insert cards representing various Logo commands into three colored racks. This idea of tangible programming was revived nearly 2 decades later (Suzuki & Kato, 1995), and since then a variety of tangible languages have been created in a number of different research labs around the world (e.g., McNerney, 2004; Smith, 2007; Wyeth, 2008).

In almost all cases, the blocks that make up tangible programming languages contain some form of electronic components. And, when con-

Figure 4.2.   This picture taken from a pilot study show kindergarten students using the tangible programming language developed at Tufts to program a robot to act out a short story.

nected, the blocks form structures that are more than just abstract representations of algorithms; they are also working, specialized computers that can execute algorithms through the sequential interaction of the blocks. Unfortunately, the blocks that make up these languages tend to be delicate and expensive. And, as a result, tangible programming languages have seldom been used outside of research lab settings. At Tufts we have taken a different approach (Horn & Jacob, 2007). Programs created with our language are purely symbolic representations of algorithms—much in the way that Java or C++ programs are only collections of text files. An additional piece of technology must be used to translate the abstract representations of a program into a machine language that will control a robot. This approach allows us to create inexpensive and durable parts, and provides greater freedom in the design of the physical components of the language. Our current prototype uses a collection of image processing techniques to convert physical programs into digital instructions. For the system to work, each block in the language is imprinted with a circular symbol called a TopCode (Horn, 2008). These codes allow the position, orientation, size and shape, and type of each statement to be quickly determined from a digital image. The image processing routines work under a variety of lighting conditions without the need for human calibration. Our prototype uses a standard consumer web camera connected to a laptop computer. Children initiate a compile by pressing the spacebar on the computer, and their program is downloaded onto a robot in a mater of seconds.

TANGIBLE PROGRAMMING CURRICULUM FOR KINDERGARTEN

Research has shown that mere exposure to computer programming in an unstructured way has little demonstrable effect on student learning (Clements, 1999). For example, a 1997 study involving the visual programming language, KidSim, found that elementary school students failed to grasp many aspects of the language, leading the authors to suggest that more explicit instruction might have improved the situation (Rader et al., 1997). Therefore, an important aspect of our work is to develop curriculum that utilizes tangible programming to introduce a series of powerful ideas from computer science in a structured, age-appropriate way. The term *powerful idea* refers to a concept that is at once personally useful, interconnected with other disciplines, and rooted in intuitive knowledge that a child has internalized over a long period of time (Papert, 1991). We introduce these powerful ideas in a context in which their use allows very young children to solve compelling problems.

Table 4.1 lists example powerful ideas from computer programming that we have selected to emphasize in our curriculum using tangible programming. Based on these powerful ideas we developed a preliminary 12-hour curriculum module for use in kindergarten classrooms that introduces a subset of these concepts through a combination of whole-class instruction, structured small-group challenge activities, and open-ended student projects. We piloted this curriculum in three kindergarten classrooms in the Boston area, using the tangible programming blocks described above and LEGO Mindstorms RCX construction kits. Initially, we provided students with pre-assembled robot cars to teach preliminary computer programming concepts. As the unit progressed, students disassembled these cars to build diverse robotic creations that incorporated arts and craft materials, recycled goods such as cardboard tubes and boxes, and a limited number of LEGO parts. Table 4.2 provides a brief overview of the activities that we included in the curriculum.

RESEARCH QUESTIONS

The research presented in this chapter is guided by the following questions: given access to appropriate technologies and curriculum, are young children capable of learning how to program their own robotics projects? How much direct adult assistance do they need? Can young children understand the underlying powerful ideas behind computer programming? Finally, should we revisit assumptions about what is developmentally appropriate for young children when designing curriculum—can we leverage new technologies to introduce more complex concepts?

Table 4.1.   Powerful Ideas From Computer Programming and Robotics Emphasized in Our Curriculum

Powerful Idea	Description
Computer Programming	This is the fundamental idea that robots are not living things that act of their own accord. Instead, robots act out computer programs written by human beings. Not only that, children can create their own computer programs to control a robot.
Command Sequences & Control Flow	The idea that simple commands can be combined into sequences of actions to be acted out by a robot in order.
Loops	The idea that sequences of instructions can be modified to repeat indefinitely or in a controlled way.
Sensors	The idea that a robot can sense its surrounding environment through a variety of modalities, and that a robot can be programmed to respond to changes in its environment.
Parameters	The idea that some instructions can be qualified with additional information.
Branches	The idea that you can ask a question in a program, and, depending on the answer, have a robot do one thing or another.
Subroutines	The idea that you can treat a set of instructions as a single unit that can be called from other parts of a program.

These ideas are not entirely new. Researchers at MIT's Lifelong Kindergarten Group have suggested that with new *digital manipulatives* children are capable of exploring concepts that were previously considered too advanced, in part because of the ability of technology to bring abstract concepts to a concrete level (Resnick et al., 1998). However, for the most part, this claim has not been empirically validated with children as young as 5-years-old. And, as noted above, it can be difficult in this research to distinguish what young children truly understand and can do on their own, versus what was done by the supporting adults (Cejka et al., 2006). In the end, the functioning robotic projects tend to hide the challenges faced by children in the process of making them.

METHODOLOGICAL APPROACH: DESIGN-BASED RESEARCH

Design-based research (DBR) is an approach to studying novel tools and techniques for education in the context of real-life learning settings (Design-Based Research Collective, 2003). As a methodology, DBR acknowledges the substantial limitations of conducting research in chaotic environments like classrooms; however, in exchange researchers hope that the resulting designs will be effective and practical for future use in class-

Table 4.2.   Kindergarten Computer Programming and Robotics Curriculum Activities

Robot Dance: In this introductory activity, we introduce students to the concept of robots and programming. Children participate in a whole-class activity in which they use the tangible blocks to "teach" a robot to dance the *Hokey-Pokey*.

Experimenting with Programming: Students work in small groups to create and test several programs of their own design. At this point they combine simple command blocks (no sensors or control flow blocks yet) into sequences of actions that are acted out by the group's robot. Robots can perform simple movements, make sounds, blink a light, and perform dance moves (such as shake or spin around).

Simon Says: In this whole class activity, students pretend that they are robots and act out commands presented by the teacher. For example, the teacher holds up a card that says *SHAKE,* and the students all shake their bodies. The point of this activity is to help students, who may or may not be able to read, learn the various programming commands that are available to use. As this activity progresses, the teacher will begin to display two or more cards at the same time that the students will act out in order. This activity is repeated on several occasions throughout the unit.

Hungry, Hungry Robot: In this challenge activity, we introduce the idea of loops as students work in small groups to program their robot to move from a starting line (a strip of tape on the floor of the classroom) to a finish line (marked with a picture of cookies). Children are prompted with the challenge: *Your robot is very hungry. Can you program it to move from the start line to the cookies?* As this activity progresses, students quickly realize that the robot needs to move forward several times in succession to reach its goal. Because they are only provided with a small number of blocks to move the robot forward, they learn to create programs that incorporate a simple counting loop.

If you're happy and you know it: The teacher reads a story in which different animals show that they are happy in different ways. Students are then asked to work in small groups to program a robot to act like one of the animals in the story.

Bird in a Cage: In this whole class activity, the teacher tells a story about a bird that sings when it is released from a cage. The "bird" is a robot with a light sensor attached. When the bird is removed from a cardboard box (the cage), the increase in light intensity triggers it to sing. The teacher then introduces the concept of sensors and shows the class how to write the program that causes the bird to sing. This activity is repeated on two separate occasions, once as a whole-group activity, and once as a small group challenge activity.

Final Projects: Students work in teams of two to design and build a robot animal that includes one motor and one sensor. Students are encouraged to create a story that involves their robot animal. This activity is open-ended and student projects are completed over a period of several days.

rooms. DBR is based on an iterative process of design, evaluation, and test-ing. By collecting both qualitative and quantitative data in nonlaboratory settings, design-based research has the additional goal of developing the-ories of learning that will inform future research.

STUDY

We have conducted a 2-year design-based research study exploring the use of tangible programming technology in kindergarten classrooms. Both the curriculum and the technology have evolved substantially as a result of each iteration. This research was conducted at two public schools in the greater-Boston area, one urban K-8 school and one suburban K-5 school. In all, we have worked with 56 children and 6 teachers. Data were collected through observation notes, photographs, and videotape. We also collected student work (both the programming code as well as the robotic artifacts) and conducted one-on-one interviews with children and teachers in the classroom. Our first intervention consisted of 2 sessions (4 hours total), with 20 students and 2 teachers at the urban school. After-wards, we made substantial revisions to the technology (described in detail below) and expanded the curriculum. Our second intervention con-sisted of a 8-hour curriculum module in 2 classrooms at the suburban school with 36 children and 4 teachers.

RESULTS

In this study, we had two primary hypotheses. First, given access to appro-priate technology, young children are capable of programming their own robotics projects without direct adult assistance. In other words, through a combination of unstructured exploration, structured activities, and scaf-folding, children will learn how to build and program independently. Second, children are able to understand the underlying powerful ideas of computer programming and robotics through the curriculum.

Based on observation notes and an analysis of videotape, we found that children were able to easily manipulate the tangible blocks to form their own programs. And, for the most part, students were also able to differen-tiate the blocks and discern their meanings. Not all of the children could read the text labels on the blocks, although we saw evidence that children who could not read the blocks were able to use the icons as a way to inter-pret meaning. For example, in the initial sessions, we asked children to look at the blocks and describe what they saw. Some children were simply able to read the text labels on the blocks. Other children said things like:

"mine says arrow" or "mine says music." In reality the text on the blocks reads "Forward" and "Sing." We used the *Simon Says* activity to reinforce the meaning of each block in terms of the robot's actions.

The children also seemed to understand that the blocks were to be connected in a sequence and interpreted from left to right. For example, one student in the introductory session pointed out, "they connect; some have these [pegs] and some have these [holes]." Another student added, "the End block doesn't have one [peg]," with another classmate adding, "the Start block doesn't have a hole." The blocks were designed using physical form factor to enforce language syntax. The students noticed that blocks could not be inserted into a program before the Start block or after the End block. During the second session, researchers asked individual children to describe their programs. One girl explained, "my program is: Begin *then* Beep *then* Forward *then* Sing *then* End." Here she was reading the text labels on the blocks in her program from left to right, resting her finger on each block in turn. The use of the word *then* suggests that she might have understood not only the implied left-to-right ordering of the blocks but also the temporal step-by-step sequence in which the blocks would be executed. Understanding the idea of sequencing is powerful, not only in the domain of computer programming but for most analytical activities that children would encounter in schooling as well as life.

In the second intervention round, we moved beyond programs consisting of simple sequences of actions and introduced more advanced constructs including loops, sensors, and numeric parameter values. Through these activities we found evidence that children could engage these concepts, reasoning about possible outcomes of different blocks and forming and testing solutions to challenge activities. For example, in our *Hungry, hungry robot* activity, we prompted teams of four students with this challenge: *Your robot is hungry. Can you program it to drive to the cookies?* We had placed the robot on a starting line, represented with a strip of tape on the floor. The *cookies* were represented with a picture taped on the wall approximately two meters from the starting line. Groups were provided with a small collection of blocks, including two Forwards, a Repeat, an End Repeat, and a number parameter block. The number parameter block was labeled with the numbers two through five, with one number on each face of the cube. This number block could be included in a program after a Repeat block to specify how many times a robot should repeat a sequence of actions. Each Forward block would cause the robot to drive forward approximately one half meter. So, for example, one solution to the challenge would be the following program:

Begin -> Repeat (4) -> Forward -> End Repeat -> End

Many other possible solutions exist, and students could add creative elements to their programs. For example, one group included a Sing block to indicate that the robot was eating its cookies after it arrived at the wall. Many groups started this challenge by creating programs that consisted of all the blocks provided to them arranged in a seemingly random order. However, after testing these programs, the groups quickly decided that the Forward block was necessary to drive the robot towards its goal. After one or two additional trials, groups discovered that they didn't have enough Forward blocks to drive the robot all the way from the starting line to the wall. Here, often with prompting in the form of leading questions from a teacher, the groups began to experiment with the Repeat blocks, creating programs that incorporated the Forward blocks inside of a loop.

Later in the unit, we introduced students to the idea of sensors through the *Bird in the cage* activity. Here the cage was a cardboard box, and the bird was a robot with a light sensor attached. The lead teacher told a story of a bird who liked to sing when released from her cage. We used this program to have the robot act out the story.

Begin -> Repeat(forever) -> Wait for Light -> Sing -> End Repeat -> End

The students were curious how the robot was able to sing when it was removed from the cage. The teacher used this curiosity to prompt students to explore the idea of sensors and to develop hypotheses about how the robot is able to sing when it emerges from the box. Finally, the teacher demonstrated how she had created the program that controls the robot:

Teacher:	Do you recognize all of the blocks?
Student 1:	No. The moon one. [Wait for Dark]
Student 2:	The sun and moon [Wait for Light]
Teacher:	Can one of you read this?
Student 2:	Wait for light
Student 1:	It means you're going to wait for the dark to come.
Teacher:	What are these?
Students together:	Repeat
Teacher:	What do they do?
Student 3:	Start all over again.
Teacher:	The bird is outside.
Student 2:	The witch catches the bird
Student 1:	If we turn this block over we could make him sing when it's dark outside. It might be shy so he sings in the dark.

Here the child was pointing out that it would be possible to use a *Wait for Dark* block instead of a *Wait for Light* to achieve the opposite effect, a bird that sings only when it is inside the cage.

For the remainder of the curriculum unit, the children worked in pairs to create robotic creatures that ideally incorporated one moving part and one sensor. The children struggled with many aspects of this activity and required substantial help from the teachers. The lead teacher described her interactions with one group:

> I worked with M. and N. for the majority of the time. They struggled with understanding that the RCX [LEGO computer] was what would power the robot. M. spent most of the time searching for materials, and I sat with N. trying to understand her plan for their robot (a parrot that snaps it's beak). She had an egg carton, and was decorating it with stickers. When I asked her where the beak was, she pointed to the egg carton. When I asked her how it would move, she picked up two large pompoms and said that the motors (the pompoms) would make it move. N. had little interest in the RCX and how it worked. When pressed, she said that the buttons and the wires would make the beak move.

We believe that these problems were due to our curriculum, which did not include enough time for children to explore the RCX brick and understand how a computer (although small) can be connected to a physical construction and how that construction needs to have moving parts that could be controlled by the computer.

As part of the final project presentations we asked students not only to demonstrate their robots, but also to show the class the blocks they used to program it. In many cases, students selected blocks that had little to do with their actual programs. We believe that in the current version of the curriculum, students were not given enough time to experiment with programming on their own, either individually or in small groups. In many cases, the programs were loaded quickly by the teacher in order to finish projects in time for the final presentations. This might explain some of the difficulty students had recreating their programs during the final project presentations.

In other cases, however, students were able to recreate programs more accurately. For example, in this transcription, two girls described their *toucan* robot during the final project presentation:

Teacher:	So what does it do?	
Student 1:	We have to make the program first	
Student 1:	[Starts connecting blocks] Begin. Wait for Dark...	
Teacher:	Can you tell us what we're doing while you're doing it?	

Student 2:   Yes. I think we should use a repeat block
Student 1:   Great idea
Teacher: [Student 2], why don't you show us your robot while [Student 1] builds the program.
Student 2:   This is our robot ... [she starts to demonstrate how it works]
Student 1:   The program isn't done yet!
Student 2:   [Looking at the blocks] It's supposed to repeat the shake
Student 1:   Yes. It's going to repeat the shake over and over again.

[The program student 1 has created is: Begin -> Wait for Dark -> Beep -> Turn Left -> Repeat -> Shake -> End]

Student 2:   [Runs the program on the robot for the class to see. The actual program waits for dark, turns, beeps, and then shakes once.]
Student 1:   These are the three blocks we used [She puts these blocks in the middle of the rug: Begin, Wait For Dark, Beep]

Here it is clear that there is some confusion on the part of the students about the concept of a program being stored on the RCX robot. However, the blocks the students chose to explain their robot are consistent with the program that they had actually loaded on the robot earlier in the day. Moreover, they seemed to understand the notion of repeating an action.

TECHNOLOGY EVOLUTION

The technology used in this project, including both the software and the tangible programming blocks, has evolved substantially as a result of our iterative testing with children. For our first intervention, we used wooden blocks shaped like interlocking jigsaw puzzles (see Figure 4.3). These blocks had several drawbacks that became obvious to us when we observed children using them in classrooms. First, the blocks are only big enough to allow space for a computer vision fiducial (the circular black and white symbols) and a small amount of text. This is problematic for children who are still learning to read. As we discovered with our current prototype, children rely heavily on icons as well as text to interpret a particular block's meaning.

Second, although children have little difficultly chaining these jigsaw puzzle blocks together to form programs, the blocks tend to fall apart when children try to carry their programs around the classroom. Unfortunately, children need to be able to carry their programs to a specific location in the classroom (the computer with the web camera attached) in order to download their programs to the robot. Finally, these blocks are designed to lie flat on a table surface. As a result, in order for the computer vision system to function properly, we had to suspend the web camera above the table pointing down. This relatively elaborate setup limits the system's portability, increases the teacher's preparation time, and limits the number of stations that can be set up in the classroom for children to use.

To address these problems, we redesigned the blocks using wooden cubes with interlocking pegs and holes instead of jigsaw puzzle tiles. These cubes provide a slightly larger surface area on which to include both text and an icon in addition to the computer vision fiducial (see Figure 4.1). Furthermore, because the cubes interlock, they are easier for children to carry around the classroom. Finally, because we place a computer vision fiducial on every available face of the cube, we are able to take pictures of programs from the side rather than from above. This allows us to simply place the web camera on a table rather than suspending it above.

As expected, the prototype based on wooden cubes was much easier for students to use. However, for our next round of evaluation, we plan to make several additional improvements, including creating slightly smaller and lighter cubes and exploring better ways to represent the syntax of flow-of-

Figure 4.3.   In our first round of evaluation in classrooms we used wooden blocks shaped like jigsaw puzzle pieces.

control structures such as loops, parameters, and branches. Children also struggle with the mechanics of downloading their program to a robot. This process involves several discrete steps: (1) turning the robot on; (2) placing the robot in front of an infrared transmitter; (3) placing their program in front of the web camera; (4) pressing the space bar on the computer; and (5) waiting several seconds for their code to download to the robot. From our experience, this process is still too complicated to be practical for young children. It is easy to forget a step, and there are multiple points of possible failure. For example, a child might do everything right but have the robot pointing in the wrong direction. Or, a child might accidentally cover up one of the computer vision fiducials while the computer is taking a picture of the program. In these cases, it is difficult for children to diagnose and fix the problem without the help of an adult. We are investigating a number of potential improvements to this system to simplify the process and reduce the amount of adult assistance necessary.

CONCLUSION

We face a challenging time in early childhood education. On the one hand, there are stepped up federally-mandated academic demands and a growing concern to respect children's developmental stages. On the other hand, there has not been yet a profound re-thinking of what young children can learn in terms of technology, nor do we have research-based evidence to evaluate children's developmental capabilities with innovative technologies. The emphasis on developmentally appropriate practice and the lack of adequate technologies have severely limited our approach to early childhood education. Our work brings together contributions to the fields of child development, early childhood education, and human-computer interaction. The overarching goal is to provide an empirical foundation for the development of future curriculum and technology for use in early childhood education. The project also proposes to take an unprecedented look at what young children can accomplish with technology when given tools that are truly age-appropriate, and what kind of powerful ideas they are able to learn when programming robots. Furthermore, by conducting the evaluation in the context of a curriculum that introduces increasingly sophisticated concepts of computer programming, our work hopes to build a broad understanding for the scope of young children's abilities to engage in computer programming and robotics activities that can inform educational reform in early childhood.

ACKNOWLEDGMENTS

We thank our collaborators at the Tufts University Developmental Technologies Research Group and the Human-Computer Interaction Laboratory including Laura Beals, Kathryn Cantrell, Clement Chau, Jordan Crouser, Rachael Fein, Robert Jacob, Nauman Khan, Emily Lin, Keiko Satoh, and Erin Solovey. Mary Murray from the Massachusetts College of Art and Design provided refreshing insights and designs for our tangible programming language. Finally, we thank the National Science Foundation for support of this research (NSF Grants IIS-0414389 and DRL-0735657). Any opinions, findings, and conclusions or recommendations expressed in this article are those of the authors and do not necessarily reflect the views of the National Science Foundation.

NOTES

1. As of 2006, 37 states have included engineering/technology standards in their educational frameworks.
2. http://www.legoengineering.com/

REFERENCES

Beals, L., & Bers, M. (2006). Robotic technologies: when parents put their learning ahead of their child's. *Journal of Interactive Learning Research, 17*(4), 341-366.

Ben-Ari, M. (1998). Constructivism in computer science education. In *Proceedings of the Technical Symposium on Computer Science Education SIGCSE'98* (pp. 257-261). Atlanta, GA: ACM Press.

Bers, M. U. (2008). *Blocks, robots and computers: learning about technology in early childhood.* New York: Teacher's College Press.

Bers, M. U., Ponte, I., Juelich, K., Viera, A., & Schenker, J. (2002). Teachers as designers: integrating robotics into early childhood education. *Information Technology in Childhood Education,* 123-145.

Bers, M. U., Rogers, C., Beals, L., Portsmore, M., Staszowski, K., Cejka, E., et al. (2006). Innovative session: early childhood robotics for learning. In *Proceedings International Conference on Learning Sciences* ICLS'06 (pp. 1036-1042). Bloomington, IN: International Society of the Learning Sciences.

Cejka, E., Rogers, C., & Portsmore, M. (2006). Kindergarten robotics: using robotics to motivate math, science, and engineering literacy in elementary school. *International Journal of Engineering Education, 22*(4), 711-722.

Clements, D. (1999). The future of educational computing research: the case of computer programming. *Information Technology in Childhood Education Annual,* 147-179.

Clements, D., & Sarama, J. (2002). The role of technology in early childhood learning. *Teaching Children Mathematics, 8*(6), 340-343.

Clements, D., & Sarama, J. (2003). Strip mining for gold: research and policy in educational technology: a response to "Fool's Gold." *Association for the Advancement of Computing in Education Journal, 11*(1), 7-69.

Copple, C., & Bredekamp, S. (2009). *Developmentally appropriate practice in early childhood programs: serving children from birth through age 8* (3rd ed.). Washington, DC: National Association for the Education of Young Children.

Design-Based Research Collective. (2003). Design-based research: An emerging paradigm for educational inquiry. *Educational Researcher, 32*(1), 5-8.

Gershenfeld, N. (2000). *When things start to think*. New York, NY: Henry Hold and Co.

Haugland, S.W. (1992). The effect of computer software on preschool children's developmental gains. *Journal of Computing in Childhood Education, 3*(1), 15-30.

Horn, M. S., & Jacob, R. J. K. (2007). Designing tangible programming languages for classroom use. In *Proceedings TEI'07 First International Conference on Tangible and Embedded Interaction*. Baton Rouge, LA: ACM Press.

Hourcade, J. P., Bederson, B. B., Druin, A., & Guimbretière, F. (2004). Differences in pointing task performance between preschool children and adults using mice. *ACM Transactions on Computer-Human Interaction, 11*(4), 357-386.

Kelleher, C., & Pausch, R. (2005). Lowering the barriers to programming: A survey of programming environments and languages for novice programmers. *ACM Computing Surveys, 37*(2), 83-137.

McKeithen, K. B., Reitman, J. S., Rueter, H. H., & Hirtle, S.C. (1981). Knowledge organization and skill differences in computer programmers. *Cognitive Psychology, 13*, 307-325.

McNerney, T. S. (2004). From turtles to tangible programming bricks: Explorations in physical language design. *Personal and Ubiquitous Computing, 8*(5), 326-337.

Norman, D. (1986). Cognitive engineering. In D. A. Norman & S. W. Draper (Eds.), *User centered system design: New perspectives on human-computer interaction* (pp. 31-61). Hillsdale, NJ: Erlbaum.

Papert, S. (1991). What's the big idea: Towards a pedagogy of idea power. *IBM Systems Journal, 39*(3-4), 720-729.

Perlman, R. (1976). Using computer technology to provide a creative learning environment for preschool children. *Logo memo no 24*, Cambridge, MA: MIT Artificial Intelligence Laboratory Publications 260.

Rader, C., Brand, C., & Lewis, C. (1997). Degrees of comprehension: children's understanding of a visual programming environment. In *Proceedings ACM Conference on Human Factors in Computing Systems CHI'99* (pp. 351-358). Atlanta, GA: ACM Press.

Resnick, M. (2003), Playful learning and creative societies. *Education Update, 8*(6). Retrieved May 1, 2009 from http://web.media.mit.edu/~mres/papers/education-update.pdf

Resnick, M., Martin, F., Berg, R., Borovoy, R., Colella, V., Kramer, K., et al. (1998). Digital manipulatives: New toys to think with. In Proceedings ACM *Conference on Human Factors in Computing Systems CHI '98* (pp. 281-287). Los Angeles, CA: ACM Press.

Richardson, K. (1998). *Models of cognitive development.* East Sussex, England: Psychology Press.

Rogers, C., & Portsmore, M. (2004). Bringing engineering to elementary school. *Journal of STEM Education, 5*(3,4), 17-28.

Smith, A. (2007). Using magnets in physical blocks that behave as programming objects. In *Proceedings First International Conference on Tangible and Embedded Interaction, TEI'07* (pp. 147-150). Baton Rouge, LA: ACM Press.

Suzuki, H., & Kato, H. (1995). Interaction-level support for collaborative learning: algoblock–an open programming language. In *Proceedings Computer Support for Collaborative Learning CSCL'95* (pp. 349-355). Hillsdale, NJ: Erlbaum.

Wang, X. C., & Ching, C. C. (2003). Social construction of computer experience in a first-grade classroom: social processes and mediating artifacts. *Early Education and Development, 14*(3), 335-361.

Wyeth, P. (2008). How young children learn to program with sensor, action, and logic blocks. *International Journal of the Learning Sciences, 17*(4), 517-550.

CHAPTER 5

DEVELOPING A CYBERSAFETY PROGRAM FOR EARLY CHILDHOOD EDUCATION

A New Zealand Case Study

Richard Beach

Young children are our most precious resource. As role models, parents and educators have both a moral and legal responsibility to ensure all practical measures are taken to provide a physically and emotionally safe environment in which young children may flourish. Information and communication technology (ICT) is opening up new opportunities for learning and discovery. It is changing the way people communicate, and it is allowing families to become more involved in their children's learning, even when distance separates them. The use of ICT in the learning environment does, however, come with some risk. Nevertheless, that risk can be managed and need not detract from the ultimate goal of ICT in education - to improve learning.

NetSafe has been working with the early childhood education (ECE) sector in New Zealand since 2005, developing model cybersafety policies,

High-Tech Tots: Childhood in a Digital World, pp. 71–92
Copyright © 2010 by Information Age Publishing
All rights of reproduction in any form reserved.

professional learning opportunities, and guidance and advice in the areas of ICT use and infrastructure, as well as cybersafety education. This chapter begins with an initial explanation of the NetSafe organization. The context is then set by introducing the New Zealand ECE environment, the setting, the curriculum, the diverse nature of services, and the regulatory system. A brief overview includes how ICT has been introduced into the ECE environment, how ICT is used in a typical New Zealand ECE service, how and why such use is promoted, and how teachers and educators access professional development. The chapter provides a summary of various risks to services themselves and to young children, which have become apparent through both research and anecdotal evidence. The chapter concludes by discussing the development of the NetSafe response to these identified risks. This response was largely comprised of the Net-Safe Kit for ECE and associated resources, including professional learning opportunities. Answers to how and why the Kit took the shape it did, and what evidence exists backing up the information and strategies it contains, are detailed.

THE NETSAFE PROGRAM FOR ECE

NetSafe is a not-for-profit organization and is recognized as New Zealand's independent provider of cybersafety advice, resources, and education. NetSafe is designated as a lead organization in the government's digital strategy under the "confidence" strand.

The Internet Safety Group Inc. (ISG) was founded in 1998 and began as a small group of interested and concerned citizens who wished to confront issues in Internet safety for New Zealanders. The group has grown steadily over the years, and there are now approximately 65 members. The ISG is managed by a six member board of directors and a full-time executive director. In 2008 the ISG changed its name to NetSafe Incorporated.

Since its inception, NetSafe's work has been supported by the New Zealand Ministry of Education. In what is believed to be a unique relationship internationally, NetSafe is contracted by the Ministry to provide cybersafety education and advice to the compulsory education sector, schools catering to students from year 0 through to year 13. Although many cybersafety organizations exist in other parts of the world, NetSafe's relationship with the New Zealand Ministry of Education and the compulsory education sector is recognized internationally as an innovative example of a positive and proactive approach to cybersafety.

NetSafe has been effective in developing a comprehensive national cybersafety initiative because of the broad range of its membership, its moderate and consistent messages, and its collaborative consultation style. NetSafe takes a positive approach to technology, seeking to enable users to experience the benefits technology brings, while raising awareness of and helping to minimize the associated risks.

NetSafe's work in the education sector is based on the premise that cybersafety is a learning enabler. From the outset, NetSafe has been supportive of the use of ICT in education. The degree to which the benefits can be realized, however, is impacted negatively in situations where unnecessary risk exists and is not managed effectively. Cybersafety incidents can have severe implications for the confidence of teachers and learners to engage with and use ICT to maximize learning.

The development by NetSafe of a cybersafety program for Early Childhood Education (ECE) began in 2005, almost two years before the NetSafe survey of ECE services was carried out. NetSafe had long intended to move into the ECE sector, and in August of that year, IBM presented a proposal to develop a cybersafety resource to accompany the Kidsmart computers the company donates to ECE services. A contract between NetSafe and IBM was drawn up, the deliverables being a cybersafety resource (which eventually became the "First Steps to Cybersafety" pamphlet), and a set of cybersafety policy and acceptable use agreement templates which would be made freely available to ECE services.

The New Zealand ECE Environment

New Zealand is a country of slightly over 4 million inhabitants (4,027,947 as of the 2006 census) and like many Western countries, has an aging population. Seven percent of the population is under 5 years of age. Five is the usual enrollment age into the compulsory school system, and all children must attend school by age 6. Enrollment in early childhood education is voluntary.

Despite it being voluntary, statistics from the Data Management Unit of the Ministry of Education (2008) show a 100% enrolment rate for 3- and 4- year-olds at an ECE service. This figure is slightly inflated as many children attend more than one service and are therefore included twice. Indeed, one of the biggest barriers to participation at the ECE level, particularly in populous, lower socioeconomic areas, is capacity. This problem has been highlighted more recently with the introduction of the Labor Government's 20 Free Hours policy, which entitles every 3- and 4- year old to 20 free hours of enrollment at an ECE service per week.

In all, there were 4,649 ECE services in July 2008. These range in type from kindergartens (which are lead by trained teachers), to play centers (led by volunteer parents), to education and care Services (privately run services), and to home based networks and playgroups. Also included in the total were 470 Kohanga Reo in which Te Reo (the language of the indigenous Maori) is used exclusively.

At this time, the regulatory system is in a state of flux. New ECE regulations were introduced in July 2008. The regulations cover a wide range of standards including health and safety, which must be met in order for a service to hold a license. All ECE services must be licensed with one exception; services which operate for less than 3 hours per day, and at which more than half of the children attend with their parents, are classified as "license exempt."

Services also have the option to become "chartered," which binds them to additional Ministry of Education guidelines, but in turn attracts central government funding. As of July 2008, there were 3,881 licensed and/or chartered services.

The national curriculum for ECE is Te Whāriki. It was released in 1996 and at the time of writing this paper, is also subject to review. The purpose of Te Whāriki was to bring consistency to the curriculum and programs in chartered early childhood services. Te Whāriki follows the New Zealand tradition of comparatively nonprescriptive curriculum statements and focuses on developing the "whole child." Strands are used to describe different areas of learning and development such as "wellbeing," "contribution," and "communication."

The Place of ICT in New Zealand ECE Services

The first substantial research into the use of ICT in New Zealand ECE services was carried out by the New Zealand Council for Educational Research (NZCER) in 2003 (Mitchell & Brooking, 2007). A full discussion of the findings appeared in Bolstad's (2004) *The Role and Potential of ICT in Early Childhood Education*. The research found that most ECE professionals had access to the Internet in their centers; although 42% said such access was very poor or nonexistent. Approximately 52% stated that children do not use the computers at the center at all. When the computer was used, the main activities involved pattern or alphabet recognition and games. Nearly 90% of teachers reported using photography to gather information about children's learning, but less than 30% said this information was used to help children reflect on their own learning. About 41% reported using a computerized Early Childhood Management System.

These findings were used to inform a strategy document that was published by the New Zealand Ministry of Education in 2005. *Foundations for Discovery* was intended to provide a guide to inform effective ICT development, use, and investment in the ECE sector. The document was accompanied by a DVD showing (as described on the DVD pocket) "innovative ways in which technology is being used with and by children, educators, and administrators in the New Zealand context." *Foundations for Discovery* was distributed widely to the sector and was built upon a number of principles, which included recognizing and addressing issues of safety and appropriateness (p. 19). The inclusion of this principle is important, as it provided a link between the work of NetSafe and the Ministry of Education's work in the ECE sector.

One of the issues identified by the 2003 NZCER survey was a perceived lack of knowledge, confidence, or expertise on the part of ECE staff. To address this issue, the Ministry of Education has funded an ICT professional learning program for early childhood educators. CORE Education (core-ed.net) was contracted to run the program, which involved 60 ECE services nationwide, and began in late 2006. A posting on the project website reports that at the midpoint of the 3-year program, the vast majority (80%) of the teachers involved were either "confident" or 'very confident' about their own and/or children's use of ICTs. More specifically, their levels of pedagogical ability increased the most in relation to using ICTs to support creativity, innovation, and fostering higher order thinking in children.

Technical infrastructure is also reported to have increased markedly:

> Over the first 18 months of the program, services have significantly increased their stocks of computers and other ICTs, and most of this increase has been in relation to ICTs located in play areas and/or for children's use. In this period, the number of laptops available for children's use in play areas has more than doubled, the number of digital still cameras, printers, scanners and video cameras have tripled, and the provision of webcams, TVs, and digital microscopes, have increased by even greater proportions. The least prevalent educational technologies in services for children's use are interactive whiteboards, data projectors, cell phones and mobile devices such as iPods, MP3, palmtops etc. (Hatherly, 2008)

With regards to the use of ICT with or by children, the most frequent activity was reported to be the documentation of learning through the use of digital cameras and the "co-writing" of learning stories. Two-thirds of the teachers reported using ICTs for this purpose.

The production of learning stories using ICTs has value in allowing children to reflect on their learning, as well as providing an authentic audience for their creative work. While at the service with parents and other family members, the child can effectively share his/her experience through these coconstructed learning stories.

As cybersafety consultants to the education sector, NetSafe has worked with services regarding both activities. NetSafe advice has been sought in incidents where personal photographs taken by staff or family members have become mixed up with photographs taken for learning stories. The most disturbing of these have involved cases where the photographs were of an inappropriate nature.

Despite the success of the professional learning program provided by CORE Education and technical assistance provided by NetSafe, educators report infrequent opportunities for professional development in ICT and training is difficult to access. This appears particularly true for regional ECE services as opposed to those in the larger cities. Issues of cost, including backfilling staff who are absent for service delivery, are also often described.

Early Childhood Education Services and Risk

A common question asked by those not familiar with cybersafety, especially with relation to the ECE sector, is whether there is really any risk. After all, ECE services are closely monitored environments, and the children are surely far too young to cause any concerns. The response requires some knowledge of what use is made of ICT in ECE services and by whom, such as recording of sensitive and confidential personal and financial details, the degree to which personal ICT is used for service duties, and the access to reliable technical support that ECE services may or may not have.

In addition to this, it is worth considering the term "risk" itself. A common understanding of risk is "something that is dangerous." However, risk can have a more specific meaning such as "the potential loss that can occur." In information security circles, two other terms are often used alongside risk; vulnerability and threat. Vulnerability is a characteristic of a system which may potentially provide an avenue for attack; for example a bug in a piece of software may be considered a vulnerability, as it could be exploited by a malicious party to compromise the system itself. One vulnerability in an ECE environment may be unsupervised Internet access by children. A threat is the potential danger that a vulnerability will be exploited by a threat agent such as a hacker, malware, or online predator. Therefore, plugging vulnerabilities reduces exposure to threats, reducing potential losses (risk).

NetSafe surveyed New Zealand ECE services in 2007, in order to understand what vulnerabilities may be present with the use of ICT in the ECE sector. The findings would assist NetSafe to work with services on mitigating the associated risks.

The Early Childhood Council (ECC) agreed to pilot an initial online delivery of a cybersafety survey to its members at no cost. With over 1,000 licensed education and care centers as members of the ECC, the organization is the largest representative body of early childhood centers in New Zealand. Although the response rate was not high, the feedback was extremely useful in the development of the final survey methodology and tool.

Following the pilot survey, the Ministry of Education agreed to fund the development and distribution of a national survey, and in February 2007, 205 services responded to a mixture of paper and telephone based survey formats. The survey had six objectives:

1. To gather and analyze data on:

    (a) The basic set up and use of computers in centers, including connection to the Internet.
    (b) Measures in place regarding security and safety practices including:

        (i)   Administrative controls
        (ii)   Electronic security
        (iii) Cybersafety education

2. To use the data obtained to assist the further development of cybersafety practices, procedures, and professional learning within this sector.
3. To use the data to assist development of a consistent approach to cybersafety best practice across the sector and the variety of services.
4. To use the data to identify issues and concerns requiring follow-up (e.g., intervention, more in depth research).
5. To inform the sector and wider society of the state of play with regards to cybersafety practices and issues for ECE.
6. To provide a baseline for comparison with a similar survey in 2-3 years, which would help stakeholders identify trends and evaluate the efficacy of projects and initiatives.

The survey revealed ICT appeared to be almost universally integrated into the ECE sector in New Zealand. About 95% of the sample used ICT in their center/work, 73% of all centers had Internet access, and 65% of those accessed the Internet via a broadband connection. This information was in line with what was expected and demonstrated an increase of the integration of ICT into ECE environments from the NZCER survey mentioned earlier.

Approximately 60% of children were likely to be using ICT in the learning environment. Among the respondents, 40% of centers with computers had Internet filtering in place, and 23% reported including the "safe and responsible use of ICT" in their teaching program.

Implications of the Survey Data

Policies and Procedures

In an ideal world, a policy which outlines the expectations, responsibilities, and procedures that will help ensure that safe and responsible use is made of an organization's ICT would be in place in every service prior to the introduction of any ICT. Just 36.1% of all the ECE services reported actually having any form of cybersafety policy in place. Even fewer services (17.6%) reported a requirement for staff and volunteers to sign a use agreement before using service ICT.

Despite feedback given by NetSafe during the review of the ECE regulations, it is not compulsory for ECE services to have a cybersafety or acceptable use policy. The fact that so few services have proactively introduced a policy covering the safe and responsible use of ICT arguably demonstrates that most services were taking advantage of the benefits of ICT before consideration was given to cybersafety.

In the event of a cybersafety incident, the details of the incident and of the responses taken by the organization should be documented. This log can then be used during a review of cybersafety policy and procedures, or possibly in any resulting investigation that may take place. Nearly 22% of services reported having some form of register which may be used to fulfill this function. This would seem to be low, given that incidents of another nature, such as traditional health and safety issues, are generally well logged.

These figures prove that by far, the majority of services did not have any guidelines or procedures in place governing the safe and responsible use of ICT. Of those that did, less than half were following best practice in informing educators of how these policies apply to their day to day use of the technologies. Furthermore, less than a quarter of services had a place to document cybersafety incidents and their associated response, making subsequent review and investigation extremely difficult.

Electronic Security

The survey revealed some worrying vulnerabilities with regards to electronic security. Research carried out by NetSafe in 2006 found that a computer that went online via a broadband connection could expect to be scanned (unauthorized attempt to identify vulnerabilities on the system) by an unknown, potentially malicious attacker, within 30 seconds. However, basic electronic security was lacking in 9 out of 10 ECE services. Basic electronic security requires regular updates to the operating system, antivirus and antispyware software, and firewall. Given that 73% of services had Internet access (65% of those via broadband), it was worrying that the incidence of basic electronic security was so rare.

The vast majority of services (95%) reported using their ICT for administrative work. This work potentially involves the collection and storage of sensitive data, such as personal or financial details. Under the NZ Privacy Act 1993 (New Zealand Government, 1993), any organization that collects personal information is required to protect that information, using such security safeguards as is reasonable to implement under the circumstances. Just over one quarter of the centers were not backing up their data and were therefore potentially at risk of losing most or all of this data in the event of a serious system failure, theft, or destruction.

Current versions of Microsoft Windows XP, Vista, and Windows 7 all have a firewall, antispyware product, and automatic update capabilities built in. Various antivirus products are readily available either for purchase or as free downloads. Mac OSX also has a built in firewall and automatic update capability, and antimalware packages are also available for this platform. Considering the availability of basic electronic security, it is reasonable to expect an ECE service to have such measures in place. A service facing legal action as a result of a cybersafety incident may have difficulty explaining why such measures were not in place.

Over 22% of services with computers utilized individual user accounts. In addition to the basic electronic security measures already mentioned, the use of strong passwords and individual user accounts can also assist in the prevention and/or investigation of cybersafety incidents. Individual user accounts have the added benefits of allowing workspaces to be customized to a user's needs, tracking the use made of network resources, and enabling resources to be organized and accessed according to user or role.

Just over half (51%) of the sample were using "shared accounts" (where two or more people share the same account name and password). For each person who uses a shared password, there exists a possible point of compromise. That person may write down the password, or share it with an unauthorized user either knowingly or unknowingly ("shoulder surfing" for example is when a person obtains a password by watching a user log in). In addition, over 30% of centers were using no passwords whatsoever to restrict or monitor access to their computers or network.

The survey also asked whether children attending the service were using passwords. Most (90%) were not. Less than 2% of services indicated that children had individual passwords. Teaching small children to use passwords may be an important early step towards developing safe cyber-citizens. Throughout their lives, children will encounter an increasing array of instances where they will be required to "authenticate" themselves to a system, person, or organization. While technology may develop to a point where remembering a password is no longer necessary (e.g., through inexpensive and reliable biometric authentication such as thumb-print or retinal scanning), there will always remain a need for an awareness about such security measures, as well as some strategies for protecting the "keys" (passwords, pin-codes, cards, secret questions, etc.) that allow access.

Three and 4-year-olds can be trained to use simple passwords. A child's logon can then also be used to separate the learning resources available for the children, from the "administrative" resources used by educators, thus simplifying the environment for children and providing an extra layer of security.

Filtering

Among the respondents to the NetSafe survey, 40% of services indicated that some form of filtering was in place. There is some debate within Internet safety circles about the effectiveness of filtering. Some opponents of filtering argue that without exposure to risk, users (including children) will not have the opportunity to learn how to react to potentially harmful material in a safe way. This, in turn, could engender a false sense of security where too much trust is put in electronic security measures, rather than efforts to educate about risk management/avoidance strategies.

Content filtering is an effective means of avoiding accidental access to inappropriate material from the Internet. Falling victim to cybersquatting (where a website is set up with an address that is very close to a legitimate website's address), spam e-mail that contains inappropriate images or content, or clicking on a link within a set of search results that turns out to be inappropriate, are all scenarios that could possibly be avoided through effective filtering.

That said, strategies for circumventing filtering products do exist and are easily discovered online. NetSafe has dealt with cases of primary school children thwarting filtering systems in place at schools. Also, false-positives (blocking legitimate content) do occur, and not all inappropriate content finds its way into an organization via the Internet.

Education

Nearly 24% of services surveyed said that "safe and responsible use of ICT" was included in their teaching program. Even if this teaching was comprehensive enough to include strategies for dealing with risky situations online, when considered together, these results suggest that more faith was being placed on technological solutions than educative opportunities.

Issues arise when privately-owned ICT is used for work off-site; for example, a teacher using their home computer for planning, creating learning stories, and so on. This appeared commonplace, with 70% of services reporting that privately-owned ICT is used for service work. This would seem to indicate that the ECE sector relies heavily on the goodwill of educators and volunteers. While it is pleasing that such generosity of time and resources is available, as services rely more and more on ICT, conflicts between security, convenience, and generosity of personal time arise. When educators use their home computers or other equipment to complete their work, they may unwittingly expose their own, or the service's computers, to viruses and other malware as they transfer files. They may also be moving sensitive or confidential data to their own computers. If their home computer is compromised or damaged in some way while performing service work, the ECE service may possibly be asked to cover some or all of the costs. Other family members may also have access to the home computer and possibly any sensitive or confidential information it may contain.

First Steps

In August 2005, an initial consultation meeting was held at the NetSafe offices. Attendees were invited from every major ECE umbrella organization, several individual services, the Ministry of Education, as well as a number of key contributors to NetSafe's work in schools, such as forensic and other ICT experts, and school principals. The purpose of this initial meeting was to introduce the concept of cybersafety to the ECE sector, and to begin to engage the sector in the creation of the deliverables of the contract with IBM.

The day was spent sharing NetSafe experiences in the school sector, and it was also an opportunity for the NetSafe team to learn more about the ECE sector in general, and how services were using technology. Much sharing of anecdotes took place, and by the end of the day, a positive atmosphere had been developed full of promise for the future development of a comprehensive cybersafety program for ECE.

Three months later, the consultation group met again, this time for 2 days to plan in more detail the content of the *First Steps* pamphlet and the policy and use agreement templates. As part of the initial round of welcomes, the members were asked to describe how their thoughts and perceptions on cybersafety and the use of ICT in their sector had changed in the intervening weeks since the first meeting. Almost everyone had a story to tell, usually related to situations that had existed previously, but were only recognized now that they were looking with a new awareness of the risks. The stories included such situations as visitors to the services caught prying through staff mobile phone contents or taking photographs of children without permission, backup disks of administration data being found to be completely blank, and even inappropriate websites being saved as favorites on the computers being used by staff with children.

Much of the second day was spent discussing the feasibility and content of cybersafety professional learning opportunities for the sector. As the session drew to a close, it was decided that such was the need for the ECE sector to be made aware of cybersafety issues that NetSafe would develop professional learning, regardless of the fact that there was no funding immediately available.

This approach was not unfamiliar to the organization, as this was how the original 2000 Internet Safety Kit for schools came about. It was written and put together through the goodwill and expertise of a range of people in the education, community, and commercial sectors. Child, Youth and Family Services and the Ministry of Education joined as sponsors in the latter stages to enable the kit to be distributed as a free resource to all New Zealand schools.

One of the most significant observations in this process was the willingness of such a diverse range of organizations and individuals to come together with the intention of putting in place a plan of action. This spirit of collaboration has continued throughout the development of the cybersafety program for ECE.

On Wednesday, March 22, 2006 the First Steps resource (NetSafe, 2006) was officially launched. The resource takes the form of a color trifold pamphlet aimed at services, as well as parents and caregivers of young children. An illustration on the cover was modeled on a drawing by one of the NetSafe ECE Manager's children, and the green and blue colors throughout have been used as a theme for subsequent ECE cybersafety resources.

20,000 copies of *First Steps to Cybersafety—Online Safety for the Early Years* pamphlet were printed, and several copies each were distributed to all ECE services, along with a cover letter announcing the launch of the NetSafe cybersafety program for ECE. Printing and distribution costs were met using funding from the contract with IBM and a separate contract with the Ministry of Education. This marked the first contribution by the Ministry into cybersafety initiatives for the ECE sector.

At the same time as the brochure was launched, NetSafe published a Cybersafety Policy template and an acceptable use agreement (AUA) template for employees and volunteers working in ECE services. An AUA for parents and visitors to services was also published. Prior to publication, these documents were subjected to rigorous consultation with education law specialists (both independent and within the Ministry of Education), IT professionals, a senior advocate from the Office for the Commissioner for Children, the NZEI, and members from the consultation group. The documents are available for free download from the NetSafe website and are reviewed on a regular basis. Services are encouraged to customize the documents to their individual requirements. Some umbrella associations, such as the Auckland Kindergarten Association and the Canterbury Playcenter Association, have taken these documents, modified them, and distributed them across their member services.

Professional Learning for ECE Educators

Development of ECE cybersafety professional learning modules began on December 8, 2005 with a full day workshop held at NetSafe. The workshop was again attended by representatives from across the ECE sector, as well as NetSafe staff and other professionals previously involved with the development and delivery of NetSafe training modules in the compulsory school sector.

Some main points for consideration when developing the ECE modules, which the consultation group identified, were:

- The modules should focus on positive prevention of risks, rather than reactive measures.
- The training should include practical resources to help keep ECE services cybersafe (e.g., checklists, templates).
- Skills such as safe searching and effective back-ups should be included.
- The training should be presented in plain English.
- There should be a consistency of message through the resources.
- Attendance costs need to be kept down to encourage good participation.

Drafting of the training modules began in April 2006 once a tentative delivery schedule was known. Two modules were produced. The first focused on managerial and educational aspects of cybersafety, such as policy development and the integration of cybersafety into learning programs. The second module focused on technical aspects including electronic security, network documentation, and technical support issues.

In an attempt to encourage maximum participation from across the ECE sector, it was decided that places in the trial workshops should be available at little or no cost to the attendees. A funding proposal was lodged with the Ministry of Education, who contributed a significant amount toward the costs of running the trials. The Ministry's contribution allowed the workshop to be provided free to attendees, who were also able to claim travel costs and the cost of relief staff back at their respective services where necessary. This offer contributed significantly to the successful running of the trials.

Encouraging Participation

A variety of methods were used for coopting attendees. In Manukau, NetSafe worked with COMET (City of Manukau Education Trust), who had already established some links with ECE services through previous projects. In Southland, an ECE ICT support/training facilitator, employed under a contract with the Community Trust of Southland, was asked to rally participants using her local links. Christchurch was targeted using an e-mail campaign, Bay of Plenty through umbrella association links, and Northland initially via e-mail and then using hard copy flyers through the post, followed up by numerous phone calls.

As well as these methods, interest in the trials was raised via conferences and presentations to association meetings. For example, a cybersafety seminar was held as part of the Early Childhood Council conference in Rotorua in April 2006, and a presentation given to the Kindergarten Inc. meeting in Wellington at the beginning of May. At these events, registration of interest forms were distributed and collected.

Feedback was sought both during the sessions and following them by way of a response form which was available electronically and in hardcopy. This feedback was considered when modifying the modules for the subsequent sessions. Much of the feedback was extremely useful for adapting and improving both content and delivery.

Informal and formal feedback was also received following the delivery of the final session. This feedback proved invaluable when producing a final version of the materials and delivery plan, prior to the official launch of the training modules.

Most comments were extremely positive about both the content, and the opportunity for training provided by the trial project;

> Found this course thoroughly enjoyable, user friendly, easy to follow course content but above all INFORMATIVE. I got a lot of practical information that I could take back to work and use.

NetSafe is meeting a need in the education community—I think the more education you can give us the better. Thanks.

Brilliant—a boost to get me up to the mark!

For me it identified outcomes of appropriate and inappropriate practices and how they can impact on the centre—not only the children but staff, parents, students and visitors. It has created for me such awareness that I will be observing and questioning many more practices. (names withheld)

As part of the funding contract with the Ministry, NetSafe produced a final report at the conclusion of the trials. The report included a number of recommendations for the final rollout of the training to the sector. On October 11, 2006, a review and planning meeting was held at IBM in Wellington. Key sector representatives were invited to hear about the results of the trials and to advise in the direction of further development of cybersafety initiatives for the ECE sector. Many issues were discussed at the meeting, including the feasibility of providing a centrally funded software or laptop program to the sector, the safety and security benefits of having up to date hardware and software, and how the professional learning modules might be delivered.

Feedback from the trial had suggested that there was crossover in the content of the workshops that could be trimmed out. The conversation turned to the possibility of shifting some of this online, and on January 31, 2007 the first participant registered for what is believed to be the world's first e-learning cybersafety course specifically designed for ECE educators. In fact, the course is designed as a prerequisite to attendance on either of the 2½ day workshops which evolved out of the full day workshops developed for the trials.

Since January 2007, there have been over 1,000 completions of the online cybersafety course; each one representing an ECE educator who now has a basic foundation knowledge of cybersafety. Most of those have also taken part in the guided workshop sessions, further strengthening their understanding of the topic as well their ability to transfer this knowledge into action.

The NetSafe Kit for ECE

When NetSafe began developing the cybersafety program for schools, one of the first resources to be produced was the Internet Safety Kit in 2000. The 2003 NetSafe Kit for Schools was used as a blueprint for Becta's e-Safety resource which was distributed to U.K. schools in 2005. The 2007 version of the NetSafe Kit for Schools is available online and is considered the reference point for developing and maintaining a cybersafe learning environment for schools. The state of Georgia has obtained a license to adapt and redistribute the 2007 NetSafe Kit to schools in Georgia. Over time, professional development, a helpline, printed materials, and other resources have been developed to help schools implement the advice given in the NetSafe Kit.

NetSafe's work with the ECE sector took a slightly different approach. The advice and support that NetSafe has had from various ECE sector organizations, coupled with a real willingness on the part of the sector to see some tangible outcomes, meant that many of the resources which would otherwise support a "Kit for ECE" were in fact created independently prior to writing of the kit itself. Resources, templates, professional learning, articles in sector publications, presentations, a helpline, and research were all implemented before any such overarching guidelines or advice in the form of a "NetSafe Kit for ECE" existed.

This is reflective perhaps of both the scope and the speed with which those on the ground in the ECE sector have integrated ICT as a powerful learning and administration tool. For any number of reasons, educators in all sectors find themselves under pressure to use the latest ICT tools. This is sometimes driven by policymakers wanting to show a commitment to introducing the latest technology. Other times it is education "thought leaders" who enthusiastically proselytize the use of ICT because in their view it assists learning.

Rarely does such pressure come hand in hand with meaningful offers of training in the use of such technologies, or practical, timely assistance in planning for their integration into the learning environment. Consequently, the implications, particularly where the safety and privacy of children and educators is concerned, can easily be overlooked.

Eventually the time came for the publication of a practical toolkit to help busy ECE educators grapple with the sorts of safety and security issues that this rapid uptake of technology brings. The NetSafe Kit for ECE was launched in April 2008, again with the funding support from the Ministry of Education. The kit itself is a forty page document in two sections. Section one introduces the concept of cybersafety, and outlines some of the risks as well as the legal and regulatory requirements facing ECE services. Section two then presents the comprehensive NetSafe approach to implementing a cybersafety program in an ECE service.

Several thousand copies of the kit were printed, and at least one was distributed to every ECE service in New Zealand. Attendees at the professional learning workshops all receive their own personal copy of the NetSafe Kit for ECE, which is also available as a free download from the NetSafe website.

Recent Developments

Looking back at the objectives of the 2007 survey, there can be no doubt that the results have contributed to the ongoing development of cybersafety support and services to the ECE sector. With the support of the Ministry of Education and many stakeholders within the sector, both individuals and organizations, NetSafe has continued to produce resources, training, and support for ECE services across New Zealand. The work has also encouraged the Ministry of Education to develop its own resources focusing on cybersafety.

In December 2008, the Ministry released a DVD titled *Cyber-Citizens & Cybersafe*. The 24 minute film interviews a number of information security professionals as well as ECE professionals, including practicing teachers. Much of the advice within the film mirrors the strategy outlined in the NetSafe Kit for ECE.

The Ministry of Education has also developed its own policy and guidelines for ECE services with regards to cybersafety (Ministry of Education, 2008). It is currently unclear as to whether the recommendations in this document will become incorporated into the ECE regulatory system. The document has been written in a style which reflects information security guidelines designed for use by government departments. It will be interesting to see how the document is received by the sector once it is more broadly promoted.

A Learning Pathway for Cybercitizens

A broader piece of work from NetSafe, which is designed to be utilized in both the ECE and compulsory school sectors, is the Cybercitizenship Pathway. Both the NetSafe Kit for Schools and the NetSafe Kit for ECE base their programs on a three pronged model of cybersafety: appropriate policies, use agreements, and procedures; an effective electronic security system; and a comprehensive cybersafety education program for the school or service's community. Much of the advice contained in the kits relates to setting up the administrative and technical infrastructure of the cybersafety program.

Although NetSafe representatives spend countless hours promoting cybersafety within schools, and have developed training materials for educators in both sectors, the creation of cybercitizenship resources for teachers to use with their students has not previously been a feature of NetSafe's work. In 2008 this was addressed with the release of the Cybercitizenship Pathway. The document provides a curriculum overview for teachers. It is presented as a table of seven columns by three rows. The columns relate to a progression of learning stages beginning at ECE level and ending with year 11-13, which is usually the final 3 years of a student's secondary education. These seven columns are further described by four stages: beginner, apprentice, practitioner, and master. The rows reflect three attributes of cybercitizenship: "connected" which implies having an understanding of the impacts and potential of technology for individuals and society; "safe" which means having and applying personal safety strategies; and "responsible" which requires an understanding and willingness to follow and promote cybersafety guidelines which support community safety and wellbeing.

Table cells contain learning objectives, which progress as one moves through the table from left to right along each row. Clicking on the cell takes the user to a second level page that contains links to resources, which teachers may find useful to facilitate teaching the related learning objective. The resources include printable lesson plans and online resources such as websites, video clips, and other materials produced by NetSafe and other organizations from New Zealand and international sources.

The Cybercitizenship Pathway is intended to provide an easy to use framework which serves also as a tool to aid teachers as they plan their programs. The pedagogical emphasis is on the integration of cybercitizenship into teaching programs across all subjects rather than as a set of cybersafety lessons taught in isolation.

At the ECE level, the focus falls on identifying and naming some fundamental technologies and their uses, identifying people who can help, seeking their help when appropriate, and following family and group guidelines for using ICT. While the pathway does provide starters for early childhood educators wishing to incorporate cybercitizenship education into their programs, NetSafe also places significant emphasis on the place of educators as role models. This is outlined in the NetSafe Kit for ECE which provides several examples of how educators can model cybercitizenship:

- Asking children if it's okay to take their photograph
- Being seen to be using passwords when accessing computers
- Demonstrating effective searching by discussing key words before using search engines
- Exhibiting discretion when viewing search results
- Using "nicknames" when entering details into websites which require users to log on
- Seeking help if they are having difficulty using the ICT
- Showing consideration for others when communicating online

- Thinking carefully about how they present themselves online
- Demonstrating calm and appropriate responses to incidents which may occur.

A Moderate Approach—A Positive View of Technology

Internationally, cybersafety has become a multimillion dollar industry. Dozens of organizations vie for funding and sponsorship. Experts abound, some seeking rock star status using their name like a brand. Net-Safe is the sole organization in New Zealand providing cybersafety advice as its core business. Although it depends on media coverage to disseminate its messages of safety and responsibility, NetSafe does not promote scare tactics, or position itself as an expert on subjects it is not. Without buy in from a sector, NetSafe cannot hope to operate there. In education, a moderate message and a collaborative approach have enabled NetSafe to earn respect from stakeholders, ranging from the Ministry of Education to individual schools, teachers, and ECE services.

Collaboration—We All Have Something to Offer

Effective cybersafety requires group responsibility. The development of the NetSafe cybersafety program for ECE has modeled this point. From the beginning NetSafe sought input from across the ECE sector at all levels. Consultation groups included educators, managers, government agencies, and parents. Even young children were involved in the development of some of the resources. A comment was made at the initial consultation meeting that this was the first time some of these sector groups had sat across a table from one another. The veracity of this comment might be questioned, but what cannot be ignored was the enthusiasm and willingness to contribute that was felt by every person during those initial gatherings. As the program has developed, and the views and advice of other professionals and stakeholders were sought, this willingness to be part of such a unique and important project was evidenced time and again.

Education at the Core—Not Self-Serving

NetSafe harbors a strong belief that education is key to online safety and that the education sector is one logical place to engage with children and young people. From its inception, the organization has involved education professionals, and there is still a practicing teacher on the board. Rather than existing as a cybersafety organization which "by the way" publishes lesson plans for teachers, NetSafe has invested heavily in developing credibility and relationships within both the ECE and compulsory education sectors. NetSafe team members visit schools and ECE organizations nationally on a cost recovery basis. Through sponsorship from Vodafone, educators have access to a toll free helpline which is often used to provide incident support and referral to other experts, such as computer forensic investigators. These and other services demonstrate a commitment to education, and NetSafe has been able to form strong bonds with the Ministry of Education because of this philosophy.

Sound Principles and Evidence

The NetSafe model outlined in both the NetSafe Kit for Schools and the NetSafe Kit for ECE presents a three pronged approach focusing on policies and procedures, electronic security, and education. Although the model may have been groundbreaking in the education sector, it is really a more descriptive version of a common triad used in information technology circles—people, process, and technology. The assertion behind the NetSafe model in education is that by attending to all three points, an organization closes more vulnerabilities which may have allowed the safety of staff, children, or their families to become compromised. Conversely, attending to only one factor leaves the others wide open for exploitation.

Educational providers that deal with children also have a duty of care both from a legal and ethical standpoint. While it is not possible to anticipate all possible situations, following a model of best practice provides a level of assurance with which a school or early childhood service can claim to be cybersafe.

While confident that the information NetSafe provides to the education sector reflects current best practice, the organization also publicly encourages constructive criticism and debate about axioms held by both itself and the cybersafety "industry." The effectiveness of content filtering (Smith, 2008), and the complicity of children who become victims of online sexual abuse (New Zealand Herald, 2008) are two examples where NetSafe has challenged widely held assumptions. These assertions are made following research conducted by NetSafe itself, or from analyzing other research.

As mentioned earlier, NetSafe is often questioned about whether ECE services or educators, children, and their families really do face any risk. The NetSafe ECE survey along with the malware experiment shows that most ECE services are in fact vulnerable and threats do exist. While these may center around the loss of data or the compromise of ICT systems, the risk of identity theft, exposure to inappropriate material, and possible subsequent litigation by parents or other agencies are also possibilities. By critically evaluating the assertions made by other cybersafety agencies, and making comment based upon evidence rather than assumptions, NetSafe itself models responsible behavior in a connected world.

NetSafe deals on a daily basis with New Zealanders who are falling victim to harassment, scams, identity theft, and other malicious activity. To say that this does not occur, or that threats to ECE educators, young children, and their families do not exist, whether by malicious intent or through ineffective management of ICTs, is to deny reality. ECE services are an ideal place to begin the work of educating young children to be safe and responsible cybercitizens, and the services themselves must also model safe practices. The process NetSafe has taken in developing the cybersafety program for ECE is reflective of the NetSafe philosophy in general: a moderate, collaborative approach focused on education and based upon sound principles and evidence.

Of all the characteristics of the NetSafe approach, collaboration is perhaps the most important. Since the initial workshops in 2005, NetSafe has sought to include wide representation from the ECE sector when developing and reviewing components of the program. This continues with a current review of the training modules. Without buy-in from stakeholders, including governance, educators, technology vendors, and families, NetSafe could not have been successful in providing a comprehensive program of cybersafety for the ECE sector.

REFERENCES

Bolstad, R. (2004). *The role and potential of ICT in early childhood education.* Wellington, NZ: New Zealand Council for Educational Research. Retrieved from http://www.educationcounts.govt.nz/publications/ict/4983

Hatherly, A. (2008, September 9). ECE ICT PL *programme resources and capability surveys.* Message posted to http://core-ed.net/ece-ict-pl-programme-resources-and-capability-surveys

Ministry of Education. (2005). *Foundations for discovery—Supporting learning in early childhood education through information and communication technologies: A framework for development.* Retrieved from http://www.educate.ece.govt.nz/~/media/Educate/Files/Reference%20Downloads/foundationsfordiscovery.pdf

Ministry of Education. (2008). *ICT infrastructure security & cybersafety—Policy and guidelines for early childhood education services.* Retrieved from http://www.lead.ece.govt.nz/ICTInfrastructure/SecurityAndCybersafety/default.htm

Ministry of Education. (2008). *Licensed services and licence-exempt groups 2008.* Retrieved from http://www.educationcounts.govt.nz/statistics/ece/ece_staff_return/licensed_services_and_licence-exempt_groups/34821

Mitchell, L., & Brooking, K. (2007). *National survey of early childhood education services 2003–2004.* Wellington, NZ: National Council for Educational Research. Retrieved from http://www.nzcer.org.nz/pdfs/15318.pdf

NetSafe. (2006). *First steps to cybersafety.* Retrieved from http://www.netsafe.org.nz/Doc_Library/IBM-NetSafe_First_Steps_to_Cybersafety_06.pdf

NetSafe. (2008). *NetSafe kit for ECE.* Retrieved from http://www.netsafe.org.nz/Doc_Library/NetSafeKitforECEwebversion.pdf

New Zealand Government. (1993). *Privacy act 1993.* Section 6, Information Privacy Principals. Retrieved from http://www.legislation.govt.nz/act/public/1993/0028/latest/DLM296639.html

New Zealand Herald (2008, 31 July). Kiwi kids become online sex victims. *New Zealand Herald.* Retrieved from http://www.nzherald.co.nz/technology/news/article.cfm?c_id=5&objectid=10524554

Smith, B. (2007, May 18). Cyber filters give "false confidence." *The Age.* Retrieved from http://www.theage.com.au/news/national/cyber-filters-give-false-confidence/2007/05/17/1178995324570.html

CHAPTER 6

HECTOR'S WORLD™

Educating Young Children About Life Online

Liz Butterfield

Hector's World is a New Zealand online safety education resource now being used in a number of different countries. This chapter offers a review of the evolution of Hector's World (HW) and some of the key factors that influenced its development. This is a chronicle of how a New Zealand charity identified the need for cybersafety education for 'digital tots' as a serious priority. The organization then developed an ambitious educational response while endeavoring to keep pace with rapid technological and social change. The challenges that were encountered during this development were sometimes formidable. This account of the decisions made and the lessons learned during the development of Hector's World may be helpful to those involved in the education and protection of the very young online, and of particular interest to those already using the resource.

High-Tech Tots: Childhood in a Digital World, pp. 93–123
Copyright © 2010 by Information Age Publishing
All rights of reproduction in any form reserved.

HECTOR'S WORLD BACKGROUND

To understand the evolution of the Hector's World program and its components, it is helpful to know the status of the resource today.

Resources Online (All Can Be Accessed For Free)

Episodes. The first five, streamed, animated episodes (8 minutes each) are focused on personal information online. A new 4 minute interactive episode and a music video on cyberbullying has been produced. Future episode topics include: computer security, intellectual property, and media literacy.

Hector's World Safety Button. This software is a free download which empowers young children to deal with unwanted content online. There are versions for different operating systems: Windows 2000, XP, Vista, and soon Mac OS10. With the Windows Deluxe XP version, there are also character, accessibility and language options (Māori, Japanese, Portuguese, German, etc.).

Activities and posters. There are jigsaw puzzles of the characters that can be played online and downloadable storybooks and special "character hats" for children to make themselves. New games and downloadable songs with song sheets are being produced. In New Zealand only, "Connect with Hector" posters in English and Te Reo Māori (Māori language) can be ordered.

For adults. Parents are encouraged to view episodes alongside their children and discussion points are offered to help them amplify their children's learning. For teachers, there are lesson plans for each episode at three different age levels: 5-6 years, 7-8 years, and 9-11 years.

Hector's World resources are created for 2- to 9-year-olds using digital technology (core episodes are animated using Flash technology and the Safety Buttons are software devices), and are delivered via digital technology from the website www.hectorsworld.com.

The Organization

Hector's World Limited (HWL) is the company that manages this education initiative today. HWL is a registered New Zealand charity and a separate subsidiary of NetSafe Incorporated (previously known as the Internet Safety Group). NetSafe is an independent nonprofit organization that educates all New Zealanders about safe, secure and responsible use of information and communication technology (ICT).

Figure 6.1.   Group shot.

SETTING THE STAGE IN NEW ZEALAND 1998-2003

A coalition of organizations in New Zealand, including representatives of the New Zealand Police, Auckland Rape Crisis, an Internet service provider, Mt Roskill Grammar School (an Auckland high school), and others, began in 1998 to address the issues of safety on the Internet. This coalition later became the Internet Safety Group (ISG). The group's first focus was helping schools institute sound Internet safety management systems, and educate their entire school community (staff, children and parents) about the risks on the Internet. The ISG partnered with the Department of Child, Youth & Family Services and the Ministry of Education to produce the *New Zealand Internet Safety Kit*, which went to every school in the country in 2000. The website www.netsafe.org.nz was developed at the same time, and a national toll-free helpline and e-mail query service was offered for easy access to advice and information. The kit referred to "children and young people" with no specific discussion of issues related to young children, though a handout with an "easy to read" format for younger readers was a part of the kit (Internet Safety Group [ISG], 2000).

Young children were not featured in the thinking of many cybersafety organizations at that time. For example, a large U.S. study of online victimization of young people interviewed children about three kinds of victimization—harassment, sexual solicitation, and unwanted exposure to sexual material. Participants were 10 years or older, and only 12% of the

1,501 youth interviewed were under 12 years (Finkelhor, Mitchell, & Wolak, 2000).

New Zealand's first research on Internet risk for children was a joint effort of the ISG and Pat Bullen and Niki Harré of the University of Auckland's Department of Psychology. This study included consultation with U.S. researchers Ilene Berson and Michael Berson from the University of South Florida. The "Girls on the Net" survey was limited to girls between 11 and 19 years of age (Bullen, Harré, & ISG, 2001). Early in 2002, another New Zealand survey "The Net Generation" (Duddy, Harré, & ISG 2002) looked at children 7 to 19 years old. With 2,582 respondents this was one of the largest internet safety studies at that time. Thirteen percent of the 7- to 10-year-olds used the Internet every day, and 23% of that age group had already met someone face to face that they first encountered online. Twenty-five percent of 11- to 12-year-olds had their own cell phone, but questions about cell phone use were not asked of younger children.

Use of computers and the Internet by children was included in the media education policy statements of organizations like the American Academy of Pediatrics (AAP, 1999), although the emphasis in such statements was more on television. In the commercial sector, according to marketing consultants Dan Acuff and Robert Reiher (1997), computer programs that use popular animated characters aimed at 3- to 7-year old children lead to "the reinforcement of interest in those characters as they appear on other products and programs" (p. 183). Regarding computer programs for a child under two, "What the future holds that will match the abilities of this young child is left for us to discover" (Acuff & Reiher, 1997, p. 180)

In mid-2002, the Internet Safety Group began work on a comprehensive Internet safety "manual" for schools on safety and security with ICT. The "convergence" of computer and cell phone technology was very much a part of the issues addressed in this *NetSafe Kit for Schools*, and the organization's approach of minimizing risk in order to maximize the benefits of ICT came into maturity. The ISG recommended that all schools institute a comprehensive cybersafety program that included an infrastructure of policies and use agreements, a sound electronic security system and cybersafety education for the entire school community, including parents. The kit also reflected the whole school approach that the ISG recommended be instituted from the first year of primary (elementary) school.

The practical education in the kit was informed by the many incidents ISG staff had responded to since 2000, and the contributions of a growing coalition of ISG members. Though the majority of the incidents reported related to adults or teenagers, an increasing number involved children under 10 years old, with the more serious issues for this age group ranging from cyberbullying, hacking, and stalking to online sexual victimization and criminal threatening. In some cases, young children were the perpetrators of the alleged crimes. This highlighted for the ISG that young children's level of cognitive development could affect their ability to manage risk effectively and to understand the sometimes serious consequences for others of their online behavior.

The *NetSafe Kit* included two printed handouts. One was dubbed "The Online Safety Rule Card," and the cybersafety themes on the card included: convergence ("when I'm on the Internet or a mobile phone"), critical thinking ("I stop and think about what I'm being asked to do", etc.), and ethical decision making ("could this hurt me or someone else?"). Several hundred thousand of these were distributed to schools and families across New Zealand (ISG, 2002). The second handout was a pamphlet for parents produced jointly by the ISG and the Police Youth Education Service (at this time 130 police officers were teaching in schools). The pamphlet encouraged parents to use the Internet themselves, empowered them to build a trusted relationship with their child about the child's use of ICT, and offered the ISG as a source for help and information (ISG and New Zealand Police, 2002).

The Ministry of Education strongly endorsed the "publications and activities" of the ISG in their published ICT policy document that same year (Ministry of Education, 2003). There was also a great deal of international interest in the kit after its release in 2003, and it was later adapted for all British schools by the U.K. government agency Becta, which advocates for effective use of technology in U.K. schools.

As a part of the kit, the ISG decided to develop a cartoon character to help communicate cybersafety content to primary school children. There was quick agreement that the character should be an animal, not a person; and there was much discussion about the possibility of using a New Zealand native animal. The group kept coming back to the qualities associated with a dolphin: intelligent, playful and fun, yet loyal and caring. One member of the group who was a primary teacher suggested the name "Hector Protector." The group then debated making the character a Hector's dolphin, one of New Zealand's endangered species. The final decision was to make Hector Protector a bottlenose dolphin, because it is almost universally recognized by children around the world, while the Hector's Dolphin has a more whale-like gently sloping snout. There was another reason a sea creature like a dolphin appealed and that was because the ocean—vast, fascinating and sometimes requiring caution—was a perfect metaphor for the Internet. As well, many children understood about the threat of pollution in our oceans, which was a useful metaphor for putting negative content out in cyberspace and the potential damage it can cause to even those far away.

In 2003, the *NetSafe Kit for Schools* was successfully launched in New Zealand with the debut of Hector Protector on a poster included in the kit, and with a link on the website so visitors could learn more about the plight of the Hector's dolphin (ISG, 2003).

Computer use by very young children was only starting to appear in research in 2003. One U.S. study focused on children 0-6 years of age, and concluded that 73% lived in a home with a computer and 18% were using a computer in their typical day, though particulars about computer use were often lost in more general discussion of screen media. The researchers commented specifically on the paucity of research on computer use by very young children and in their conclusion went so far as to suggest topics to encourage further investigation (Rideout, Vandewater, &

Figure 6.2.   Early Hector.

Wartella, 2003). Very young children were also beginning to appear on the radar of cybersafety organizations.

In New Zealand at the end of 2003, *NetGuide Magazine* donated the proceeds of its web awards event to the ISG. The sum of just over N.Z.$11,000 was specifically earmarked for the animation of Hector Protector, and an introduction was made to the three partners of Inkspot Digital Ltd., an Auckland animation and production company. This was a quiet start to what became an enormous undertaking for the Internet Safety Group, creating a resource that would have a positive impact on the lives of thousands of young children.

BUILDING THE "WORLD" 2004-2005

NetSafe, now the more common name for the Internet Safety Group, had a growing number of projects in development to meet the wide range of online safety needs of New Zealanders, from improving computer security and prevention of the trading of child sexual abuse images, to training of school personnel and community organizations about cybersafety. The animation of Hector began in 2003 as a small project aimed at children 5 to 10 years old, and was managed by NetSafe's executive director (the author of this chapter).

Mark Saunders of Inkspot Digital became an important collaborator on this project. He had previously worked as a senior animator on projects for Warner Brothers and Disney, and also had a background in community theater. Mark's talent for hand-drawn animation, and his faith in the communication power of this art form, had a great influence on the early direction of the Hector character. As Walt Disney himself said, "I take great pride in the artistic development of cartoons. Our characters are made to go through emotions" ("Disney Quotes," n.d., para. 5).

Disney producer Don Hahn, who worked with several of Disney's legendary "nine old men" animators, explained in an interview in 2005 the link between animation and emotions.

> I always feel like in animation, you can go somewhere emotionally that maybe you can't in live action—it might feel a little saccharine or sweet in live action. In animation there's a sincerity to it that's kind of germane to the art form. ("A Chat with Cinderella and Don Hahn," 2005, para. 2)

He continued, "There's a great old saying that great animators don't just move drawings, they move people" (2005, para. 6).

There was little precedent for a charity in New Zealand taking on a project of this complexity. Quality Flash animation was labor-intensive

Figure 6.3.   Photo of Mark Saunders and storyboards.

and costly to produce, even when utilizing ICT to make the process much more efficient. Commercial rates at that time were approximately N.Z.$1,200 a second. In a country of 4.3 million people, charitable grants were very rarely over N.Z.$500,000 and more likely to be in the range of N.Z.$20,000-$50,000. To raise sufficient funds to undertake a project like this was daunting for both the management and board of NetSafe.

After much discussion, NetSafe's goal slowly evolved from creating an animated cybersafety mascot to creating a character called Hector, who lived in a magical underwater community where he and his friends had many adventures that involved technology. Most importantly, this character would have emotions.

There were not many models for NetSafe to emulate in order to educate about a particular safety issue using strategies of communication with children that were usually the terrain of commercial children's brands. Such brands use the emotional bond that children have with the characters to sell merchandise, tickets to theme parks or movies. Though the intent may also be to entertain and delight children, the bottom line is profit for owners or shareholders. The stronger the emotional bond or brand loyalty is, the greater the chance of better sales.

For NetSafe, the intent was to build an emotional bond between young children and the characters so those children listened and learned more from the messages, perhaps even using the characters as role models. The hope was that role-modelling could offer young children useful safety strategies online until their own critical thinking about safety and security was more fully developed (through resources and activities). One excellent source of inspiration was *Sesame Street* which so successfully developed the literacy skills (and social skills) of children around the world. As expressed by Malcolm Gladwell, "Sesame Street was built about a single, breakthrough insight: that if you can hold the attention of children, you can educate them" (Gladwell, 2000, p. 100).

There were several critical issues NetSafe needed to resolve to be able to move forward. There was a need to determine the learning focus the content was to have, the personalities of Hector's friends, and if the resource was to be very local or to be designed from the start for a wider market.

The Focus of the Content

NetSafe was using phrases like "building skills" and "fostering critical thinking" regarding its education of children and young people. A larger context for those phrases was desired and an article in a National Council for the Social Studies publication helped suggest a theoretical and practical framework—cybercitizenship (Berson & Berson, 2004). The concept had the potential to unify diverse issues such as ethical decision making, computer security, validity of information and privacy. Although not fully developed for NetSafe yet, this new framework helped guide decisions about what content should be a part of Hector's World.

The Group of Friends

The development of the group of characters who were Hector's friends began in late 2003. NetSafe developed a list of personalities or roles for these characters:

- one who thinks there is a technological solution for every problem,
- one who is a bit bossy and conservative about the Internet,
- one who enthusiastically loves everything online and will try anything,

- one who is very young and follows the older friends, which offers opportunities to remind older children about the need to watch over younger ones online,
- a police constable (or officer character), to remind viewers of the seriousness of some of the criminal activity online, but also to build a notion of community policing in cyberspace,
- and a wise, older character that could be sought out for advice.

Roots in New Zealand

From the start, there was the decision to give Hector's World a "Kiwi" flavor—a reflection of the society in which it was created. It was almost an impulsive decision at first to make the characters reflect the diversity of New Zealand, though this turned out to have unanticipated implications.

A Global Resource

There was the potential for Hector's World to become a global resource —one used in a number of different countries. This was a wistful goal—an idealistic hope that children in the connected world of the Internet could share a fundamental resource for starting life online. Also, it was hoped that somehow cybersafety organizations could share resources to avoid expensive and needless duplication. However, the logistics of such cooperative sharing, culturally, linguistically and monetarily (who would pay for the cost of creating the resource?), were daunting. There was also a very practical reason why NetSafe looked beyond the New Zealand shores; the budgets of funding organizations and sponsorships by businesses were much larger outside New Zealand.

With the help of Inkspot Digital, the concept and design of the creatures came together quickly and was very appropriate for the key messages NetSafe needed to communicate. There was a techno crab (Ranjeet), a conservative clam (Ming), an enthusiastic fish (Sprat), a sweet and naïve young jellyfish (Tama), a friendly seahorse (Constable Solosolave) and a wise old whale (named Kui). The seahorse was specifically chosen for the police character because of its upright posture, and because of the message that size is not a reliable measure of integrity and authority. Several of the names were Māori, from New Zealand's indigenous culture, and the whale character honored the Māori tradition of respecting the wisdom of elders. In fact, the Māori word for a wise older woman is *kuia*.

Rough drawings of a core group of characters, a model pack for Hector (needed for animation), and a beautiful image for a 3' x 4' poster were produced with the NetGuide funding to inspire everyone working on the project. NetSafe now had something more tangible to show those whose support it wanted to enlist.

This was a great start and everyone at NetSafe was very excited, including the board members. A vision was starting to take shape of an education resource that could effectively communicate complex cybersafety topics to young children, using engaging and fun animated characters. The resource could deliver the education online through a website using animated episodes. The educational impact would be strengthened by offering lesson plans for teachers and materials for parents.

Figure 6.4.   First poster image.

Getting this far required a lot of consultation and cooperation, particularly with representatives of the Ministry of Education and New Zealand Police. NetSafe was supporting some of this development with a portion of its annual funding from the Ministry of Education, as the education resource being developed met their need for cybersafety materials for primary schools. To build a website and complete all of the character development required a serious commitment of time and money. NetSafe could go no further without funding dedicated to this purpose, so the search began for a foundation sponsor. Any hope of becoming a global resource seemed likely to hinge on working closely with multinational corporations and other organizations that had a global reach, particularly those with a focus on ICT. From NetSafe's perspective, there could be no better company for this role than Microsoft.

Development continued in 2004 at a slower pace as NetSafe focused on other initiatives, and discussions progressed with Microsoft's New Zealand office about becoming the first major HW sponsor. Other sponsorship was sought for creating sets of episodes (four episodes per set), but the funding required was exceeding most commercial companies' marketing budgets (over N.Z.$400,000 a set was needed). NetSafe also started the process of protecting its intellectual property with the filing of trademark applications in New Zealand (and later in the United States and Australia).

Two small shifts occurred during 2004. One was that the target age for Hector was lowered to include from 2 to 10-year-olds. The other change was the need to give the website and the resources being developed a sense of place or community—Hector's World was born.

One interesting project at this time that the Ministry of Education helped fund through their support of NetSafe was the creation of what was termed "the Hector Safety Button." This little piece of software was built to run on computers with Windows 98, 2000 and XP operating systems. Once downloaded and installed, a software file would run an animation of Hector in the corner of the computer screen. Hector would swim there quietly until a child clicked on the animation, then the screen would be covered with an entrancing underwater scene. Hector was there with a written message that read, "Well done!!! I'll keep the screen covered until an adult can come and help you. Remember I'll always be there to help you when you need me." This was basically a screensaver, and a button in the screensaver's corner could be clicked to return to the original screen so the problem could be addressed. The Safety Button was a very simple device born out of a desire to empower children to quickly cover up whatever comes on the screen that makes them uncomfortable, such as a violent or pornographic image.

In October 2004, Microsoft and NetSafe signed a foundation partnership agreement and launched the partnership and the button in November. The Hector Safety Button was a free download from the Net-Safe website but also from the international downloads section of the Microsoft site, a very unlikely scenario for a small New Zealand charity. Other sponsors helped out, including a generous donation of two high capacity servers from Hewlett Packard.

As it turned out, the button was a helpful response to a problem a number of parents and schools reported to NetSafe at that time. Threatening email chain-letters were making the rounds in New Zealand. Receiving these chain-letters was quite traumatic for some children. The recipient of the email was warned to forward it to 10 friends in 5 minutes or they would be murdered that night when they were asleep in bed. To illustrate the threat, the email included photo images of rotting or dismembered bodies. Unfortunately, the e-mail bypassed any content filtering software because the images were actually hyperlinks to U.S. websites not actual attachments, and the e-mails were coming from a friend of the recipient, so not likely to be caught by the spam filters of that era. The button gave children a quick way to respond to such material.

As NetSafe's Annual Report for 2004-2005 reflected, "Foundations were carefully laid for the ISG's most ambitious and complex project—Hector Protector and his friends" (NetSafe/ISG, 2005). During this same time period in the commercial world, marketers continued to explore the new terrain of the Internet and the access to children that this medium offered.

> The World Wide Web also represents a whole new world of marketing to children. First of all, most of the restrictions for marketing to kids using television are not applicable to the Internet, so almost anything goes in that medium. Two other Internet marketing monsters have popped up as well: invasion of privacy and unfair and deceptive advertising. Young people are offered free gifts like T-shirts and CD players in exchange for filling out online surveys. The goal is to be able to "microtarget" individual youngsters … advertisers have free reign to capture hours of children's attention at their Web sites where commercials and content including branded cartoon characters and games are seamlessly interwoven. (Acuff & Reiher, 2005, p. 43)

An interview in 2005 illustrated how even though the needs of young children online were starting to register with those providing safety education, it was still a challenge for all organizations to keep up with the impact of ICT on children under 6 years. Paul Jackson of U.K. media literacy group Media Smart was asked why children older or younger than children aged 6-11 were not targeted by their school program. "It is at that vulnerable age in primary school—ages six to eleven years—where children are absorbing advertising, and need to make informed judgements, that we wanted to concentrate" (Clarke, 2005, p. 23).

In New Zealand, there was a very important positive development that directly related to the downward trend in the age at which children started using ICT. The Ministry of Education launched a policy document in 2005, *Foundations for Discovery*, which provided a clear framework for the use of ICT in New Zealand in the early childhood (preschool) sector. This sector is quite diverse and different from the compulsory education sector. Managers of early childhood centers can range from boards of trustees to loosely organized parent or *whanau* (Māori extended family and community) groups. This new framework was collaboratively developed and included consultation with NetSafe. The report acknowledged the ongoing work needed to expand the applications for ICT within centers while evolving safe practices that recognized the potential risks to the very young children in their care (Ministry of Education, 2005).

The First Episode

NetSafe had not succeeded in finding sponsorship or grant funding for production of episodes by mid-2005, so there was no content with which to activate the website that had been built. Microsoft gave permission to re-allocate the last funds of their foundation sponsorship to produce a pilot episode. This pilot would illustrate how the characters interact and prove (or not) NetSafe's contention that creating characters with the power of those from the commercial world would help young children learn and remember important online safety skills. The pilot would also confirm the appeal or "stickyness" of Hector's World and its ability to move past New Zealand borders.

This was a lot of pressure on a small organization. Much larger cybersafety organizations like the National Center for Missing and Exploited Children (NCMEC) and IKeepSafe, both in the United States, had created animation components for their excellent education programs, as well as organized lesson plans that used the animation. None, however, had tried the character-based entertainment crossover that NetSafe was poised to try.

In the meantime, feedback was starting to come in about the Hector Safety Button. E-mail queries and compliments about the button were being received in the NetSafe Contact Centre from schools in New Zealand and overseas. In New Zealand, the button was being installed on individual machines (what it was designed for), but also on school networks and in computer labs in primary schools. Network installation caused a few hiccups but they were fairly easily resolved. The very positive feedback from schools, libraries and the general public helped formulate a more articulate policy statement about the use of the button. One advantage of the button that had not previously been considered was that it was child-activated. Many online safety strategies involve an active response by parents (like installing filtering) for passive children. The fact that young children could actually be active in their own defence, as with the e-mail chain-letter scenario, fit well with the maturing NetSafe philosophy about cybercitizenship skills and responsibilities.

A consultation process was established with the pilot episode that worked well. A topic was chosen for the episode which seemed the most pressing for young children—personal information online. The NetSafe team developed a list of cybersafety points to be integrated into the 5 minute storyline, and Inkspot Digital used that list to create a draft story outline. The NetSafe team then amended the outline and sent it out to a group of colleagues—online safety experts in New Zealand and the United States, a New Zealand social work lecturer, and representatives from the Ministry of Education, the Commissioner for Children's Office and the Police Youth Education Service. Comments came back, amendments were made, the final script was written and the episode went into production. Part of the production included the creation of the episode introduction, with the catchy Hector's World theme song—the first foray into music. The production was on a very tight timeline and more funding had to be found to complete the editing.

The tight timeline meant that there was not a lot of deliberating about certain production decisions. One such issue was accents. With characters of implied Chinese, Māori, Samoan, Indian, Australian and North American background, the traditional approach would be to give them all a nonspecific accent. The decision was made to have a wide range of accents—not to make fun of any character, but to make them more individual and enjoyable. This issue turned out later to be quite important as the resource moved out of New Zealand.

The creation of content like Hector's World is an incredibly delicate balance. A trusted relationship between the commercial animator and the charitable organization is imperative because each naturally seeks compromise from the other. These are very serious topics, but they must be presented in a fun and entertaining format. There must be educational integrity in how cybersafety themes are presented, yet the final product must be "sticky" enough to encourage repeat viewing. NetSafe's ability to raise funds hinged on how well this episode got across the vision. In animation, every second costs money to produce. In that five minutes of storytelling, there had to be enough time for the characters to be developed so they could have their desired impact.

Figure 6.5.   Scene from episode 1.

As the final production was being completed, the NetSafe team created lesson plans for three different age groups of children using the same episode. These too were sent out for comments from colleagues. Other components were also completed for the website: a downloadable storybook based on the pilot episode and four jigsaw puzzles using the characters. Such puzzles are a way to build a child's relationship with the characters rather than teach about cybersafety. The hope was that such play could help make other materials with specific messages more effective, and could be a part of that delicate balance of serious safety issues and fun.

The Hector's World website quietly went live in November 2005 with the button, lesson plans, storybook, puzzles and first episode. Parents and teachers were encouraged to use HW alongside the cybersafety resources of other organizations, to offer children as much reinforcement of cybersafety messages as possible.

The animated and text portions of the site actually sat on separate servers and NetSafe was not able at that time to collect statistics from the animated section on how many people were visiting and what they were doing. The text portion of the website (information about HW and resources for parents and teachers) was actually part of the larger NetSafe website. Monthly statistics from that site showed that a few HW pages were almost always in the top ten most visited pages for the site as a whole. The response from teachers and parents about the range of resources offered was also quite positive. Word was even getting out overscas, with queries and comments coming in from Canada, the United States, Australia and elsewhere. The pilot episode and website were achieving what they were designed to do.

In 2006, research offered a clearer picture of very young children's use of ICT with first use of computers starting between the ages of 1 and 3, and 4% of 2- to 3-year-olds using a computer every day. By the age of 4 to 6 years, daily use of computers jumped significantly (13%). For those 4- to 6-year-olds, 26% used the computer in a typical day, 35% had a parent with them supervising the whole time, but 27% did so without a parent in the room (Rideout, Hamel, & Kaiser Family Foundation, 2006). By 2007, 78% of New Zealanders used the Internet and 66% of users with a connection at home had broadband. Age, income and location did influence the likelihood of access to broadband (Bell et al., 2007), but the opportunity for very young children to have access to high speed Internet at home, potentially unsupervised, was definitely increasing. At the same time in New Zealand, use of ICT in early childhood centers was expanding, as was NetSafe's work with the Ministry of Education to develop online safety resources for the sector.

A DREAM OF SOCIAL ENTREPRENEURSHIP— HECTOR'S WORLD LTD

In September 2006, the board of NetSafe and the executive director began planning an important step in Hector's World development—the creation of a new company that would be a subsidiary of NetSafe. In October 2005, Hector's World Limited (HWL) became an independent charitable subsidiary of NetSafe, and NetSafe's executive director moved to a new role as managing director of HWL.

Part of the dream for HWL was that a business structure could be found that would allow the project to become a self-sustaining entity while also being a New Zealand charity. In May 2006, HWL became one of the first non-profit organizations to take up a residency in the Start-up "incubator" program of the Icehouse, a government-backed business development initiative. A residency at the Icehouse gave budding entrepreneurs mentoring and intensive training on business growth. Once again, HWL was going to try a cross-over for which there was not much precedent in New Zealand. This time the cross-over was evolving from a small national nonprofit organization to a growing, exporting social entrepreneurship venture.

In business parlance, HWL's goal of creating a social entrepreneurship business model that would sustain a global cybersafety education program while offering core resources online for free was a "BHAG"—a big, hairy audacious goal (first used by James Collins and Jerry Porras).

> A true BHAG is clear and compelling, serves as a unifying focal point of effort, and acts as a catalyst for team spirit. It has a clear finish line, so the organization can know when it has achieved the goal; people like to shoot for finish lines. A BHAG engages people—it reaches out and grabs them. It is tangible, energizing, highly focused. People get it right away; it takes little or no explanation. (Collins & Porras, 1996, pp. 9-10)

Well articulated core values are very important to keeping a company on course. This is probably even more critical for a social venture than for a more conventional business. HWL's core values were identified as:

- Communicate cybersafety with creativity, imagination and humour.
- Offer high quality and reliable products.
- Respond to the needs of families and educators as they teach cyber-safety.
- Work with passion, commitment and integrity.
- Create trends, don't follow.

In the early stages of residency at the Icehouse, between seminars on sales pipelines, business strategies and marketing plans, HWL received word of new funding. The Community Partnership Fund of the Government's Digital Strategy was funding N.Z.$423,000 for production of four episodes and the associated education materials. These episodes were produced by HWL during the residency using a similar consultation process as NetSafe did with the pilot episode. They were launched by the Minister of the Community and Voluntary Sector, the Honorable Luamanuvao Winnie Laban, in mid-2007, shortly after the Icehouse residency concluded.

Additional funding was secured to create new, improved versions of what was now called the Hector's World Safety Button. The Microsoft Vista operating system button was funded by Microsoft and was one of the first pieces of software globally to actually be integrated into the Parental Controls option on several versions of that operating system. A New Zealand funding body, the Tindall Foundation, supported development of buttons for other operating systems. A new XP version added languages other than English and accessibility options. Development also began on an Apple Mac OS10 version, but this has been hindered by a bug in the Mac code. The bug has been logged with the Apple development team in the United States, but unfortunately still remains unresolved.

All of the new buttons were launched at Parliament in late 2007 by Minister Laban, including a message read out from the Minister of Education naming Hector as "New Zealand's cybersafety ambassador" (S. Maharey, personal communication, October 24, 2007). Funding was also raised for a national "Connect with Hector" poster campaign that included all early childhood centers and primary schools. The building of the HW "core content" and the integration of that into the programs of New Zealand schools, early childhood centers, and nonprofit organizations working with families was moving forward rapidly.

The business model that was forged at the Icehouse included securing more funding from charitable sources like foundations to sustain the organization until revenue could be generated to self-fund development. Distribution of the resource was to be achieved with the help of Education Partners. A partner would sign a licence for use of HWL intellectual property (conservatively valued at N.Z.$1.7 million). For the first three partners the licence would be free as they would be very active collaborators, sometimes even sponsoring content; but for later partners there would just be a reasonable annual fee. Through their distribution of HW resources in their country, the partners help create a market for HW educational merchandise such as books. The revenue from the merchandise and the licence fees is then used to create more content for the partners to share.

Figure 6.6.   Hector icon for notification area of taskbar.

The beauty of this business model is that the merchandise that creates the revenue is also helping to reach more children and have greater educational impact with the online safety messages. The challenge of the model is that it moves a charitable entity like HWL into closer competition with commercial children's brands. Such brands have far more spending power and marketing reach than a charity would ever have (with the notable exception of the Children's Television Workshop). Also, conventional start-up businesses can court investment from venture capital firms, while HWL cannot take such investment because it cannot risk having to compromise its charitable goals to maximise investor returns.

THE CONSTANT QUEST TO BE MORE EFFECTIVE

In 2006, the HWL and NetSafe teams collaborated on an evaluation of the HW pilot episode, conducted at an Auckland primary school. The evaluation participants were all from Year 2 classes (most were 6 years old). In an attempt to learn how best to structure the use of Hector's World materials, two groups were studied. The Study A group first watched the episode in class, then enjoyed a lesson using one of the online lesson plans, and finally watched the episode a second time before they were interviewed. The second group (Study B) were given a disk and a letter for parents requesting the child view the episode 3 times over the course of that week. Those children were then interviewed using the same interview schedule as Study A. The findings included that 88% of the students in the classroom-based viewing (Study A) were able to recount Hector's suggestion to use a nickname compared to 50% of Study B. Responses like "the dolphin told his friend not to type his name, address and school" (NetSafe, 2006, p. 14), "he wanted a new friend but didn't know if it was safe or not" (p. 18) and "to keep other people from seeing the information" (p. 25) indicated the messages were getting through. On all comprehension questions the classroom group had a significantly better understanding of the content. From this small study was gleaned that the lesson plans and repeated viewing in the classroom helped comprehension, but certainly the best outcome is for a child to have both.

There were specific questions about character identification, with 70% rating Hector as one of their favorite characters, many describing him as "cool" and "helpful." Ranjeet and Ming were the least liked characters in that question response, yet in a separate question Ranjeet was selected as the second favorite character for Study A group. Ming was the only female character of the friends and was what New Zealanders would describe as stroppy or outspoken, with nothing unusual in her accent. Some of the young participants seemed a little confused by the name of the whale; some called her "the queen" instead of Kui (NetSafe, 2006). Some children assumed Tama was female, perhaps because this jellyfish character is pink, but the name is actually a Māori boy's name.

The results of this study were presented in a session, "An Examination of Animated Video to Shape Young Children's Perceptions and Perspectives about Cybersafety," by Berson, Berson and Fenaughty (author of the study) at the American Educational Research Association (AERA) conference in the United States in 2007. One person who attended the session queried whether the depiction of Ranjeet in the pilot episode, where he has a noticeable Indian accent and he seems to get in the most trouble, might be interpreted in the United Kingdom as racist.

The first step in response to that feedback was for HWL to check with cybersafety colleagues that were either directly or indirectly involved in the use of the first episode in classrooms, especially in communities where there was a significant Indian population. At that time, there had been no other feedback about Ranjeet being a racist depiction in the United Kingdom, United States, Australia or New Zealand. The next step was to look at the characterization. HWL knew that Ranjeet's character would unfold over subsequent episodes,—that he would be smart, gifted with ICT, exuberant and loyal. Yet in this condensed pilot it was not possible to see all this. The animation was reviewed carefully to see if any minor changes might alter any negative perceptions of the character. There was a very short sequence where Ming is being a bit strident with Ranjeet, and he taps the little clam to the side in irritation. It was concluded that this sequence *could* negatively color Ranjeet's character (by hitting a friend ...), so the sequence was removed. The issue has never been raised again, perhaps because later episodes helped clarify Ranjeet's character for viewers. As for Tama's color, the idea of the characters running counter to stereotypes was appealing, so Tama the male jellyfish remained pink.

The issue of accents was looked at again. All of the characters but Hector (to New Zealanders he sounds vaguely American) had strong accents of one type or another. The strongest were Ranjeet and Constable Solosolave. Advice had been given to HWL that dubbing would be required to export this education or to offer it to overseas broadcasters. For the U.S. market, the recommendation was that mild, vaguely mid-Western accents would be required. HWL's decision was that this norm was rapidly being redefined by the Internet. Children would be interacting online with other children, sometimes far away, and sometimes via web cam or classroom link-up. If everyone is speaking English, sometimes that English will be accented and not always perfect (though the speaker may also speak several other languages). Online friends may also have names that are long or hard to pronounce, and English names may be awkward for them. It seemed to HWL that to change Ranjeet's or the

Constable's accents to something bland, or to shorten a name so viewers don't need to learn how to pronounce it, would be a repudiation of the wonderful diversity of the online community. Later, when negotiating with a U.S. state government agency about possible partnership, HWL was delighted when they decided they would not change any accents or names, as from their perspective there was none that could be used that was not represented in their state population, and they completely concurred with the celebration of diversity.

There was one other aspect of this internal debate worth mentioning and that was the issue of difference online, and that it may be beneficial to help children understand that difference by itself does not indicate risk. A new friend's accent or an unfamiliar name need not be a flag to a child of potential risk, as the real risk may be from someone who seems quite similar, enjoys the same sports as they do, also has parents just divorced, and so forth. Thus HWL made the decision to continue to incorporate strong accents and ethnic names where possible while reinforcing the message that caution with *all* new online friends is wise.

In 2009, a new evaluation of the use of all five episodes in the classroom will be completed. This incorporates repeat viewing and use of some of the online resource materials designed to amplify the learning outcomes.

Getting the Best Results

If cybersafety organizations only change awareness and not behavior, then the impact of the education, though positive, may be less than hoped-for. This issue was also highlighted in the *Byron Review: Children and New Technology* released in Great Britain in 2008. Byron encourages more of a social marketing approach where messages are very specifically targeted to relevant groups or individuals (Byron, 2008, p. 118).

The Rubric: An Important New Tool

In 2007, researchers Berson, Berson, Desai, Falls, and Fenaughty developed a rubric to be used to evaluate the effectiveness of cybersafety resources and published the results of the study in *Contemporary Issues in Technology and Teacher Education*. This development was achieved through a careful analysis of prevention effectiveness literature, an analysis of behavioral decision making theory as it relates to young children, and a focus on electronic media as a means of delivery of cybersafety messages (Berson et al., 2007). In this study, the rubric was used to evaluate seven online cybersafety education resources. Hector's World was one of the programs evaluated using the rubric and did very well in the results.

HWL intends to use this rubric not only in ongoing program evaluation, but in project planning as well. An Appendix to the study lays out the rubric grid, with criteria on the vertical axis and four graduated stages that measure the level of success at meeting the criteria on the horizontal axis, with the fourth stage exemplifying the greatest success. The criteria are as follows:

- Based on a coherent theoretical framework.
- Includes active, systematic and specific skill training.
- Integrates multiple program components (i.e., classroom training combined with parent involvement).
- Includes interactive instructional components.
- Provides intensive training.
- Addresses protective factors as well as risk factors.

With new projects, HWL will look at the rubric criteria and have the fourth stage outcome as the goal. Thus, using Project X as an example, if Project X is truly "based on a coherent theoretical framework" (first criteria), then Project X will have a goal of "a theory of behavioral change (that) is clearly articulated and integrated into the program activities"— the highest level of success (Berson et al., 2007, pp. 242-243).

HWL will continue to consult with other cybersafety organizations about some of the challenges evaluating programs aimed at this very young age group. If an organization succeeds at reaching a child with online safety education simultaneously or even prior to the start of their use of ICT (HWL's ideal), then there are not entrenched online behaviors to be modified. Also, it can be challenging to evaluate children who may not be confident readers, and their young age may make evaluation problematic.

REACHING MORE CHILDREN THROUGH EDUCATION PARTNERSHIP 2007-PRESENT

In the HWL business model developed at the Icehouse, education partnership is the mechanism for HWL to get its online safety education to thousands, even millions, of children quickly, efficiently and with the endorsement of respected government agencies. Partners also have the option of sponsoring the creation of new resources such as episodes, which all partners can then share.

In New Zealand there are two partners—the Ministry of Education (as previously outlined in this chapter) and New Zealand Police, which promotes HW as effective cybercrime prevention. An article by Police Commissioner Howard Broad about HW was published in *Police Chief* Magazine, which went to over 20,000 senior law enforcement executives worldwide. New Zealand Police had direct in-put into the development of the constable character, and Commissioner Broad serves on both the NetSafe and HWL boards (Broad, 2008). Hector's World has been integrated into the new Junior Primary *Keeping Ourselves Safe* Program which 130 Police Youth Education Service officers are now delivering in schools and early childhood centers.

The Child Exploitation and Online Protection (CEOP) Centre is part of the Serious Organised Crime Agency, and HWL's exclusive partner in the United Kingdom. HW is CEOP's ThinkUKnow resource for children 5-7 years old (the youngest age group for their program)—http://thinkuknow.co.uk/5_7/. CEOP launched HW across Great Britain on May 8, 2008. By August, CEOP had delivered HW training to over 30,000 children, and packets of HW posters and promotional materials were sent to 22,000 schools. Feedback from CEOP indicates HW is very popular with children and teachers, and use of the resource is becoming widespread (CEOP, personal communication, August 29, 2008). Jim Gamble, Chief Executive of the CEOP Centre, commented in a launch press release:

> Teachers have asked us for this material because it is never too early to start giving children "safety first" messages: in the same way that we teach small children to cross the road safely, there is a need to ensure that young children learn good habits for a future life online. If we give them early lessons in a way that is engaging, relevant and fun, we can help to safeguard young children online not only now but well into the future. (CEOP, 2008, para. 5, quote 2)

In Australia, HWL's Education Partner is the Australian Communications and Media Authority, the content regulator for Australia charged with providing all of their cybersafety education. The Australian Federal Police may later become partners, and HWL is also negotiating with a state government agency in the U.S.. Partners have much to contribute to the development of this resource internationally and can help get the HW resource distributed to a very large group of children, families and schools as a part of their own local resource.

Figure 6.7.   Connect with Hector poster in Māori.

ACCELERATING TOWARD A
COMMERCIAL HYPER-REALITY FOR THE VERY YOUNG ONLINE

Given the wider range of online activities children over 10 years are more commonly engaged in, Hector's World Ltd. decided to amend the age range for its education to 2-9 years. By the age of 10, HWL decided many children will be ready for more detailed safety and security messages. Also, the 2-9 age range better reflects the role of HW material as a child's introduction to online safety—laying the groundwork or building blocks for the more complex information children will need as they grow up online.

Children are now able to watch television through a variety of ICT devices including portable media players and gaming consoles. In addition, children's broadcasting has become an extremely interactive medium. The Kids' Choice Awards (KCAs) on the Nick-MTV networks is an example.

> This year's KCAs will let kids vote for their favorites and take part in the show through more platforms than ever. In addition to Nick.com, votes can be cast on the TurboNick broadband site as well as a cell-phone friendly Web site … and in a special area of its Nicktropolis virtual community, where kids can hang out on the orange carpet, go backstage, visit the after-party and chat with buddies. (McLean, 2008, para. 4)

The use of social networking sites by young children has escalated. Recent UK research found that for children 8-17 who use the Internet, almost half (49%) have set up their own profile, and 41% of those had their profile set so it was visible to anyone. Twenty-seven percent of 8- to 11-year-olds who are aware of social networking sites say that they have a profile on a site, though some are on sites intended for children (Ofcom, 2008).

Yet social networking is but one face of the increasingly interactive activities designed for young children online, many with a commercial focus. There are a number of websites that are commercial brand sites, sometimes with multiple sites for one brand (such as www.barbie.com and www.barbiegirls.com). There are also social networking sites and interactive virtual worlds, often dubbed "virtual playgrounds." The distinction between these three types of sites is rapidly blurring. It is estimated that by 2011, virtual worlds will attract over 20 million children. Many of these environments are built by businesses generating revenue through ads, the sale of virtual items like furniture, or subscriptions for premium access. These businesses can also use the site as a marketing channel for other lines of merchandise owned by the business. The membership and revenue numbers for these sites is staggering. Club Penguin, at the time it was acquired by Disney (for up to $700 million), had 700,000 subscribers and estimated annual revenue of $50 million (Chmielewski & Pham, 2008). The Finnish company Sulake generated revenue of $100 million in 2008, 25% through advertisers and 75% from the sale of virtual furniture for outfitting virtual Habbo Hotel rooms (McIntyre, 2008).

The toy company Mattel has recently announced a new phase of development as it launched the Mattel Digital Network that will further enhance loyalty to its brands (and challenge its competitors). It unites all ages of Mattel users (including parents and adult collectors) with a tailor-made online experience that meets their individual needs. The activities offered will "provide tools to harness the creativity of brand fans." New products announced at the same time include mind games that use a lightweight headset with sensors for the forehead and earlobes to measure brainwave activity and a new Barbie "Beautronics" line that allows a user to print custom designs onto nails. Other new products being marketed include FAMPS (Feelings, Attitudes, Moods and Personalities) that combines social networking and collectible figures—"each figure creates a unique emotional makeover" (Business Wire, 2009).

When looking at the commercialization of childhood, the American Psychological Society (APA) Task Force on Advertising and Children observed,

> the ability to recognize persuasive intent does not develop for most children before 8 years of age. Even at that age, such capability tends to emerge in only rudimentary form, with youngsters recognizing that commercials intend to sell, but not necessarily that they are biased messages which warrant some degree of scepticism. (APA, 2004, p. 9)

That research was focused on television, but brand websites and virtual worlds offer a much more compelling form of brand immersion, complete with music, video, games and interactivity.

In New Zealand, the Advertising Standards Authority handles any complaints about possible breaches of an industry self-regulatory code for advertising to children. Sample guidelines include "2(c)- Children should not be urged in advertisements to ask their parents, guardians or caregivers to buy particular products for them," "2(e)- Advertisements should not suggest to children any feeling of inferiority or lack of social acceptance for not having the advertised product," and "3(a) if there is any likelihood of advertisements being confused with editorial or program content, they should be clearly labelled 'advertisement' or identified in a clear manner" (Advertising Standards Authority, 2006). Such guidelines clearly illustrate how digital environments like virtual worlds aimed at young children have outpaced the mechanisms designed to protect such children from unbridled commercial exploitation.

PRIORITIES FOR HECTOR'S WORLD

Hector's World Ltd. must continue to develop its primary mechanism for delivery of education—its website. HWL has now embarked on a complete re-design of www.hectorsworld.com to make it much more interactive for children and to mirror as much as possible the atmosphere of some of the virtual worlds. There may not be the financial capacity to compete in look and feel with major commercial sites for children, but there must be at least an attempt to mirror the environment in which children are now spending so much of their time. Funding for this important core development (as well as for further development of HWL's business model) came from InternetNZ, the charity that manages the .nz domain name.

There is another challenge for HWL and that is to set a high standard for the way in which it markets its education to children, parents and teachers. There will never be any educational merchandise marketed in the children's section of the HW site. The children's section will only offer free activities and downloads, with no "pester power" tactics. Not only will any HWL marketing be done ethically and responsibly, but there will be clear information for parents and teachers about the way HWL conducts its charitable business (and why). Then when those visitors look at other websites, they will have the ability to more critically evaluate the suitability of those sites for their child or student. Links to other helpful sites will also be offered.

The development of new content for Hector's World is a priority and that content must address some of the compelling issues for young children online, such as –

- Cyberbullying
- Online friendships and social networks
- Intellectual property
- Computer security
- Online gaming
- Media literacy
- Privacy (also covered in the first five episodes).

Such content must be augmented with interactive online resources for testing new knowledge and rehearsing new skills that are relevant to the fast-paced, user-generated world of children today. For example, recent research indicates children's skill with the technology may obscure their lack of competency with effective searching. Most are performing quick and easy searches using common search engines and spending little energy evaluating the information they find for "relevance, accuracy or authority" (British Library and JISC, 2008).

Teaching skills such as searching, as well as the ability to discern the commercial intent of a website, would certainly fall within the common definition of media literacy, but perhaps such skills could equally be associated with Internet safety or cybersafety, information literacy, digital literacy and cyber or digital citizenship. Harmonizing these terms is an important step to unifying the education, and the organizations, needed to keep children safe in this rapidly changing environment. Yet these topics are often considered distinct disciplines, sometimes firmly established in different educational silos. The complexity of the online environment is now forcing this situation to change. In the view of HWL, children's early years are where it is most important to have a holistic, seamless education foundation which can then diversify and specialize as children grow older. To this end, HWL will now use the term "digital citizenship" for its education that will include elements of media literacy, cybersafety, digital literacy, and information literacy.

Only through partnership and collaboration can government, charitable, education, law enforcement and industry organizations offer young children the positive start they need to life in this borderless online world, and the age-appropriate information and support they need to become confident and capable online citizens. This is an ideal to which Hector's World Ltd. is firmly committed.

REFERENCES

A chat with Cinderella and Don Hahn. (2005). Retrieved from http://www.ultimatedisney.com/cinderella-interview-3.html

Acuff, D. S., & Reiher, R. H. (1997). *What kids buy and why*. New York, NY: The Free Press.

Acuff, D. S., & Reiher, R. H. (2005). *Kidnapped: How irresponsible marketers are stealing the minds of your children*. Chicago, IL: Dearborn Trade.

Advertising Standards Authority. (2006). *Code for advertising for children*. Retrieved from http://www.asa.co.nz/code_children.php

American Academy of Pediatrics. (1999). *Policy statement: Media education*. Retrieved from http://aappolicy.aappublications.org/cgi/content/full/pediatrics;104/2/341

American Psychological Association. (2004). *Report of the APA Task Force on Advertising and Children*. Retrieved from http://www.apa.org/releases/childrenads.pdf

Bell, A., Crothers, C., Goodwin, I., Kripalani, K., Sherman, K., & Smith, P. (2007). *World Internet Project New Zealand: The Internet in New Zealand Final Report Executive Summary*. Retrieved from http://www.aut.ac.nz/resources/research/research_institutes/ccr/wipnz_2007_final_report.pdf

Berson, I. R., Berson, M. J., Desai, S., Falls, D., & Fenaughty, J. (2007). An analysis of electronic media to prepare children for safe and ethical practices in digital environments. *Contemporary Issues in Technology and Teacher Education, 8*(3), 222-243.

Berson, M. J., & Berson, I. R. (2004). Developing thoughtful "cybercitizens." *Social Studies and the Young Learner, 16*(4), 5-8.

Bullen, P., Harré, N., & Internet Safety Group. (2001). Girls on the net. Retrieved from http://edorigami.wikispaces.com/file/view/girls+on+the+net.pdf

British Library and the Joint Information Systems Committee. (2008). *Information behaviour of the researcher of the future*. Retrieved from http://www.bl.uk/news/2008/pressrelease20080116.html

Broad, H. (2008). Cybercitizenship for the very young: An evolution in cybercrime prevention education in New Zealand. *The Police Chief*, LXXV(4). Retrieved from http://policechiefmagazine.org/magazine/index.cfm?fuseaction=display&article_id=1464&issue_id=42008

Business Wire. (2009, January 8). *Mattel to expand online focus in 2009 with development of Mattel Digital Network*. Retrieved from http://www.businesswire.com/portal/site/home/permalink/?ndm-ViewId=news_view&newsId=20090108005536&newsLang=en

CEOP. (2008, May 8). *Media Release – Dive in to Hector's World*. Retrieved from: http://www.ceop.gov.uk/mediacentre/pressreleases/2008/ceop_08052008.asp

Chmielewski, D., & Pham, A. (2008, January 28). Disney adds fantasy lands. *Los Angeles Times*. Retrieved http://articles.latimes.com/2008/jan/28/business/fi-virtualdisney28

Clarke, B. (2005) Children are getting media smart in the UK. *Young Consumers, Quarter 3*, 20-25.

Collins, J., & Porras, J. (1996). Building your company's vision. *Harvard Business Review*, 1-13. Retrieved from http://www.idbisc.com/building%20vision.pdf

Byron, T. (2008). *Byron review: Children and new technology*. Nottingham, England: Department of Children, Schools and Families & Department of Culture, Media and Sport.

Duddy, M., Harré, N., & Internet Safety Group. (2002). *The net generation: Internet safety issues for young New Zealanders*. Retrieved from http://www.netsafe.org.nz/Doc_Library/net_gen_report.pdf

Finkelhor, D., Mitchell, K. J., & Wolak, J. (2000). *Online victimization: A report on the nation's youth*. Retrieved from http://www.unh.edu/ccrc/internet-crimes/papers.html

Gladwell, M. (2000). *The tipping point: How little things can make a big difference*. London: Little, Brown and Company.

Internet Safety Group. (2000). *The New Zealand Internet safety kit*. Auckland, NZ: Author.

Internet Safety Group. (2002). *Online Safety Rule Card* (updated since 2002). Retrieved from http://www.netsafe.org.nz/Doc_Library/download/06safety_card.pdf

Internet Safety Group. (2003). *NetSafe kit for schools*. Auckland, NZ: Author.

Internet Safety Group and New Zealand Police. (2002). *Keeping Kiwi kids safer on the Internet* (updated since 2002). Retrieved from http://www.netsafe.org.nz/Doc_Library/download/cybersafetyfinal.pdf

McIntyre, P. (2008, October 9). Boom in virtual playgrounds for kids. *The Sydney Morning Herald*. Retrieved http://www.smh.com.au/news/biztech/virtual-playgrounds-for-kids/2008/10/09/1223145499071.html

McLean, T. (2008, March 26). Nick broadcast gets interactive. *Variety*. Retrieved http://www.variety.com/index.asp?layout=print_story&articleid=VR1117982954&categoryid=1983

Ministry of Education. (2003). *Digital horizons: Learning through ICT* (Revised ed.). Wellington, NZ: Ministry of Education.

Ministry of Education. (2005). *Foundations for discovery* (Extended version). Wellington, NZ: Ministry of Education.

NetSafe/Internet Safety Group. (2005). *Annual report 2004-5*. Auckland, NZ: Author.

NetSafe. (2006). *Hector's World evaluation: Pilot episode "Details, Details ..."* Auckland, NZ: Author.

Ofcom. (2008). *Social networking: A quantitative and qualitative research report into attitudes, behaviours and use*. Retrieved from http://www.ofcom.org.uk/advice/media_literacy/medlitpub/medlitpubrss/socialnetworking/

Rideout, V., Hamel, E., & Kaiser Family Foundation. (2006). *The media family: Electronic media in the lives of infants, toddlers, preschoolers and their parents*. Retrieved from Kaiser Family Foundation website: http://www.kff.org/entmedia/7500.cfm

Rideout, V. J., Vandewater, E. A., & Wartella, E. A. (2003). *Zero to six: Electronic media in the lives of infants, toddlers and preschoolers*. Retrieved from http://www.kff.org/entmedia/upload/Zero-to-Six-Electronic-Media-in-the-Lives-of-Infants-Toddlers-and-Preschoolers-PDF.pdf

Walt Disney quotes on animation. (n.d.). Retrieved from http://www.disneydreamer.com/walt/quotes.htm

CHAPTER 7

IS SOCIAL NETWORKING THE NEW "ONLINE PLAYGROUND" FOR YOUNG CHILDREN?

A Study of *Rate* Profiles in Estonia

Andra Siibak and Kadri Ugur

INTRODUCTION

The Convention on the Rights of the Child (1989) recognizes every child's right "to rest and leisure, to engage in play and recreational activities appropriate to the age of the child and to participate freely in cultural life and the arts." Playing in childhood is not only a human right but also a precursor for developing a strong identity, healthy relations, and adequate self esteem. Some researchers have noticed significant changes in the structure and content of children's play (Jenkinson, 2001), while others have noticed that the environment in which children play is changing as well (Sutton, 2008). Compared to children in the early 1980s, present day children are spending much less time outside or engaged in orga-

High-Tech Tots: Childhood in a Digital World, pp. 125–152

nized sports, and studies have noted a progressive increase in time spent in front of the computer (Swanbrow, 2004).

This chapter analyzes the use of online social networks, one of the most popular means of communicating online, by young children so as to understand whether these popular online platforms could be viewed as new versions of playgrounds with concrete rules, regularities, structure as well as expectations about the participants. The chapter begins with a theoretical discussion about the concept of playground and the importance of play and types of games in children's peer cultures as well as their possible influence on their identity constructions. The chapter then moves on to give an overview of the most popular social networking site in Estonia, rate.ee and its users as well as the methodology of the empirical study. This is followed by the analysis of various types of games the children tend to play on their social networking site profiles and profile images. We also focus on the differences in how parents and peers interpret these games. The chapter concludes with some pedagogical recommendations.

PLAYGROUND AS A PLACE FOR ANTICIPATORY SOCIALIZATION

Theorists have described a playground in different ways. For example, Sutton-Smith (1990) has viewed playground as children's "cultural and recurrent festival" (p. 6) whereas others have defined playground "as an environment where children are empowered to participate, create and develop in a unique and fundamental way" (Ota, Erricker, & Erricker, 1997, p. 19). Both of these descriptions are accurate and useful for understanding the importance of playground in children's lives. However, in this chapter we would like to promote another perspective in defining playground by comparing it to Pierre Bourdieu's (1993) concept of the "field." According to Bourdieu, a field is a structured place of positions that imposes a specific determination on all who enter it. In other words, fields form distinct microcosms endowed with their own rules, regularities, and forms of authority.

We suggest that the aforementioned features that actually make fields functional also characterize the playgrounds of children. According to Veronika Kalmus (personal commuication, October 12, 2009), we can distinguish between at least three types of processes and influences in building up the structure and rules of a playground. First, some of the children's playgrounds, both in online as well as offline settings, are built by adults. Second, children themselves interpret the actions, rules, and roles of grown-ups while playing on the playgrounds. Third, children's peer culture is a significant agent in creating new rules or modifying the rules of adults according to children's own standards. Play enables the children to change, emphasize, or reduce the position of different under-standings, rules and hierarchies apparent in all of the fields of society. Therefore, we claim that children's play on the playground could be viewed as a certain type of "anticipatory socialization," that is, a prepara-tory activity in order to be able to function within other fields (economic, social, cultural, etc.) in their later life (Merton, 1965).

Playgrounds are used for unstructured play as well as structured play (games), both of which are important tools in identity building. Unstruc-tured play can be viewed as a voluntary, intrinsically motivated activity that is significant to the socialization of young people. The limits of unstructured play are wide. They include a mother's funny facial expres-sions that are supposed to amuse an infant, preschoolers playing home or shopping, but also adolescents practicing extreme sports; unstructured play can be solitary or played together with one or more playmates. The benefits of free, unstructured play are also affirmed in the study of the American Association of Pediatrics: It promotes brain development, teaches interaction, gives an opportunity to practice adult roles, helps to develop confidence, fosters conflict resolution skills as well as other abili-ties (Ginsburg & the Committee on Communications, 2007). In addition, when engaged in social play with playmates, children are able to receive feedback about their actions from their peers and reform their actions according to the feedback received.

Games, however, are more connected to the processes Bourdieu described (1993) when analyzing agents' involvement in the fields. He claimed that "in order for a field to function, there have to be stakes and people prepared to play the game, endowed with the *habitus* that implies knowledge and recognition of the imminent laws of the field, the stakes, and so on" (p. 72). Likewise children's playgrounds can be viewed as are-nas for struggle where all the players would like to overturn or preserve the existing distribution of capital. Therefore, it could be claimed that the children who are involved in the playground share a certain number of fundamental interests that are all connected to the mere existence of the playground. According to Kalmus (personal communication, 2009), status hierarchies are constantly formed and reformed on the playgrounds, and these formations are often influenced by biology (e.g., gender), forms of capital received (e.g., brand clothing, pocket money, cultural capital, etc.), as well as the children's own abilities and skills (e.g., social skills). These elements all influence the tacit structures formed on children's play-grounds. For instance, based on Moreno's (1997) method of *sociometry*, we can fairly well distinguish between the "stars" and the "outcasts" as well as other peer relations occurring on the playground. By sociometry Moreno meant a system of measuring human relations. In the group of people (children or adults) he asked everybody to choose one person they liked the most (or they wanted to spend a day off, or to travel with etc). "Stars" were people in the group who were chosen often; "outcasts" were not chosen at all, or very rarely. Moreno also described "chains"—a structures of relations where person A chooses B, B chooses C, and so forth. Relation structures like this form spontaneously in every group even before participants are able to reflect on them.

THE INFLUENCE OF PEER CULTURE ON IDENTITY CONSTRUCTIONS

Childhood sociologist William Corsaro (1992) stated, "Childhood socialization must be understood also as a social and collective process" (p. 162) as part of peer culture; that is, "A stable set of activities or routines, artifacts, values and concerns that children produce and share in interaction with peers" (p. 162) that is produced collectively with peers. Gaining control of one's life and sharing this control with others are two basic themes in peer cultures. Children acquire control through play and games that serve a crucial role in young children's lives.

In the present day context, these initial peer cultures are not only formed in play groups and nursery schools, as Corsaro (1992) proposed, but also in the online world while communicating and playing together in different online environments. As children do not fully grasp the social knowledge of the adult world, they try to "creatively appropriate information from the adult world to produce their own unique peer cultures" (p. 168). In this way children also become part of the adult culture as they reproduce the elements and information gained from the adult world in their own creative manner. Jean Piaget (1999) noticed that a child's attitude towards the person he or she imitates plays a great role; young children will imitate only adults or older children who are admired by a child (p. 73). This tendency seems to continue in further developmental stages; for example, in role play children "aim older" when choosing the roles. In that way both imitation and role play have a significant role in the process of socialization.

While communicating in offline as well as online worlds, people are always trying to obtain information about each other in order to be able to know in advance what to expect and what kind of response to give. Goffman (1990) was the first to emphasize the importance of impression management, that is, people often engage in activities in order "to convey an impression to others which it is in his interests to convey" (p. 4). Whenever other persons are present, people tend to emphasize aspects of the self that typically correspond to norms and ideals of the group the person belongs to, or wishes to belong to. Therefore, in order to find out what kind of qualities and features are thought to be sought by potential partners a person may have to "perform" several acts before receiving the approval they were looking for. In case of communicating online, the impression management is formulated into a constant worry of how to construct one's virtual identity so that it would be appreciated and accepted among one's peer group.

Lemke (2008) proposes that people have two kinds of identity concepts: "identity-in practice" and "identity-in-timescales" (p. 24). The former is similar to Goffman's (1990) theory about identity performances and is used to refer to identity constructions on the short timescales that take place as small-group activities (e.g., role-playing computer-games or participating in Internet communities). The latter is a more long-term identity that is not determined by a single identity performance in a single situation, but is made up of several actions and different types of situations we encounter and therefore connected to our *habitus*. Both of these identity notions cannot exist without the other as the two different views upon the same concept are interchangeably linked together. It could be claimed that while constructing profiles for a social networking site, young people practice several identity performances that need not be taken up for a long period of time. Therefore, constructing online profiles could also be viewed as an "auxiliary ego" (Moreno, 1978) which was created in psychodrama in order to allow the protagonist to see "oneself" from aside (p. 603). Auxiliary ego as well as one's online profile, can work as any other kind of mask as they hide and protect the real identity of the person. Negative feedback or rejection will not hurt as much when it is addressed to the mask, not the real identity of the person.

According to Larsen (2007), who used the identity notions proposed by Lemke (2008) to analyze the identity performances of youngsters in *Arto*, a Danish social networking site, youngsters are using "many different identity performances which are all linked to the individual, social, and historical lives of Arto users" (p. 16). Larsen claims that in the context of social networking websites youngsters use their friends and the feedback received from them as "mediational means" in order to reconstruct one's identity (p. 16).

ONLINE ENVIRONMENTS AND YOUNG CHILDREN

Nursery school children are reported to be the newest group of Internet users amongst whom 32% has used the Internet before they go to kindergarten (Feller, 2005). Children who are 2 to 5 years old are usually using the Internet under the supervision of an adult when viewing interactive stories or animated lessons that are launched for teaching numbers, letters and rhymes online (Feller, 2005).

As children grow older, the time spent online also increases. A recent study by Double Click Performics found that 83% of the children between the ages 10 to 14 spent daily an hour or more online (Mildin, 2008). Children in this age bracket were found to be more engaged in some online environments and less interested in others. According to the results of the DoubleClickPerformics study, for example, 72% of the children online had a profile in a social networking websites whereas 60% rarely or never read blogs (Mildin, 2008). Frequent engagement in social networking sites by this age-group, has also been reported by other studies (e.g., RIT Cyber Survey, see McQuade & Sampat, 2008). The numbers of social networking site users among 10- to 12-year-olds has been growing rapidly over the last couple of years. For instance, findings of the Harris Poll "2007 Youth Pulse" suggest that more than twice as many children from the 10-12 age group reported using social networking sites in 2007 than in 2006 (Oppenheim, 2008). Furthermore, according to the eMarketer estimates 1.9 million 3- to 11-year-olds are using the social networking sites by the year 2011 ("Teen Social Marketing," 2008).

The immense popularity of social networking websites among the age group could be explained not only because of the fact the sites offer convergence among the previously separate activities of e-mail, downloading videos or music, diaries, and photo albums, but also because these means offer children an opportunity for self-expression, sociability, and creativity. According to Livingstone (2008), "creating and networking online content is becoming an integral means of managing one's identity, lifestyle and social relations" (p. 394).

Our interest in social networking sites is related to the fact that young people consider these new platforms as " 'their' space, visible to the peer group more than to adult surveillance" (Livingstone, 2008, p. 396). Without the recognizable surveillance of adults, children not only start to "explore the social matrix of relating to others," but they also feel safer when trying out and displaying different constructions and reconstructions of their identity (Ota, Ericker, & Ericker, 1997, p. 21). Many features (e.g., freedom, entertainment, communication with peers, competition and change of roles) as well as the activities which are typical to the ordinary playgrounds are also visible on the social networking website. Previous research (Livingstone, 2008, p. 407) has indicated that especially younger children are the ones who "relish the opportunities to play and display" on their SNS profiles.

THE ROLE OF ADULTS ON THE PLAYGROUND

The role of adults on the playground is mostly controversial. On the one hand, children need freedom and independence for the types of play that are relevant for identity building. Besides, the exclusion of adults helps also to maintain "the secret nature of the playground world" (Ota et al., 1997, p. 22). On the other hand, however, both in the real surroundings and on the Internet there can be risks or harmful factors that are too powerful for children to deal with. Nevertheless, even in this case we have to bear in mind that the activities which an adult observer may consider risky are often precisely the opportunity that the youngsters themselves seek (Livingstone & Helsper, 2007).

Jenkinson (2001, p. XV) suggests that the controversy of the adult's role goes even deeper: "Adults are simultaneously children's protectors and their greatest detractors. Children learn to look to us for protection, yet they are also taught to fear us. A stranger is a potential source of danger, not someone to ask for help." To minimize risks there is definitely a need for adult in supportive role: "chaperones," or "drama directors" who are aware of limits and can contribute to the well-being of every participant. However, adults' reactions to new forms of social interaction reflect their indetermination, and they struggle to fulfill the role of supportive person in the background. Furthermore, adults may feel more "lost" in online playgrounds than when serving in the capacity of keeping an eye on the offline playgrounds. Comparative studies in Europe indicate that parental interest and control over children's media activity (watching TV, surfing in the Internet) is a little bit stronger in the countries that did not undergo big social changes during the last 20 years. In transition societies adults are slightly less concerned what the children do online (Hasebrink, Livingstone, & Haddon, 2008).

TYPES OF PLAY

Play is a complex activity that can be understood and defined in different ways. Evaldsson and Corsaro (1998) distinguish between four major types of play: spontaneous fantasy play, sociodramatic role play, games with rules, and games where cultural and economic resources have to be appropriated. During spontaneous fantasy play children manipulate their toy figures in order to turn them into imaginary characters or take on themselves the roles of monsters or other figures of fantasy. In sociodramatic role play children experiment with the behaviors of different types of people in society; for example, how different genders should act and what kind of roles and expectations are connected with each gender. In these role-plays children are "creating images of the adult world and reflecting on their place in that world in the present as well as projecting to their futures as adults" (Corsaro, 2003, p.126). In games with rules, such as card and board games or various chasing games, children often make up their own rules as they progress in the games. Games that involve trading of some goods (e.g., marbles) are also popular among children. These types of games are focused on "an ongoing specification of standards of value as well as the mutual assessment of the relative value of objects, and the determination of the general preferences and situated motives of children" (Evaldsson & Corsaro, 1998, p. 167). Still, all these different types of play are made up of various elements, such as humor, verbal chanting and rhyming routines as well as other types of collective fun, which are communally shared and spontaneously generated among the peers (Corsaro, 1992).

Online communities can possibly be (or have potential to become) online playgrounds. The basic functions of playing (having fun, supporting one's identity and social relationships, recreating) can be acted out in social networking and communities. It is possible that online communities are, to a certain degree, replacing interactions that traditionally were carried out in the same physical space. We assume that children feel the adult control to be less strong in the case of online communities and, therefore, experience more freedom in choosing roles and expressing themselves. Since feelings of freedom are very important for role play, we assume that most playful activities in online communities can be described as sociodramatic games. Nevertheless, due to the influence of adult culture, we also expect to find various instances of gendered play and mimicry practiced on the most popular online playground for Estonian children called *Rate*.

SOCIAL NETWORKING SITE RATE.EE AS AN ONLINE-PLAYGROUND

The social networking website *Rate* is an adult-created online playground which has more than 290,000 active users (www.rate.ee). The number is huge for a tiny nation like Estonia with a population of 1.3 million. A questionnaire survey "Youth and the Internet" (Siibak, 2007), carried out among 11- to 18-year old pupils ($N = 713$) in autumn 2007 revealed the immense popularity of the site. Approximately 71% of the 11- to 12-year old sample were users of *Rate*.

Compared to some other social networking websites that are mostly focused on networking, most of the users of *Rate* are foremost interested in being rated and rating others. The majority of the agents acting on this field are hoping to gain positive comments and points for their profile images accompanying the textual parts of the profile. The ones who receive the highest points have the opportunity to become members of one of the numerous popularity charts created on the site (e.g. "TOP 100 of the most remarkable men and women in Rate," "TOP 100 of the most famous users," "TOP 100 of the most popular dates," etc.). These kinds of popularity charts help the users to distinguish between Moreno's (1937/ 1997) "stars" and "outcasts." However, when actively taking part in this kind of struggle for recognition and acceptance by peers, the users of *Rate* also help to "reproduce the game by helping to produce belief in the value of the stakes" (Bourdieu, 1993, p. 74). Furthermore, just as in the case of agents participating on a certain field (see also Bourdieu, 1993), the new users of *Rate* have to fully recognize the value of the game and learn the practical principles about its function.

The website provides the users with various opportunities for spending their free time, including sending e-mails, chatting in forums, keeping a blog, reading horoscopes, and converging among different communities. Several other advantages (e.g., to upload one's photos to the site before others, to get a VIP status in a chat room, to use the Compatibility-Meter in order to test one's compatibility with certain users from the opposite sex, etc.) are made available for the users who have purchased SOL's, the monetary unit only applicable on the *Rate* website. Therefore, similar to a typical playground, the players on an online playground also need to have various types of capital (e.g., economic, social, and cultural) in order to succeed in the game.

At the same time, *Rate* not only functions as an online playground for children but also as part of the economic field of adults. Dedicated *Rate* users, who constantly want to keep track of changes in their profile, can use the services of a special Rate mobile phone. Whenever something of importance happens on their profile (e.g., in case someone has added them as a friend or if they were selected for one of the popularity charts), they will receive a *Rate*-SMS (short message service) message. Furthermore, with the help of this special phone card all calls made and SMS messages sent to other *Rate* users are free of charge (www.rate.ee/mobiil).

Adults have also created additional offline games for the *Rate* users. The most active users of the site may continue playing according to the adult rules, even on the traditional media field. One can take part in a weekly radio show "Choose me!" or become the star of a TV dating show *The Right Choice* on a private TV channel. Therefore, we claim that *Rate* is not only an online playground where children can appropriate their games to fit with the rules and values of the peer culture, but also a place for production and reproduction of the adult culture and the economic field.

METHODS AND DATA

In the following sections of this chapter we apply the theoretical framework related to the concept of "playground" to the analysis of data drawn from an empirical study analyzing the Rate profiles of 11- to 12-year old boys and girls. In this age group most of the children move from a relatively peaceful developmental phase (in psychoanalytical tradition called latent phase) and enter a phase of preadolescence, where all the aspects of personal development (e.g., sexual development, social relations with peers, gaining independency from parents, etc.) are extremely vivid and rapid. Being "inconsistent and unpredictable" at this age is rather a norm than pathology (Freud, 1958). Furthermore, as preadolescent children are also said to have "a heightened control of acceptance" (Parker, Rubin, Erath, Wojslawowicz, & Buskirk, 2006, p. 428), our intent was to capture this boundary between "childish" and "adolescent" games.

The search engine in rate.ee was used for sampling. The age range and gender were inserted in the engine in order to find profiles of youngsters belonging to the 11-12 age group. The engine displayed only the first 300 girls or boys, depending on the search, who were currently online and whose age matched the search criteria. Random selection was used for compiling the sample of 11- to 12-year-olds who happened to be online on that moment. Being online on the site was an important aspect as we assumed that these children therefore could be viewed as active users of the site who thus could be well aware of the expectations and norms of the community. Ten profiles of girls and 10 profiles of boys were selected. The sample consisted of 6 girls and 5 boys who were 12-years-old; 4 girls and 5 boys were 11-years-old.

Content analysis was used in order to analyze the data provided in the textual parts of the profiles. The main focus of the analysis was to find out what kind of interest and tastes young children proclaim to have as well as what kind of communities they had joined. The labels which represented the interests and various communities on the site are created by the users. The search engine can be used for looking for the interests and communities children would like to include on their profiles or new labels can be created by everyone in order to emphasize their particular interest.

The girls in the sample had enlisted 179 different interests and boys 160 interests which were grouped into 21 and 19 categories respectively. Both genders had categories which emphasized their interest in famous people/celebrities, things/objects, sports, animals, brand names or were concerned with the lifestyle of youngsters. The categories created for analyzing the interests of children were also used for analyzing the communities. All in all, 18 community categories for the girls and 15 for boys were created.

In order to study the photos accompanying the profiles, another type of content analysis was carried out. The analysis was based on the photos that were publicly available for everyone to see on the website. Photos that appeared in special photo albums accompanying the profile were not studied. However, not all the youngsters in the sample were included in the visual analysis. One girl and two of the boys from the sample presented all of their photos in albums; one boy had no photos uploaded on his profile; and the profiles of two girls were blocked because of their inappropriate behavior. Therefore, the results of the study are based on the photos collected from the profiles of seven boys and seven girls. All in all 25 photos of girls and 25 photos of boys were used for the visual analysis.

The categories used for coding the photos were based on the theories of Goffman (1979) followed up by the research of Kang (1997) and Umiker-Sebeok (1981). Furthermore, the method of "reading images" that was introduced by Kress and van Leeuwen (1996) and developed further in the studies of Bell (2001) was also used for building categories for content analysis. Although most of the categories formed for the content analysis have been originally used in order to study the representations of gender on advertisements, we suggest that photos used for self-presentation and impression management on social networking websites can be viewed as "advertising the self" in the virtual world.

The aim of the visual analysis was to find out which strategies do the young children use in order to construct their gendered selves on the photos. We were also interested in analyzing if young children mimic the visual self-presentation strategies of older youngsters on rate.ee (see Siibak, 2007). The main coding categories that were used for coding the photos were as follows:

1. Social Distance marks the distance from where the photo is taken (Kress & van Leeuwen, 1990). The category was divided into six subcategories:

   - Intimate Distance—only the face or the head of the person portrayed on the photo are visible
   - Close Personal Distance—the head and the shoulders of the person portrayed are visible
   - Far Personal Distance that—the person on the photo is depicted from the waist up
   - Close Social Distance—the whole body of a person is visible on the photo
   - Far Social Distance —the whole figure of a person "with space around it" can be seen
   - Public Distance—torsos of at least four or five people are depicted on the photo

2. Activities. The category consisted also of six subcategories which were studied in order to analyze what are the main activities young children are interested in portraying about themselves.

   *   Entertaining—contained activities like singing, dancing, playing a musical instrument, and so forth.
   *   Sport—included activities like playing basketball, swimming, surfing, roller skating, riding a bike, and so forth.
   *   Romance—included activities like hugging, kissing, embracing, and so forth.
   *   Everyday doings—included activities like talking on the phone, eating, drinking, taking photos, having conversations with their friends, and so forth.
   *   Posing—was used for photos were children were not engaged in any purposeful activities

3. Behavior: Based on the studies of Bell (2001) the Category of Behavior was used to analyze the way the person depicted on the photo looks at the camera. The category of behavior was narrowed down to four different behavior patterns represented on the person's face while posing.

   *   Demand/Affiliation—represents an angle when there is no power difference between the person on the photo and its viewer. The image is at the eye level and the model looks at the viewer directly, smiling.
   *   Demand/Seduction—the person on the photo looks up at the viewer, head canted, smiling or pouting seductively at the viewer.
   *   Demand/Submission—the person on the photo looks down at the viewer from the position of superiority and is not smiling.
   *   Offer/Ideal – person on the photo "offers" oneself to the viewer "as items of information, object of contemplation, impersonally, as though they were specimens in a display case" (Kress & van Leeuwen, 1996, p. 124).

Studies (Siibak, 2007) about the visual self-presentation of older youngsters have found that while girls use the behavior Demand/Seduction most frequently in the photos, the behavior Offer/Ideal is most often found in the photos of boys. The category was included in the analysis to test if the above mentioned strategies are also used in the younger age-group.

1. Facial Expressions: The subcategories of this category were enti-
    tled: smiling, serious, pouting, making faces, covering one's face
    (mouth).

Studies (Dodd, Russel, & Jenkins, 1999; Hall, LeBeau, Gordon Reinoso,
& Thayer, 2001) have reported that women tend to smile more often than
their male counterparts on the photos. The category was used in the analysis to test if the photos of young children correspond to this kind of gender stereotypical behavior.

2. Location: The Category was cut into four different subcategories
    depending on the location where the photo is taken:

-   Indoors—apartment, bedroom, office, classroom, nightclub,
    and so forth.
-   In the wilderness—in the woods, near a lake/sea/river, in the
    park/garden, and so forth.
-   In the city—on the street, near a (famous) building, and so
    forth.
-   Decontextualized—the setting of the photo is unidentifiable
    and does not allow any purposeful activities (Umiker-Sebeok,
    1981).

Traditionally masculinity has been associated with the public sphere,
and therefore, the representations of men often depict them in public settings, whereas women are portrayed in the private sphere. In order to
analyze if gender stereotypical posing strategies can be found in terms of
selecting a location for posing, the category was included in the analysis.

For a more in-depth study of how children and adults understand elements of play and game in a social networking site, from August to
December 2008 we interviewed three boys and three girls ranging from
12-13 years of age. Respondents were found by using the snowball sampling method (first respondent was suggested by children on a real playground, she suggested who could be next respondents, etc.), and during
the half-an-hour semistructured interviews some visual and verbal elements from *Rate* accounts were shown to respondents with a question,
"Why do you think this person uploaded this photo, joined this community…?" or "Do you think they did it seriously or just for fun?" The feeling during the interviews was very casual, and voluntary comments from
respondents often gave more detailed inside-information than directly
asked.

During the same period of time six adults were interviewed. Two of them were parents of 11- to 13-year-olds; the other 4 were teachers and parents. During semistructured interviews a list of *Rate* activities and communities was shown to respondents in order to get their reaction, and four photos were discussed.

SOCIODRAMATIC ROLE PLAY ON THE PROFILES

The analysis of the interests of young children revealed that children in the age-group are interested in portraying themselves in rebellious ways. One of the most popular categories in terms of interests was "Rebellious youth." The labels belonging to the category were made up of different rebellious expressions that could be regarded as part of the sociodramatic role-play suggested by Corsaro and Nelson (2003). Children relish taking on and expressing power with the use of expressions like

"Tell.it.straight.Up.To.My.Face.Not.Speak.Behind.My.Back,"
"schoolpetrolmatchesbomb:" "IamwhatIamIfYouDon'tLikeItThenPissOff,"

or

"Itisbettertoruinmyyouththannottouseitatall,"

and so forth.[1] These communities are created in order to develop the "strategies of resistance" (Cobb, Danby, & Farrell, 2005, p. 6) against the imposed restrictions, regulations, and rules the children have to submit to in their life-worlds. While belonging to these communities, children are performing the images of rebellious youngsters who are just trying to go past the rules created by their parents and teachers in the offline society as the online world gives them more freedom to test the boundaries between right and wrong. The youngsters seem also very much aware of the freedom of expression the online world gives them, as they see these kinds of platforms only as a place for themselves without the restrictions made by parents or teachers.

Furthermore, children had also joined in several communities that could be viewed as online spaces of sociodramatic role-play. The majority of communities of this kind such as "Help, my parents won't let me live!" "We do not break the rules, we just make them ourselves," and "I just like forbidden things," reflected the rebellious lifestyle of youngsters. By joining these communities, children seem to "use the dramatic license of imaginative play to project to the future—a time when they will be in charge and in control of themselves and others" (Corsaro & Nelson, 2003, p. 112).

Nevertheless, interviews with young experts indicated that in many cases the manifest of "rebellious youth" is a strong exaggeration or meant just to tease strangers. In some cases the young seem to rebel against the inside rules of the game; however, they still obey the rules in order to be able to stay in the game.

> Girl 12: "Communities are pointless, really. You just want to be popular and so you pick the same communities that most popular people have. If you are in the right communities, it raises your fame and you'll make it to the TOP 100 and that's the whole point of it."

> Boy 12: "Some communities or interests are picked just because you want to have them as much as possible. I have this "Burn the schools, I can't learn any more!" I wanted to have more interests in my list."

> Girl 13: "I just picked some communities for my profile, they don't mean anything. I mean, my friends and who know me, they know my interests too and they understand that I am just … joking."

Corsaro (1997) has also discussed the development of subgroups and hierarchies inside the subgroups of children that have formed due to the resistance to rules imposed by adults. Children organize these groups so as to govern themselves and maintain social order in the group. For instance, there were communities in *Rate* where children could take a role of authoritative figures in order to give advice and share their opinions and pieces of wisdom with others. Children's agency is visible in communities like "Tough men do not smoke," "All girls are worthy to be treated like princesses," "Life is too short to waste it on people who do not care about you," where children are seriously engaged in moral issues to influence their peers.

In addition to the communities where children could practice the feeling of empowerment from taking up adult roles, there were several communities where children represented different aspects related to being young and the lifestyle of youngsters. Communities like "Music is our freedom," "MSN is our freedom," or "Thinking left and laughing all the time," were popular among both of the sexes. In comparison to the communities where power and control are exhibited, there were also communities that emphasized their young age and problems connected to being young (e.g., "Help, I'm a minor!" and "I hate math!" or "We are the ones who get the strange looks").

In comparison to the communities and interests that emphasized being in control and empowerment, the communities some of the girls joined demonstrated clear evidence of the struggles children have to face while growing up. These communities that were described by sayings like "I'm sorry I can't be perfect," "sorry that I exist," or "I am ugly" refer to the pressures girls feel in their everyday lives. Joining these kinds of communities can on the one hand be viewed as public declarations of low self-esteem which seem to be a vivid result of the expectations of peers and family members as well as the existing beauty norms of the society. On the other hand, the interviews with young experts showed also other possibilities in decoding these communities. For example, it is remarkable how unanimous the respondents were when they interpreted names of some communities.

> Girl 12:   "This **Sorry I do exist**—it's because she was angry for a while. And this **Sorry, I am not a toy**, this one you pick if somebody has used you or so. **I hate mornings**—they like to sleep."
>
> Boy 12:   "I don't believe that these people who have "sex" in their interests, that they are really having sex.

Interpretations like these give us a reason to state that the use of codes and exaggerating was a popular element in children's online sociodramatic role play.

GENDERED PLAY ON THE PROFILES

As they move into middle childhood, children's understandings of friendships as well as the nature of their involvement in the relationship changes (see Parker et al., 2006). Children's friendship choices not only become more stable (see Corsaro, 1999), but preadolescent children also start to form cliques which are reported to function (see Brown & Klute, 2003) as sources of definition and identity development. The "specialized relationship with friends" (Youniss, 1999, p. 23) were emphasized on the profiles of rate.ee. In some of the cases children used expressions like "I think that friends are all that matters," or enlisted names (e.g., Karl, Sandra, Kertu) or nicknames (e.g., Ellu, Raku) of their friends in order to express the special role these friends have in their lives. Children also admitted the importance of love and close relationships in the lives of the children with different sayings like "If-you'd-only-knew-how-much-you-mean-to-me," or "When I say I care I really do," or just by including different emoticons that express love (L) or hugging (K) as their interests.

Gender segregation in children's play groups during most of the childhood has led some authors (see Zarbatany, Hartmann, & Rankin, 1990) to suggest that "girls and boys inhabit almost entirely separate worlds in childhood" (Parker et al., 2006, p. 439). Gender specific tastes emerged when speaking about one's likes and dislikes. For example, girls were interested in chocolate, strawberries and the sun, compared to the typically masculine tastes of boys which included computers, msn-messenger, Internet, money, bicycles, and so forth. In comparison to the girls, boys also emphasized stereotypically masculine interests in motor vehicles and sports, the categories that were rarely mentioned by the girls. Furthermore, the favorite activities of girls differed greatly from that of the boys. Girls claimed to be interested in very feminine hobbies like drawing, singing, dancing, writing, and so forth, while the boys preferred sleeping, jumping, watching TV, or listening music.

IDENTITY GAMES WITH THE ELEMENT OF IMITATION

While posing for the camera children were (un)consciously starting to play games that involve imitation. These games allow them to explore different identity possibilities and through this kind of pretense experiment with different roles.

In the twenty-first century world the body has become a project not just for females but also for males, and the importance of being physically fit has therefore also become a crucial element of identity management (Gill, Henwood, & Mclean, 2005; Thomas, 1996; Wienke, 1998). The influence of the advertising industry and media representations has led to the conclusion that in a present day world "body has become a source of symbolic capital, less because of what the body is able to do then how it looks" (Gill et al., 2005, p. 5) The majority of the profile images of children were taken from the far social distance or the far personal distance, that is, either the whole body of a person or at least the body from the waist up was visible on the photo. For instance, one could see girls sitting or lying on the beds smiling sweetly to the camera, or boys taking poses in order to present their masculine self on a motorbike.

Sometimes the boys were also found to be engaged in activities that explored masculine stereotypes. In several occasions boys could be found posing on motorbikes or playing football. On some of the photos, boys also stepped out of these normative masculine roles and displayed their childlike behavior when posing together or hugging their pet animals just like the girls did. Nevertheless, the analysis of photos still suggests that the children were usually not engaged in any purposeful activities while the photo was taken. The most popular activity exhibited on the photos was ordinary posing in front of the camera. When taking this kind of model-like poses the boys preferred to imitate the stars of the hip-hop culture. In their baggy clothing, peaked-caps, sunglasses and massive accessories the boys were trying to take the role of a cool and trend conscious guys.

Just as in case of the 14- to 25-year old men (see Siibak, 2006, 2007), the majority of 11- to 12-year old boys were also displaying themselves on the photos as ideal objects that seem to be unconscious of being photographed. Thus, it could be claimed that the twenty-first century boys have adopted the passive role that was previously associated more strongly with women. The only difference in posing behavior in terms of age was found in the facial expressions displayed in the photos. In comparison to older men, young boys tend to smile more on the photos (Siibak, 2006, 2007).

Model-like behavior and poses were more frequently exposed by the girls who were often found tilting their heads and seductively smiling to the camera. Using the behavior classified as Demand/Seduction, the girls are exhibiting their understanding of the feminine gender role as the latter behavior has been considered to be stereotypically feminine and frequently encountered on the covers of women's or fashion magazines.

Our young experts obviously recognized the "codes" used in photos, but they had difficulty verbalizing their experiences. However, all six respondents indicated that the pictures are mainly meant as fun, and they even confessed that the main "game" in *Rate*—rating—is mostly a game for them.

> Girl 12:   This is a typical Rate face. Everybody looks like this on Rate photos.... It's like ... I don't know ... I can't explain it.... Like you are not looking straight ahead. Or if you take your own picture. It's kind of sick. If you want to show yourself kind of higher than others.
>
> Girl 13:   If I get high points from somebody, I give him/her[2] high points too. It's like saying thanks or so. I do not get any ideas, like wow, they gave me high points, well, now I am like something ... I mean, I do understand that it's just the Internet, it's not like a question of life and death.
>
> Girl 12:   It's Rate – it's not life but it's necessary for life.

Both boys and girls liked to pose in the public places and not in the private sphere. In most of the cases nature and cityscape were selected as a place for taking a photo; therefore, we could see boys sitting on the stones or posing on pastures as well as girls hanging out on the streets. However, 11- to 12-year old children also used private settings for posing more often than 14- to 25-year old youngsters (Siibak, 2006, 2007). Besides the usual scenes with youngsters sitting on the sofas and posing on the beds, photos of children taking a bubble-bath could also be found. All in all, it could be postulated that children tried to combine different locations on their profile photos in order to portray various aspects of their selves. On the one hand, they positioned themselves as outgoing and active youngsters spending their time in the wilderness as well as in the city. On the other hand, they also invited the viewer to the intimate places in their homes.

The analysis of the visual self-presentation strategies of 11- to 12-year-olds indicated that in the majority of categories (e.g., Behavior, Location, Social Distance, Activities), the findings match the results of previous studies carried out with a 14- to 25-year old sample (Siibak, 2006, 2007). These findings also allow us to postulate that children are very well aware of the expectations of their peer group and consciously monitor the behavior of older persons on the website in order to incorporate the same kind of tendencies from the adult culture into their own presentation of self. Thus, social comparison (see Bandura, 1989) also plays an important role in the development of attitudes of personal agency and self-efficacy in online environments. Furthermore, the narcissistic self-display that would characterize a number of the photos on the sample could be explained by the visible role the media, advertising, and fashion industry play in the lives of youngsters. While imitating the roles of "real" men and women displayed in the everyday media world, the children were reproducing their own understanding of the society's norms and expectations.

ADULTS ON THE ONLINE PLAYGROUND

Spontaneous, creative play can only be born when participants feel themselves free and safe on the playground. In real physical spaces adults can identify dangers and usually respond to children's safety. This is done in many ways. First, playgrounds are designed, located, and built considering children's physical well being. Second, parents or other responsible adults are near and follow the action on the playground. However, in case of the online playground, adults are not very confident in making decisions about children's activities.

In the *Rate* environment adults are present in two ways: as moderators and as account owners. The real age of moderators is not known, but socially they try to fulfill the role of "groundkeeper" or "director." However, our young experts claim that moderators only demand that the pictures are not too obviously retouched and that the protagonist must be identified clearly. When there are more people on the photo, the protagonist must add a remark that the owner of the profile is standing on the left or on the right, hugging their sweetheart, and so forth. The moderators also have the power to choose "special ones"—the most desired status in this community.

However, since there is no age limit in participation, many adults have created their own profiles in *Rate*. They act like everybody else: uploading photos, rating others, developing their profiles, but this kind of activity is not accepted by young children.

Girl 12:   It's totally sick, if somebody like 30- to 40-years-old is on Rate.

Girl 13:   Yeah, and nagging. How sick can you get, I mean. It's totally crazy, like a fat lady on the swing.

Girl 12:   Like there is a 56-year old woman with a big fame, and she keeps begging others for high grades ... she wants to be on top 100. Totally weird.

Boy 13:   They are not disturbing ... it's just cranky to have them there.

Adults interviewed expressed their lack of experience and uncertainty about the rules and practices of online communication. However, some of the respondents tried to define children's activities on a social networking site as a game.

Teacher and mother, 48:   I feel that this online world of children is so distant from me, I just can't understand it. Therefore I struggle to understand rather than condemn. Perhaps they do not mean these things as badly as I take it. Teacher, female, 29: They are playing. It's not their real self they express on those photos.

Teacher and mother, 48:   I like when kids are making fun. These communities have quite funny names. It indicates that kids are thinking of life and understand things and.... It bothers me though a little, these obscenities, for I am the person of old times.

Teacher, female, 52:   Are they imitating somebody or have they found their own style? It would be nice if they had found their style in life.... This girl ... she is like more inviting ... kind of sexually even.... Perhaps she does not mean it like this but I get that impression.... But I am old and corrupted; perhaps she just wants to show how pretty she is.

Teacher, female, 29:   I think we overestimate the sexual load in Rate.ee. We read out of the pictures more

> than kids have put into pictures. They are just imitating, just wanting to be like adults. Like this second girl. I think she is just demonstrating her new boots.

Adults seem to recognize that there are some games going on, but often they interpret these games as "JUST a game." The relevance of social role play for children's identity building remains unnoticed. In several cases respondents expressed their double standards in real life and online, pointing out that "I would like it less; if she dressed like that in real life" or "If he came to school with an attitude like that he would get himself into trouble." It seems to be difficult for adults to understand the codes children are using in online role plays. But even in case they recognize some kind of violation of social norms, they tend to interpret those situations differently in real life and online. Adults in our study did not show any concern about differences between online and real environments, for example, the fact that a child cannot control how uploaded pictures are used by other Internet users or that one cannot really be sure what kind of person is behind a user name. If that is so, adults can hardly fulfill their role as a caregiver, teacher, or parent.

The limited role of parents was also reported by the research network EU Kids Online whose report stated that parental mediation increases with age until around the age of 10; after that there is strong decrease in mediation (Hasebrink et al., 2008). Estonian children are very active Internet users, however, compared to other countries like the United Kingdom and the Netherlands where Internet usage is also high among children, the parents of Estonian children do not pay enough attention to the online activities of their children. According to EU Kids Online report, Estonia (together with Bulgaria, Poland, and the Czech Republic) was considered a high risk/lowest coping country, which means that Estonian children have frequently encountered risks online; however, the parents' perception of their children's ability to cope with risks is low (Hasebrink et al., 2008).

This leads us to pose the following question: How can educators and families encourage positive usage and discourage negative social consequences associated with social networking? What can adults do in order to make social networking a safer playground? What kind of adult activities would be acceptable for children?

RECOMMENDATIONS FOR PARENTAL STRATEGIES

We believe that one way of overcoming the generation gap in terms of the attitude towards online activities is to create a common ground for discussing online experiences. Mutual understanding of the issue can only be reached when accepting these online experiences as a part of everyday life. Parents should be able to talk about what is happening in online communities just in the way they are interested about how their children are doing at school. In order to do so, adults must define their position clearly and also be aware of risks and dangers in online communities. Awareness about risks and dangers includes recognizing situations that need deeper investigation or discussions with a child. Adequate conversation techniques provide parents with a much-needed alternative to strong parenting methods like prohibiting or limiting Internet access in order to protect children. We will give a short list of knowledge, skills, and attitudes for parents and educators, and make some suggestions for a conversation technique that might promote a meaningful dialogue between generations (see Table 7.1).

Talking about peer culture can be difficult even for youngsters belonging to the same age group because a large part of the communication within the group is often nonverbal. For example, hair style, clothes, body language, make up style, music preferences, likes and dislikes are in many cases very important in terms of recognizing "our group," but they can hardly be verbalized. The girls whom we interviewed easily recognized "a typical *Rate* photo," but were not able to articulate what this typical photo looks like. Talking about peer culture with one's parents or discussing it at school is a serious challenge for both children and adults. Parents and educators must at first understand that online communities can form a big and significant part of children's lives. Only then should the adults let the children know that their online experience is a matter of interest for parents. It should be clear that the purpose of opening the conversation is not to ridicule or set restrictions.

Social networking can be made a topic of conversation at the breakfast table or morning circles in classes. Adults should use open questions (*Is there anything interesting or new going on? What kind of feedback have you received lately?*) and try to create an atmosphere where answering is possible, but not mandatory. Verbalizing actions on the Internet can be one way to break the wall between real life and online—and this might prevent children from creating double standards.

Furthermore, it is important that adults perform their controlling and facilitating role with a great sense of respect, especially when children are exploring the limits of their identity. A clear and personal response from an adult can help a child to understand oneself better. The most important part of this kind of message is the fact that the adult has noticed a child's activity (or change in action, etc.) and tries to open up conversation about it. Still, it must be up to the child how far this conversation goes. One possibility to formulate this kind of message is just to say what

Table 7.1.   Knowledge, Skills, and Attitudes Needed for Beneficial Acting in Online Communities

Knowledge: Person Knows That …	Skills	Attitudes
… account owners are real people who tell true and untrue facts about themselves.	Person is able to find information about online partners; s/he is able to guess what kind of information is true and what is not.	Person is willing to create meaningful human relations and be truthful without compromising anybody's safety.
… any information s/he uploads to the Internet is public, and understands the meaning and possible consequences of that.	Person knows how to upload and download desired material to the Internet, and is familiar with the possibilities of changing uploaded material in a particular community.	Person is willing to create his/her online identity in the manner that does not hurt anybody, including him/herself.
… most activities in the Internet can be traced, and that antisocial behavior is not allowed.	Person knows to whom to turn to if s/he is suspecting antisocial behavior in the Internet.	Person is willing to keep the Internet safe.
…there are rules and habits of a particular online community and is aware of consequences of violating them.	Person is able to enjoy him/herself within limits.	Person is motivated to follow the rules.
Person is aware of different aspects of human personality and communication models.	Person is able to distinguish different feelings based on partner's actions online, and different modalities of interaction (play, work, worry etc.)	Person is motivated to express him/herself in different roles and moods.

you have noticed and if one desires, the element of question can be added to that (*You look rather angry on that picture—can you tell me why? I see that you have been quite creative when describing your interests. I haven't seen this side of you yet. You have worked on your avatar quite a bit—are you happy with it yet or will you make more changes?*).

Importance of delicacy comes across again when parents or educators visit their children's accounts. On the one hand, it sometimes disturbs children who would like to have a place just for themselves. On the other hand, children must be aware of the fact that the Internet is a public sphere, and they should not upload anything they do not want to show to adults. There is a clear tension between concepts of freedom and safety, but it is possible to find creative ways of regulating young children's activities in the communities. In other words, teaching how to act online by reacting to the real actions of real kids must and should be brought to the communities rather than put into classrooms or curricula.

CONCLUSIONS

In this chapter we have argued that social networking websites provide an online playground for people in various ages and with different social backgrounds. Belonging simultaneously to children's peer culture and adult's business world, online communities are a complex social phenomenon where unstructured play, structured games, and business undergo rapid changes. The most significant forms of unstructured play occurring on the profiles of social networking sites seem to be sociodramatic role play and mimicry; both include strong elements of socialization. Furthermore, as playground can be compared to Bourdieu's concept of the field, children involved in the play are in a constant struggle for gaining the acceptance and acknowledgment of their peers.

We used the case-study of 11- to 13- year old users of *Rate.ee*, the favorite social networking site in Estonia, in order to understand if these online platforms could be viewed as online playgrounds for young children. Based on the results of the study we argue that young children tend to interpret the whole Internet environment as a playground and are therefore well aware of the playful nature of social networking websites. Children express themselves on their profiles and interactions rather freely, partly by the means of creative and interpretive reproduction of the adult culture. The instances of sociodramatic role-play, gendered play, and elements of mimicry found on the profiles allow us to postulate that social networking websites give children a much needed opportunity to experiment with their identity constructions.

While children recognize and cherish the opportunities provided by the social networking sites, the adults, in contrast, often express their uncertainty towards the online world. Adults do not fully grasp the identity play visible on the profiles and therefore often use double standards for interpreting children's activities in online compared to offline settings. In order to help the adults overcome their fears and uncertainties which have led to the "digital generation gap" (Papert, 1996), we defined basic knowledge, skills and attitudes needed for the safe usage of online communities as well as proposed some suggestions for conversation techniques.

ACKNOWLEDGMENTS

The preparation of this article was supported by the research grant No. 6968 and also by the European Union through the European Regional

Development Fund. Andra Siibak is also thankful for the Archimedes Foundation for the European Social Fund's scholarship Dora that supported the preparation of the article during her research stay at the Masaryk University, the Czech Republic. The data was collected thanks to the support of target financed projects No. 0180017S07 and No. 018002S7. Andra Siibak is also grateful for the support of the project "Construction anD Normalization Of Gender Online Among Young People in Estonia and Sweden," financed by The Foundation for Baltic and East European Studies

NOTES

1. The sayings are translated from Estonian and spelled in a way as it was done by the youngsters.
2. Interviews were conducted in Estonian which is a gender neutral language. Girl 13 used a person pronoun which stands for male and female person (*tema*).

REFERENCES

Bandura, A. (1989). Social cognitive theory. In R. Vasta (Ed.), *Annals of child development: Six theories of child development-Revised formulations and current issues* (Vol. 6, pp. 1–60). Greenwich, CT: JAI Press.

Bell, P. (2001). Content analysis of visual images. In T. van Leeuwen & C. Jewitt (Eds.), *Handbook of visual image* (pp. 10-34). London: SAGE.

Bourdieu, P. (1993). *Sociology in question*. London: SAGE.

Brown, B. B., & Klute, C. (2003). Friends, cliques, and crowds. In G. R. Adams & M. D. Berzonsky (Eds.), *Blackwell handbook of adolescence* (pp. 330–348). Malden, MA: Blackwell.

Caillois, R. (2001). *Man, Play and Games*. (Meyer Barash, Trans). Urbana, IL: University of Illinois Press.

Cobb, C. L., Danby, S., & Farrell, A. (2005). Governance of children's everyday spaces. *Australian Journal of Early Childhood, 30*(1), 14-20.

Convention on the Rights of the Child. (1989, November 20). Retrieved from http://www.unchr.org/english/law/crc.htm

Corsaro, W. A. (1992). Interpretive reproduction in peer's cultures. *Social Psychology Quarterly, 55*(2), 160-177.

Corsaro, W. A. (1997). *The sociology of childhood*. Thousand Oaks, CA: Pine Forge Press.

Corsaro, W. A., & Nelson, E. (2003). Children's collective activities and peer culture in early literacy in American and Italian preschools. *Sociology of Education, 76*, 209-227.

Corsaro, W. A. (1999). Preadolescent peer cultures. In M. Woodenhead, D. Faulkner, & K. Littleton (Eds.), *Making sense of social development* (pp. 27-50). London: Routledge.

Dodd, D. K., Russell B. L., & Jenkins, C. (1999). Smiling in school yearbook photos: Gender differences from kindergarten to adulthood. *The Psychological Record*. Retrieved from http://www.findarticles.com/p/articles/mi_qa3645/is_199910/ai_n8856394

Corsaro, W. A. (2003). *"We're friends right?": Inside kids cultures*. Washington, DC: Joseph Henry Press.

Evaldsson, A., & Corsaro, W. A. (1998). Play and games in the peer cultures of preschool and preadolescent children: An interpretive approach. *Childhood, 5*, 377-402.

Feller, B. (2005, June 5). More nursery school children are going online. *Associated Press*. Retrieved from http://earlychildhoodmichigan.org/articles/6-05/AP6-5-05.htm

Freud, A. (1958). Adolescence. *The Psychoanalytic study of the child, 13*, 255-278.

Gill, R., Henwood K., & Mclean, C. (2005). Body projects and the regulation of normative masculinity. *Body and Society, 11*(1), 37-62.

Ginsburg, K. R., & the Committee on Communications. (2007). The importance of play in promoting healthy child development and maintaining strong parent-child bonds. *Pediatrics, 119*, 182-191. Retrieved from http://pediatrics.aappublications.org/cgi/content/full/119/1/182

Goffman, E. (1990). *The presentation of self in everyday life*. New York, NY: Penguin Books

Goffman, E. (1979). *Gender advertisements*. Cambridge, MA: Harvard University Press.

Hall, J. A., LeBeau, L. S., Gordon Reinoso, J., & Thayer, F. (2001). Status, gender, and nonverbal behaviour in candid and posed photographs: a study of conversations between university employees. *Sex Roles: A Journal of Research*. Retrieved from http://www.findarticles.com/p/articles/mi_m2294/is_2001_June/ai_80805132

Hasebrink, U., Livingstone, S., & Haddon, L. (2008). *Comparing children's online opportunities and risks across Europe: Cross-national comparisons for EU Kids Online*. London: EU Kids Online (Deliverable D3.2).

Jenkinson, S. (2001). *The genius of play: Celebrating the spirit of childhood*. Hampshire, England: Hawthorn Press.

Kang, M. E. (1997). The portrayal of women's images in magazine advertisements: Goffman's gender analysis revisited. *Sex Roles: The Journal of Research*. Retrieved from http://findarticles.com/p/articles/mi_m2294/is_n11-12_v37/ai_20391904

Kress, G., & van Leeuwen, T. (1996). *Reading images: The grammar of visual design*. London: Routledge.

Larsen, M. C. (2007, October). *Understanding social networking: On young people's construction and co-construction of identity online*. Paper presented at Internet Research 8.0: Let's Play, Association of Internet Researchers, Vancouver.

Lemke, J. (2008). Identity trouble. In C. R. Caldas-Coulthard & R. Iedema, R. (Eds.), *Critical discourse and contested identities*. Basingstoke, England: Palgrave Mcmillan.

Livingstone, S., & Helsper, E. J. (2007). Gradations in digital inclusion: Children, young people and the digital divide. *New Media & Society, 9*(4), 671-696.

Livingstone, S. (2008). Taking risky opportunities in youthful content creation: teenagers' use of social networking sites for intimacy, privacy and self-expression. *New Media & Society, 10*(3), 393–411.

McQuade, S. C. III, & Sampat, N. (2008). Survey of internet and at-risk behaviors: Report of the Rochester Institute of Technology. Retrieved from http://www.rrcsei.org/RIT%20Cyber%20Survey%20Final%20Report.pdf

Merton, R. K. (1965). *Social theory and social structure*. New York, NY: Free Press.

Mildin, A. (2008, August 24). Preferring the web over watching TV. *The New York Times*. Retrieved from http://www.nytimes.com/2008/08/25/technology/25drill.html?_r=4&scp=1&sq=children%20online&st=cse&oref=slogin

Moreno, J. L. (1978). *Who shall survive?* Beacon, NY: Beacon House. (Reprint of 2nd edition 1953)

Moreno, J. L. (1997). *Gruppenpsychotherapie und Psychodrama*. New York, NY and Stuttgart, Germany: Georg Thieme Verlag.

Oppenheim, K. (2008). Social networking sites: Growing use among tweens and teens, but a growing threat as well?, *Trends & Tudes, 7*(3), 1-4.

Ota, C., Erricker, C., & Erricker, J. (1997). The secrets of the play ground. *Pastoral Care in Education, 15*(4), 19-24.

Parker, J. G., Rubin, K. H., Erath, S. A., Wojslawowicz, J. C., & Buskirk, A. A. (2006). Peer relationships, child development, and adjustment: A developmental psychopathology perspective. In D. Cicchetti & D. J. Cohen (Eds.), *Developmental Psychopathology: Theory and methods, Second Edition* (2nd ed., Vol. 1, pp. 419-493). Hoboken, NJ: Wiley.

Papert, S. (1996). *The connected family: Bridging the digital generation gap*. Atlanta, GA: Longstreet Press.

Piaget, J. (1999). *Play, dreams and imitation in childhood*. London: Routledge.

Siibak, A. (2007). Reflections of RL in the virtual world: Visual gender identity of the most remarkable youngsters in Estonian dating website Rate. *Cyberpsychology: Journal of Psychosocial Research on Cyberspace*, 1. Retrieved from www.cyberpsychology.eu

Siibak, A. (2006). Romeo and Juliet of the virtual world: Visual gender identity of the most remarkable youngsters in Estonian dating website Rate. In F. Sudweeks, H. Hrachovec, C. Ess (Eds.), *Cultural attitudes towards technology and communication 2006* (pp. 580-592). Murdoch, Australia: Murdoch University.

Sutton-Smith, B. (1990). School playground as festival. *Children's Environments Quarterly, 7*(2), 3-7.

Sutton, L. (2008). The state of play: Disadvantage, play and children's well-being. *Social Policy and Society, 7*(4), 537-549.

Swanbrow, D. (2004). U.S. children and teens spend more time on academics. *The University Record Online*. Retrieved from http://www.ur.umich.edu/0405/Dec06_04/20.shtml

Teen social marketing still growing. (2008, May 1). Retrieved from http://social-media-optimization.com/2008/05/teen-social-networking-still-growing/

Thomas, C. (1996). *Male matters: Masculinity, anxiety, and the male body on the line*. Urbana, IL: University of Illinois Press.

Umiker-Sebeok, J. (1981). The seven ages of women: A view from American magazine advertisements. In C. Mayo & H. Henley (Eds.), *Gender and nonverbal behavior.* New York, NY: Springer-Verlag.

Wienke, C. (1998). Negotiating male body: Men, masculinity, and cultural ideals. *The Journal of Men's Studies, 6,* 255-283.

Youniss, J. (1999). Children's friendships and peer culture. In M. Woodenhead, D. Faulkner, & K. Littleton (Eds.), *Making sense of social development* (pp. 13-26). London: Routledge.

Zarbatany, L., Hartmann, D., & Rankin, D. (1990). The psychological functions of preadolescent peer activities. *Child Development, 61,* 1067–1980.

CHAPTER 8

ONLINE YOUTH PROTECTION

Joint Efforts Are Needed

Jutta Croll and Katharina Kunze

AN INTERCOMMUNICABLE
SOCIOTECHNICAL APPROACH TO ONLINE YOUTH PROTECTION

The Internet is an essential part of everyday life for today's young people. Often referred to as "digital natives" (Palfrey & Gasser, 2008), today's youth were born with readily available Internet. Their parents, however, had to learn to use the Internet after several years of socialization with nondigital media, if they use it at all. Early childhood in the virtual world of today's Web 2.0 means growing up with possibilities to communicate and interact that have never been available before. It also means that parents and responsible adults have to take responsibility for their children's safety in respect of new challenges.

The ubiquitous availability of the Internet is accompanied by fear of online risks and threats. Adults responsible for minors are concerned about the negative impact the Internet can have on a child's mental development. Governments, the welfare sector, educational institutions,

High-Tech Tots: Childhood in a Digital World, pp. 153–183
Copyright © 2010 by Information Age Publishing
All rights of reproduction in any form reserved.

and companies, all call for action and agree to joint efforts to ensure youth online safety.

At the Youth Protection Roundtable, 32 members from 13 countries worked together to develop guidelines for online youth protection. The Youth Protection Roundtable is a project within the Safer Internet Programme of the European Commission. Its overarching goal is to facilitate and coordinate the exchange of views between child welfare specialists and technical experts on educational and technical measures regarding harmful content, and to develop an intercommunicable sociotechnical approach to youth protection. In this chapter, we will describe how online youth protection was defined, how different viewpoints were identified, how a common view on risks and measures was developed, and how a new approach to digital literacy was elaborated with input from young people.

MEASURING THE LANDSCAPE—RESULTS OF AN EXPERTS' SURVEY ON MATTERS OF YOUTH PROTECTION ONLINE

Common Ground

At the Youth Protection Roundtable, online youth protection was defined as the protection of children and young people from harmful content and contacts on the Internet. The project did not address the protection of a special age group of young people, but was targeted at the empowerment of minors and responsible adults. With regard to early childhood it has to be acknowledged that children are beginning to use the Internet usually around school enrollment. But even preschoolers and kindergarten toddlers are getting acquainted with the Internet more and more. The annual survey KIM-Studie revealed for Germany that 59% of children 6-13 years of age use the Internet regularly at least once a week. In the youngest age group surveyed 6-7 years old about 20% have already experienced the web (Medienpädagogischer Forschungsverbund Südwest, 2008). Eurobarometer 2008 reveals a total of 42% of children aged 6 years in 27 European countries using the Internet regularly (Flash Eurobarometer, 2008). Although there are only a few studies dealing with younger children's Internet usage[1] it can be assumed that those children who use it regularly at the age of 6 did start earlier.

About the Survey

To identify the different viewpoints of European technical experts and children's welfare specialists—pedagogues, scientists, and practitioners—

with regard to online youth protection, an international survey was conducted between January and June 2007 by the German based Stiftung Digitale Chancen, within the framework of the Youth Protection Roundtable. The purpose of the survey was to ask representatives from child welfare organizations and companies in the field of protective hardware and software how they judge the current situation of youth protection in their country.

Method

A set of questions was developed and adjusted to the technical, legal and pedagogical requirements of youth protection. The development of the questionnaire was based on the assumption that representatives from different areas and different countries might have varying conceptions of online youth protection. The purpose of the survey was to set the agenda for the further work at the Youth Protection Roundtable, to consolidate the common view of the members at the Roundtable, and also to base the Roundtable's work on the expertise of children's advocates and technical specialists from all over Europe.

The questionnaire was e-mailed to 675 contacts in preparation for a phone interview conducted between January and the end of June 2007. The questionnaire was provided on the project website at www.yprt.eu for online completion. By the end of June, 125 experts from 25 European countries, and one from Israel, completed the questionnaire, resulting in an 18.5% response rate. Of the 126 respondents, 86 were welfare experts and 40 were from companies, mostly in the area of protective hardware and software. In an effort to identify regional differences, the countries were clustered to four different regions of Europe. Sixty-six respondents were from the central region,[2] 21 from the northern region,[3] 19 from the southern region,[4] and 20 from the eastern region.[5]

The Risks From Real Life are Evident in the Virtual World

The first question "Which areas do you connote with the term youth protection?" was intended as an opener to the interview and did therefore not specifically address the Internet. Nevertheless, more than one third of the respondents (37%) stated Internet issues as being associated with the term "youth protection". Sixty-three percent of the respondents mentioned media literacy, parental control, and other activities for youth and parents to protect themselves.

Dangers and risks from real life—like abuse, violence, and so on—were mentioned as evident in reality as well as in the virtual world. Internet safety must therefore be seen as an integral part of the important task of youth protection in general (see Figure 8.1).

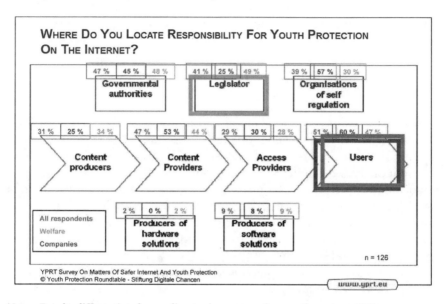

Note: Results differentiated according to the sectors of respondents (*n* = 126).

Figure 8.1.   Where do you locate responsibility for youth protection on the Internet?

Highest Responsibility for the Users Themselves

Respondents to the survey were asked to imagine a value chain from the content producer to the user comprising content producers, content providers, access providers, and the users. This chain is supported by hardware and software solutions on the one side and by political, legal, and executive authorities on the other side. Respondents were asked "Where do you locate responsibility for youth protection on the Internet?" Fifty-one percent of all respondents agree that the highest responsibility is on the users themselves; however, there are differences between the business and the welfare sector. Nearly 60% of respondents from companies agree, as compared to 47% from the welfare area. Forty-nine percent of welfare experts view the responsibility for youth protection as being with the legislator.

Great Regional Differences

The results were further analyzed for geographic differences. The answers from 26 countries were clustered into 4 regions to measure whether there are regional differences in Europe. The countries from the southern region locate most responsibility for youth protection on the Internet with the governmental authorities, while the countries from the central region see three main actors as responsible for youth protection on the Internet: content providers, self-regulation organizations, and the users themselves. In the eastern region, 75% of respondents viewed the user as the most responsible, followed by the legislator. These answers suggest that the different European backgrounds, with regard to the historical experiences and political situation, lead to different understandings about the responsibility for youth protection on the Internet (see Figure 8.2).

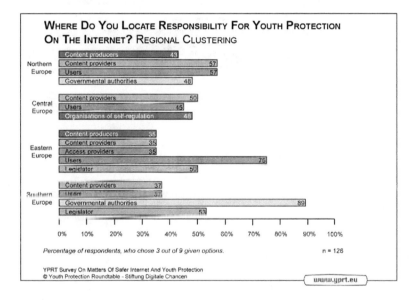

Note: Results differentiated according to four regions of Europe (*n* = 126).

Figure 8.2.   Where do you locate responsibility for youth protection on the Internet?

Interactive Areas of the Web are Estimated to be the Most Dangerous

The Internet and its available services are not only growing but also rapidly changing. Enhanced possibilities for user communication, interactivity and publishing and, especially for young people, increasing opportunities for learning and socioemotional development are accompanied by new threats and risks. The measures undertaken to protect children and young persons have to be adjusted to the new landscape of the web. It is, therefore, not astonishing that 31% of the respondents identified Web 2.0 applications as more risky than traditional websites. One-to-one communication via e-mail does not seem to bear remarkable risks, but communication with many unknown people in chat rooms is estimated to be the most dangerous activity on the web (see Figure 8.3).

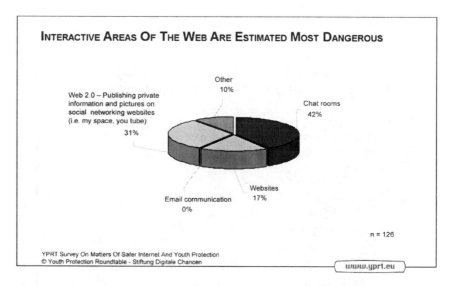

Figure 8.3.   Which areas of the virtual world do you estimate the most dangerous for kids and teens?

Inappropriate Sexual Content is Seen as Most Harmful

Sixty-eight percent of the experts fear that young people and minors are exposed to inappropriate sexual content while online, more than 55% view unsuitable contacts and exposure to violent content as being significant threats. Fifty percent of respondents view potential privacy fraud as high risk. Youth contact with politically incorrect contact (i.e., racism), potential economic fraud, and receiving inadequate advice were seen as less of a risk by responding experts (see Figure 8.4).

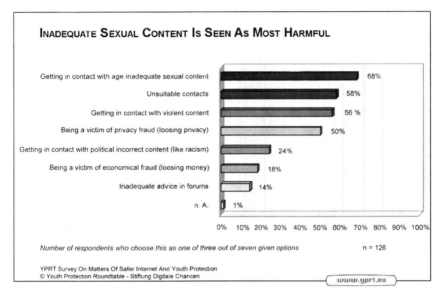

Figure 8.4.   What do you think most harmful for kids and teens?[6]

Parents, Teachers and Social Youth Workers are the Preferred Caregivers Throughout Europe

Respondents from all European regions agree that parents and peda-gogues should act as primary caregivers for online youth. Respondents from southern European regions identify companies as the least-responsible for online child welfare; they allocate more responsibility to policy makers. Both the Southern and the Eastern European region assign more relevance to actions undertaken by the police than by companies (see Figure 8.5).

When the results were then analyzed for respondent organizational background, it was apparent that, contrary to the expectations, although there were relevant differences among the experts from the different European regions in their answers to some questions, only marginal dif-ferences existed between the two groups of representatives, technical experts and child welfare specialists (see Figure 8.6).

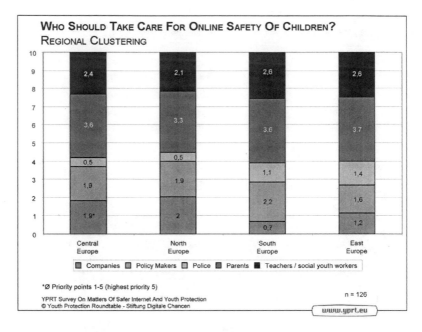

Figure 8.5.   Who should take care of children online?: Regional differences.

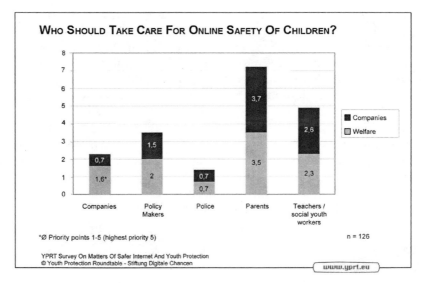

Figure 8.6.   Who should take care of children online?: Type of respondent expertise

Primary Protection Measures are Empowerment and Parental Control

When asked about protecting minors against inappropriate sexual content and violence on the Internet, parental control and the teaching of media literacy are the most frequently identified protection measures. While empowerment by educational measures, such as teaching media literacy, seems to be the most appropriate measure for young persons 14 to 17 years old; parental control is identified as the most appropriate measure to protect younger children up to 13 years. Experts report that reducing access to only age-appropriate areas is an adequate measure to protect younger children; however, youth, aged 14 years and older, are better protected with software solutions. Surveillance of the Internet by the police is seen as the least effective measure to protect young people in both age groups (see Figures 8.7).

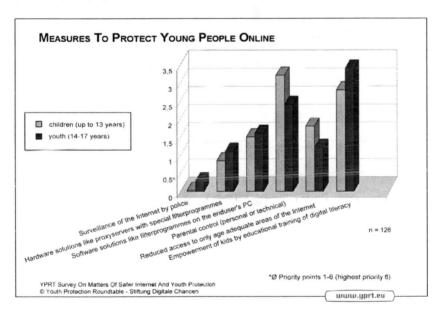

Figure 8.7.   Which measures are adequate to protect children and youth?

Vague Knowledge About the Legal Situation

About 75% of the respondents have some knowledge about their country's legal system with regard to youth protection and the authorities who are responsible for compliance with the law. Nevertheless, one quarter of respondents did not answer the question, or stated that they did not have any knowledge about the legal system. In Eastern European countries there are more people who report that they do not know about the legal situation than in the other regions, but overall there are only slight differences (see Figure 8.8).

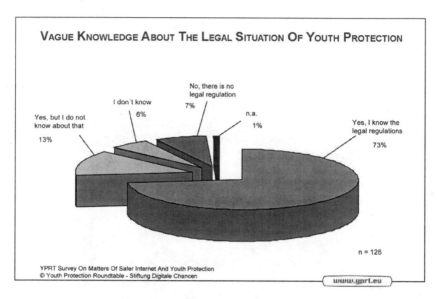

Figure 8.8.   Vague knowledge about the legal situation of youth protection.

Whereas around three quarters of the respondents have some knowledge about legal regulations, the picture looks different when it comes to knowledge about self-regulation, as the following chart shows (see Figure 8.9).

Self Regulation: Little Knowledge—Little Trust

From all respondents only one-third trusts in national instruments of self-regulation. More than one fifth of the respondents have no knowledge of such self-regulation instruments. Considering that more than half of the respondents of the Central European region trust in national instruments and almost one third trust in international instruments, the results from the Eastern and the Southern region are worrying. None of the respondents from the Eastern region trust in national instruments of self-regulation, and only 5% of those from the Southern region do so. Thirty-five percent of the respondents from the Eastern region and 16% from the

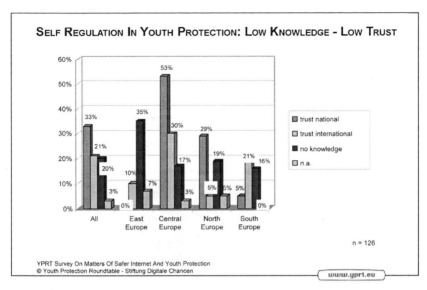

Figure 8.9. Do you have knowledge of any national or international instruments of self-regulation, i.e., Codes of Conduct?

South do not have knowledge about self-regulation on a national or international level (Croll & Kubicek, 2007).

Many Institutional Activities Undertaken to Protect Children and Youths

Eighty-six percent of the respondents undertake activities for youth protection. Educational training in digital literacy for parents, young persons, teachers and social workers was named most often. This was closely followed by awareness campaigns and projects, and efforts to influence legislation. Only 8% of the respondents report that activities for youth protection are not relevant for their target group or that they have never thought about it. These answers underline that the experts who participated in the survey have experience in the field of youth protection in practical work, as well as in theory. These results are therefore a good validation for the significance of the survey findings in general, which build the basis for the development of recommendations on how to deal with the risks and threats children might be exposed to in their newly explored digital everyday life.

3 CS—CONTENT, CONTACT, CONDUCT: A MATRIX OF RISKS

A Matrix of risks and threats shall help to gain a structured overview of the risks occurring with the rapid changes of the Internet. The Matrix shows the Internet as an inner sector divided in four main areas with a permeable inner barrier (see Figure 8.10).

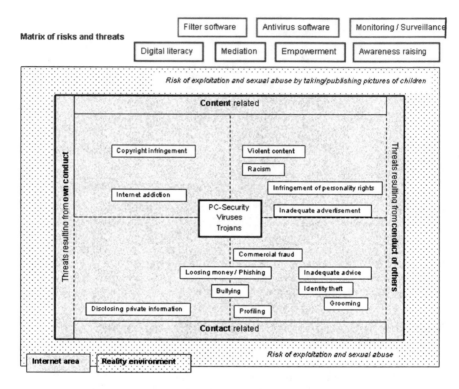

Figure 8.10.   Matrix of risks and threats.

The risks and threats related to the use of the Internet are located between digital content on the one side and digital contacts on the other. The mapped risks and threats can result from the conduct of the users themselves and the conduct of other users in the virtual world. Depending on the location of the risks and threats identified, appropriate measures shall be developed and enacted. The localization of the risks and threats varies depending on these four aspects (content, contact, own conduct and conduct of others). The inner sector is surrounded by the reality environment where risks that emerge are caused or intensified by certain online activities. Appropriate measures to combat the risks shall be developed with a focus on the Internet sector and in accordance with the area where the risk occurs. In the center of the Matrix, viruses and Trojan horses are named as general threats to PC-security.

The location of some of the risks depends on whether one takes the perspective of the consumer or the producer of content, especially when it comes to user-generated content. This underlines the need for permeability between the areas of the Matrix. Furthermore, it appears that some risks are relevant only to specific age groups of users and therefore can only be addressed by measures tailored to the user group's specific needs. While risks fixed to one area of the Matrix, for example, harmful content, can be addressed directly by supportive technologies like filter software, addressing the less clearly fixed risks seems to be similar to the attempt of meeting a moving target.

The Matrix gives a complete overview of the risks and threats identified as relevant regarding online youth protection. It is evident that not all of these risks are related to younger children's use of the Internet. Nevertheless it is important to be aware of all risks and threats in order to develop a holistic approach to youth protection comprising measures more appropriate to protect younger children and others addressing the older age group. Especially attempts to protect younger children have to take into account that the main objective should be their empowerment for an autonomous and responsible use of the Internet when growing up. This concept will be elaborated in more detail later on in this chapter.

Risks Related to Online Content

With regard to online content it is important to differentiate between illegal and harmful content. There is no general international agreement on what is meant to be illegal, harmful or inappropriate content. Nevertheless, some types of content, such as child pornography, are outlawed in many countries worldwide.

Age inappropriate content. The Internet provides a wealth of content for all groups of users. Mainstream interests are served as well as special interest groups. Nevertheless, not all content should be accessible for children and youth. Therefore, it is necessary to carefully decide which content is appropriate to which age group. Special attention should be given to content that is not illegal in general but might harm younger users. Facing age inappropriate content like adult pornography might especially harm younger children. The risk of inappropriate content can result from the user's own conduct of deliberate searching as well as unintentionally accessing the material. Content that is not appropriate for all age groups might be provided for commercial reasons but can also be generated by the users themselves. Access to the former might be restricted to closed user groups only, while user generated content is mostly publicly available and needs special attention. Since a high percentage of today's children and youth have mobile phones with multimedia functionalities and access to the Internet at their fingertips, it must also be considered that they might access age inappropriate content when on their own and without adult supervision and guidance. Mobile devices also enable children to produce their own digital content anywhere, thus contributing to the increasing amount of user generated content (Eurobarometer, 2007).

Violent content. Violent content is a type of age inappropriate content. The effect violent content has on the viewer largely depends on the viewer's age, his or her habits of consuming Internet content, and the social environment. Especially younger children should be protected from inadvertently accessing violent content by adequate means like filtering software. Their deliberate attempts to access violent content through download and purchase should be prevented. An additional focus should be put on user generated content, particularly because children and youth as producers and publishers of violent content may not be aware of the harm this content could do to others.

Illegal content, that is, racism, child pornography. The type of content classified as illegal, depends foremost on national law, albeit some type of content is outlawed in many countries. Nevertheless, illegal content is available and can be accessed unintentionally, but also deliberately, by children and youth. Attention should also be paid to children and youth as victims of illegal content, e.g. child abuse pictures or videos.

Incorrect content. The risk of accessing incorrect content, that is, within Wikipedia or as an advertisement of false products, is primarily related to the conduct of other users and is multiplied by the increasing number of Web 2.0 appliances where the correctness is at the most controlled by the users themselves, not by an editor.

Incitement of harm. There are many sites on the web inciting users to harm themselves, for example, websites promoting suicide or anorexia. With Web 2.0 and the increasing possibilities to publish a user's own content, the risk of being exposed to content inciting harm is growing. In particular children and youth are not able to make a realistic assessment of the risks arising from following the instructions given in such websites.

Infringement of human rights/defamation. In the anonymity of the web, propaganda against certain population groups or individuals can be widespread. Additionally, one can presume that people act differently online, where they must not face the reaction of their counterparts or victims directly, and therefore are not immediately confronted with the consequences of their conduct. Thus the risk of infringement of human rights and being victim of defamation is more likely to happen online than in reality. In addition, defamatory content is harmful to children and young people whose opinion might be influenced by misleading information.

Inappropriate advertisement and marketing to children. Inappropriate advertisement means the risks of receiving or being exposed to advertisement for products and/or services that are inappropriate to children, such as cosmetic surgery. The more users give away private information, that is, name, age or gender, the more likely they are to receive advertisement or be asked to participate in lotteries. Since children are in many cases not aware of the consequences of typing their names into forms and boxes on the web, they are profoundly at risk. Considering the high penetration rate of mobile phones among children and youth, attention should also be paid to this additional channel for the dissemination of advertisement.

Data persistence. Content, once published on the web, can spread rapidly around the world. Children and youth are not aware of the short-term and long-term consequences of publishing texts and pictures on the Internet. They often spontaneously upload content to their profiles they might not want to be publicly available later. Since it is impossible to totally delete this information at a subsequent time, the risk of data persistence is particularly relevant to imprudent younger people.

Data portability. Data deliberately stored on a server or a platform can easily be transferred to innumerable other servers. People who are not aware of that fact might easily lose their privacy. Even if younger people are likely to know a great deal about the technical possibilities of the web, admittedly most of them do not have the ability to estimate the consequences when their private data are mingled with other data about their own person.

Copyright infringement. Copyright infringement is a risk mostly related to the conduct of the users themselves. Irrespective of the fact whether the copyright of others is infringed deliberately or not, the infringement is an economical fraud for the holder and puts the violator in risk of penalty.

Harmful advice. Forums, blogs or other contact related areas of the Internet provide a platform for the exchange of advice among users. This can be a valuable tool; however, it can also be dangerous. The openness of the Internet increases the likelihood that children and youth might come into contact with inappropriate advice and risky advisors. The risk of receiving harmful advice for children and youths occurs more often in social community platforms or other Web 2.0 appliances than on regular websites.

Internet addiction. As people spend more time online, the risk of becoming addicted to the use of the Internet grows. In particular young people are at risk of not being able to switch off the computer. Therefore, this risk is first and foremost related to one's own conduct.

Identity theft. Obtaining and intentionally using other peoples' electronic identity (e.g., user name and password) with the purpose to cause commercial or other fraud to this person and to benefit thereof is called identity theft. Identity theft is a growing risk as the number of virtual identities is increasing with the number of people being online and in particular using personalized services.

Losing money/Phishing. Phishing means the process of harvesting bank details, in particular PINs[7] and TANs,[8] with the purpose of stealing from other people's bank account. Younger people are more likely not to recognize a fake website, and are therefore likely to give away their own or their parents' bank details.

Commercial fraud. Commercial fraud happens when sellers pretend to sell goods or services, which after payment either do not show the promised attributes or are not delivered at all. It can also result from identity theft and from phishing. Another source of commercial fraud can be the selling of digital services, for example, a ring tone, at an unreasonable and unfair price, often bound to a permanent subscription to the service that was not intended by the buyer. Children and youth are, in the majority of cases, not aware of the consequences of such contracts.

Grooming. Pedophiles use the Internet as a means to contact children and young people by concealing their adult identity. They often build their strategy on children's longing for friendship and familiarity. All areas of the Web that provide platforms for personal contact and exchange are likely to provide a basis for grooming attacks. As previously mentioned, use of the mobile phone as an additional device to contact others and to access social networking platforms should be taken into strong consideration; especially as children view their mobile phone as a particular part of their private life and are mostly on their own when using it. Thus the risk of being a victim of a grooming attack and then following a dangerous invitation is increased.

Bullying. Various types of bullying seem to be always part of young people's life. Bullying one another is certainly simplified by the Internet due to the anonymity the medium provides. Children and young people risk both being victim of bullying and being offender. Hence, bullying is related to one's own conduct as well as to the conduct of others. Even though publishing content, such as defaming pictures can be part of bullying, the phenomenon is foremost related to online contact. As mentioned before, multifunctional mobile phones are often the device used to take pictures with the intention to bully and then upload the pictures to the Internet or send them via MMS[9] to others. In view of the high penetration rate among children and youth, the mobile phone equipped with a digital camera is likely to make bullying easier.

Disclosing private information. Setting up a profile on a social community platform invites the user to disclose private information with the intent to present oneself to the community. In chat rooms and forums users may disclose private data to others, such as their address or telephone number. Typically, young people are not able to foresee the consequences of publishing their private data. They are often not aware that a chat room is not a private but a public area.

Profiling. With the increasing number of profiles a person publishes on different platforms, the risk increases that personal data published on one platform are merged with those published on others. Thus profiles are created that allow others to directly address the person with potentially unwanted content, services, and advertisement. Profiling can be accomplished from the front side of the Internet, but more dangerous from the backside when the profiles of users or parts of these are harvested and sold out from the platform provider to third parties.

APPROPRIATE MEASURES TO DEAL WITH THE RISKS: A COMBINATION OF EDUCATIONAL MEASURES AND TECHNICAL TOOLS

There are several technical tools available to address the risks and threats that might arise from the use of the Internet by children and youth. The Youth Protection Roundtable has assessed recent research and findings in regards to the effectiveness of these tools. Also, the Youth Protection Roundtable members have assessed the following technical tools and estimated their effectiveness based on their own expertise. This was done in two steps of estimation, discussion and validation, leading to a high degree of consensus.

As a result, the Youth Protection Roundtable members concluded that all technical tools need to be complemented by additional measures to be truly effective. Technical tools were therefore called supportive technologies for online youth protection. The following version of the Matrix of risks and threats aims to demonstrate in which areas those measures can be effective and thus support the efforts for youth protection on the Internet (see Figure 8.11).

Filter Software

Description of filter software and its workflow. Filter software is an electronic facility that allows Internet data to be selected and sorted. With regard to youth protection, filter software can, to a certain degree, protect children

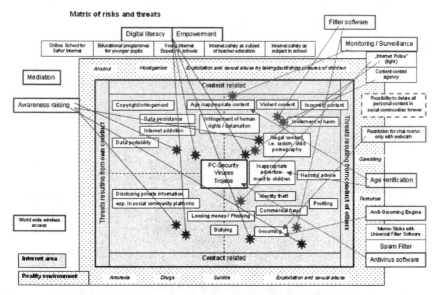

Figure 8.11.   Matrix with supportive technologies and pedagogical measures.

and young people from accidentally or deliberately accessing harmful, illegal, or inappropriate online content. Filter programs use either lists of rated content, or analyze the content of websites by semantic and statistical methods, and work as a program or module on an end-user device, on a central Internet access point like a proxy server or at the provider. Content can be rated by editorial classification (black and white lists), automatic classification (keyword blocking) and content ratings done by the content provider himself, for example, ICRA labeling. Most of the filter programs integrate different content classification methods (Luxembourg Safer Internet Helpline Project, 2006).

According to SIP Benchmark (Deloitte, 2007), filtering can be done at several levels. Filter software could be installed at the following places: at the end-user's PC, at a local server, at the Internet Service Provider, and elsewhere on the Internet, that is, proxy-server based Internet filtering service. The techniques of filter software tested by SIP Benchmark include:

- Block a request to a URL that is listed in a vendor-provided blacklist (local blacklist check) or that is blacklisted on a vendor's or provider's site (remote blacklist check)
- Block a request to a URL that is *not* listed in a vendor-provided white list (local or remote white list check)

- Block a request to a URL that contains one or more keywords blacklisted by the user
- Block content that contains one or more keywords blacklisted by the user
- Erase pieces of content that resemble keywords blacklisted by the child carer
- Block a request to a URL with an ICRA label that is blacklisted by the user (remote ICRA check)
- Block a page that contains an ICRA label that is blacklisted by the user (local ICRA check)
- Disable specific applications (possibly during specified time intervals)
- Disable specific applications outside a time slot specified by the user
- Disable specific ports.

In order to achieve effective filtering rates, several technologies need to be combined (Deloitte, 2007, p. 32f). It has to be taken into account that there are several possible side effects associated with the process of filtering, not only with regard to freedom of expression and unintended censorship, but also false positives and the negative impact on the infrastructure and the quality of services.

Effectiveness of filter software. Filter software is seen as a tool to solve many problems. With regard to the various risks previously listed, it becomes evident that the more concrete a type of content or a type of online conduct can be defined, the more likely it is to be detected by filter software. Filter software, therefore, is less effective for less concretely definable content and online conduct.

The experts at the Youth Protection Roundtable estimated that filtering software blocks about half of all websites with age inappropriate and violent content. With regard to illegal content filter software reaches a slightly higher degree of effectiveness. This is due to the fact that illegal content can be more clearly defined, and therefore it can be more easily detected than other types of content and online conduct. For the same reason—definition of content—filter software must fail with regard to incorrect content for which effectiveness is seen as fairly low. This is reinforced by the results filter software gains with regard to inappropriate advertisement to children and incitement of harm. Both types of content can be defined and therefore detected by filter software as content to be blocked in around one-third of all cases. It is more challenging to detect harmful advice often given in direct contact between users, which leads to the estimation that filter software can filter only one out of seven cases.

Online grooming cannot be sufficiently detected by filter software; the experts anticipated detection in one out of five cases. The risk of disclosing private information, which is also more likely to happen in the contact related areas of the Internet, can be addressed by filter software in only one out of ten cases, according to the experts' opinion.

Risks related to user conduct, such as copyright infringement and Internet addiction, as well as risks related to the conduct of other users, such as identity theft and bullying can be addressed by filter software only to a small degree. It was estimated that filter software can detect only one out of ten cases of infringement of human rights and defamation, which is related to both user conduct and the conduct of others. The experts at the Youth Protection Roundtable suggested that filter software can address a sixth of all cases of commercial fraud and phishing, but that it tends to lower effectiveness for the risk of profiling and nearly no effectiveness with regard to risks like data portability and data persistence.

Monitoring and Surveillance

Description of monitoring and surveillance and its workflow. A monitoring system is software that monitors content and user's activity on the Internet and reports the results to a responsible person. It is an instrument to systematically search online content for a subsequent categorization (Wikipedia Encyclopedia, 2009), for example, into harmful or harmless content. Monitoring means to automatically poll or check systems and services in an online environment (Mercury Interactive Corporation, 2004, para. 14) with a filter mechanism to achieve more sensible and qualified results. The results are reviewed by an expert who decides whether the content has to be filtered or removed. Usually the review process is carried out with a random sampling of the scanned content. A monitoring system enables review of chat sessions, blog entries, or the uploading and exchange of pictures. Technically, it can be installed on the level of the internet service provider (ISP) or the operator of an online service. In some cases monitoring and surveillance procedures are installed to review content before it is published online. Other monitoring procedures are based on the notice-and-take down approach, where online content is taken down after detection. In regard to online communication, this approach can lead to the deletion or deactivation of users' profiles once a violation of the code of conduct is reported or detected.

Effectiveness of monitoring and surveillance. Through monitoring and surveillance, the content of the Internet and the communication via the Internet can be reviewed, to a certain extent. This might happen at various stages during content storage and hosting, as well as at the access point to service. Monitoring and surveillance are more effective than filter software alone. This result is based on the assumption that monitoring and surveillance both use human review to determine whether online content should be removed or filtered.

Monitoring and surveillance are most effective for age inappropriate content, estimations are that more than half of all cases are detected. Monitoring and surveillance effectiveness for violent content, illegal content, and incitement of harm is only slightly lower, with two-fifth of all cases. Monitoring and surveillance were estimated to detect at least every third case of harmful advice, infringement of human rights/defamation, inappropriate advertisement to children and grooming. It is assumed that monitoring and surveillance can detect more than every fourth phishing attack, and more than every third bullying attack. Its effectiveness against incorrect content, copyright infringement, commercial fraud, identity theft, and disclosure of private information is seen in approximately one of every five cases. The chance to address the risk of Internet addiction by monitoring and surveillance is considered low, with only one out of six cases identified. Monitoring and surveillance score higher than filter software for data persistence, data portability, and profiling; nevertheless, the degree of effectiveness for the 3 of them is less than one out of 10 cases.

Age Verification

Description of age verification and its workflow. Various systems are used to verify the age of users of online services and to ensure that only appropriate content and services are provided to specific age groups. Age verification can take place outside the Internet, based on a one-time personal face-to-face authorization. That means after the personal identification and age verification the user receives his access token, for example, a card or USB stick, and a PIN. These tools are usually associated with paying functionalities, thus the owner oversees possible misuse to avoid loss of money. The identification and age verification is based on the concept of the togetherness of the token (card or stick) and the knowledge (PIN or password). Only the person having both at hand can be identified and thus can prove to belong to a particular age group. This type of technical age verification is highly effective; nevertheless, it requires specific technical equipment (e.g., a card reader) and also corresponding legal regulations.

Currently legislation in many countries allows age verification of adults to restrict access to adult content for minors. There are only a few examples of technical age verification for minors, like the kids card in Belgium (Anonymous, 2007), that are able to ensure to a reasonable degree that only minors have access to special Internet areas, for example, chat rooms for children. The level of many of the risks and threats depends on the age of the user. Therefore, age verification is important with regard to restricting access of minors to specific content or to platforms providing contact opportunities.

Effectiveness of age verification. As described before, age verification is a tool meant for restricting access to specific content or areas of the web. It does not come as a surprise that age verification gains higher effectiveness with regard to age inappropriate content (nearly half of all cases) and violent content than with regard to other risks. With regard to illegal content and inappropriate advertisement to children, the experts noted that age verification can detect every fourth to fifth case. It is assumed that age verification could prevent one of seven grooming attacks, which suggests a low effectiveness against that risk. Incitement of harm cannot be addressed properly by this supportive technology. Age verification has low effectiveness against risks like harmful advice, phishing and commercial fraud, and it is judged as nearly ineffective against all other risks.

Other Technical Tools

Description of other tools, their workflow and effectiveness in regard to specific risks. As with age verification, there are some other tools addressing special areas of risk. Time control can be used to restrict the usage of a computer to a fixed span of time by switching off the machine automatically at a pre-set time limit. Automatic time control is not primarily developed to fight Internet addiction, but it can be useful for that purpose. The experts at the Youth Protection Roundtable judged that time control can manage one out of every two cases of Internet addiction.

Automatic authentication processes are usually based on human authentication factors, i.e. something the person owns like an identity card, something the persons knows like a PIN or password, and something unique to the person, like a fingerprint. Authentication processes that need to meet high security demands are often based on asymmetric cryptography, that is, the digital signature. Experts at the Youth Protection Roundtable suggest that automatic authentication processes can prohibit more than one-third of cases of identity theft.

Antiphishing software is a special type of filtering software meant to detect and inhibit phishing attacks. Some experts see a high degree of effectiveness, safeguarding against approximately two-thirds of all cases. Others do not believe that it can respond to more than one quarter.

Digital watermark technology (Photopatrol, 2007) might be a solution to prevent copyright infringement. Watermark technology means the implementation of a piece of code into digital content, which enables detection of location, duplication, and distribution. A monitoring tool is required for watermark recognition. It is assumed that one out of four copyright infringements could be prevented by watermark technology.

Data persistence and data portability are not *a priori* to be seen as a risk. Both are necessary to ensure that data are unaltered and can be ported to another system. Nevertheless, data persistence and data portability can cause problems to the users. Not everybody wants all personal data retrievably stored forever. As described above, nearly all known technical tools are failing with regard to the risks of "unwanted" data persistence and data portability. Encoding can be a tool to prevent unwanted portability of data. Encoding is the process of transforming information from one format into another. Before the encoded data can be ported to another system and merged with other data, they must be decoded. Thus encoding can help to prevent unwanted porting of data in approximately one half of all cases. Setting an expiration date for all user generated content can slightly reduce the risk of data persistence in one quarter of all cases; also an irremovable tag with an expiration date might prevent unwanted data persistence. An invariably available option to delete personal data can help to minimize the risk of unwanted reduplication in one out of five cases.

A so-called Anti-Grooming Engine (Crisp Thinking Group Ltd., 2005) combines several methods to detect unusual conduct and thus prevent grooming attacks against children in chat rooms. The engine works from a database containing profiles of usual conduct of real-life groomers and real-life girls and boys. These profiles are built on an analysis of the communication with regard to vocabulary, punctuation, sentence length, typing speed and aggression level. The profiles are regularly updated, and thus the engine is able to differentiate good relationships from bad ones. If there is evidence of a bad relationship, an alert is sent to a responsible adult via SMS,[10] e-mail or a control panel on the PC. This tool is judged to be effective in around two-fifths of all cases, which means that it is likely to be as effective against grooming as monitoring and surveillance.

PROTECTIVE MEASURES:
A WALLED GARDEN FOR YOUNGER CHILDREN

For younger children, aged up to thirteen years, parental control was ranked first in protecting children in the Youth Protection Roundtable survey as described before. Parental control can be obtained by use of technical tools like filter software to a certain degree of effectiveness. A second way especially appropriate to younger children is accompanying them constantly when using the Internet. Taking into account that this is a question of time and availability, not all parents would be able to ensure that their younger children do not have access to the Internet when on their own. A third way of parental control could be the offer of a walled garden on the Internet, making sure that children can access only those websites that are part of an Internet area especially created for children. In Germany a walled garden was developed in 2008 accessible to children at www.frag-finn.de. Parents must install an easy-to-use application on their home PC ensuring that their children surfing the web do not access any other websites than those included in the service. The websites within the walled garden are quality tested by a team of media pedagogues and certified as appropriate to younger children. Only those websites that prove their appropriateness for children up to 12 years old are included into the system funded completely by industry. The German government in addition has set up a funding program for good quality web content for younger children.

The value of a walled garden on the Internet has different aspects. First, younger children learn how to use the Internet in a completely safe environment. Second, in the walled garden they train their ability to navigate the web and learn how to judge the content of websites. Up to now the walled garden www.frag-finn.de consists of more than 30,000 single documents. Thus, the third aspect of providing a special children's surf area is addressed. If the area is too small children might try to circumvent the protective barrier. Therefore, the area must be wide enough and provide a diverse range of different types of content, so that even more experienced children do not notice the borders.

The walled garden www.frag-finn.de also provides for areas of safe communication, that is, moderated chat rooms for younger children and interactive forums where they can learn how to get in contact with other users safely. The human moderators of the chat rooms also take care for use of appropriate language and address the children directly when guessing inadequate contacts or disclosure of private information. Along the way children are learning how to behave on the Internet properly and how to deal with inappropriate conduct of others. A walled garden thus contributes directly to the empowerment of younger children by training their digital literacy.

NEW SIGNIFICANCE FOR DIGITAL LITERACY

Educational training of digital literacy was judged by the experts at the Youth Protection Roundtable as the most adequate measure to protect and empower young people. For younger children, up to thirteen years old, parental control was ranked first in protecting children, which can be obtained as described previously. But parental control was directly followed by digital literacy training for the younger age group. Literacy with regard to media, formerly called media literacy, is now termed digital literacy, referring to the digitalization of media.

The Four Dimensions of Digital Literacy

Dieter Baacke (1999) identified four dimensions of media literacy: Media Criticism, Media Knowledge, Media Use and Media Design. *Media Criticism* is the user's ability to deal with media in a reflexive, analytical and ethical way. It means critical analysis of social processes with regard to media, reflection of one's own media knowledge and media action, and ethical judgment of media in regards to social responsibility. *Media Knowledge* is the user's knowledge about media and media systems. It is the knowledge about program genres and the factors of producing content, the ability to decide which media and which content suits the user's own needs best, and the knowledge of how to use media technically, that is, to utilize computer programs or to log-on to a network. *Media Use* is the user's ability to utilize and apply media in a receptive, interactive, and providing way. It means the ability to receive and to reflect the message of the media, apply programs efficiently, effectively use information/content provided by the media, and use media for interaction and transaction. *Media Design* is the user's ability to design and develop media systems in an innovative way. It is the ability to create media and media content, as well as design and innovate media. In 1999, when Dieter Baacke published the description of the four dimensions of media literacy the Internet had just begun to enter into consumers' households. The initial role of the user was, though interactive to a certain degree, a consumer of information as opposed to a producer. Hence, the dimension of media knowledge meant particularly knowledge of the systems and structures behind the production of media content has become more prominent.

With today's Web 2.0 and the dissolution of separate roles of consumers and content producers, the four dimensions gain additional significance. The dimension of media criticism becomes introspective also and calls for the reflection of the user's own conduct while being online and producing online content. Digitalization has lowered the threshold for the production of media content; users now need more detailed media knowledge about copyright and licensing, for example. Indeed media use requires knowing how to interact correctly with others. Web 2.0 provides for the opportunity for all users to design their own media. The dimension of media design requires, according to Baacke, the ability to do this in an innovative way, which means thinking beyond the beaten tracks of reproduction and developing innovative media content, making use of all production technologies available so far.

Recent developments of the Internet lead to a broader view of digital literacy and calls for an adoption into current curricula for teaching digital literacy. The role of teacher and student should be reconsidered as young people are more adept at Web 2.0 appliances than are their teachers. This became evident at the Young Roundtable and was reflected in the findings of the Eurobarometer (2007).

The Youths' Voice

In May 2008 the Youth Protection Roundtable invited 20 young people aged 15 to 19 years old to take part in a three day meeting in Nuremberg, Germany to discuss their online habits and need for support in the digital world. The young people came from seven different countries and had previously been engaged in matters of Internet safety, predominantly at school. The purpose of this meeting was to develop the Youth Protection Roundtable strategy for a safer online environment in tune with the young people's needs and expectations.

Many of the young people had been confronted previously with viruses received via e-mail or memory stick. Their fears were focused first on technical procedures outside their own control. They feel more comfortable with activities they can handle by adhering to safety rules they already know well. They pointed out that they also know how to identify Spam-Mails and how to react: ignore them and the related links.

Some users had experienced mobbing, while others admitted frankly to bullying other people in chat rooms. The participants mentioned that the use of false identities was the main problem in chat rooms. They were aware of people who use pictures of others for their profile and mentioned that this could be a danger in reality, when young people trust in the fake identity and meet with the person face-to-face.

It is crucial for the young people to be aware of who has access to their private data, for example, pictures or information about hobbies—only invited friends should be able to get these details. A lot of the participants said that in chat rooms they contact only friends and people they know. They expressed their strong desire to control who has access to their private data and pictures.

All young people at the Roundtable were aware of the risk of Internet addiction; they identified that the attractiveness of computer and Internet games is seductive to young people. The wide range of the risks and measures mentioned by the young people demonstrates a high level of risk awareness. Self-control and their own expertise regarding Internet issues have highest priority in the range of their preferred countermeasures.

Analysis and Research in Regard to Digital Literacy

From the analysis of the young people's responses during the Roundtable, it can be assumed that today's young people are more acquainted with the Internet and digital media than their parents and adult teachers, and they are highly aware of this generational gap in digital literacy. They report that their families often deem them computer experts. But somehow they know their expertise is mainly based on their skills related to the dimension of media use, while they are less skilled with regard to media criticism and media knowledge. The young people at the Youth Protection Roundtable expressed their strong demand for a safer online environment, but they have to face that their adult caregivers are not the ones to provide them with support (Croll & Lippa, 2008).

The 2007 Eurobarometer study also shows evidence that today's young people rely much more on their peers than on adults in regard to knowledge about the Internet and counseling in critical cases of age-inappropriate content and unwanted or embarrassing contacts on the Internet. The sample of the study comprised two age groups: children aged 9 to 10 years and children twelve to 14 years old. The qualitative research revealed that children, who were questioned about the problems and risks which they might experience when using the Internet or mobile phones, said they are well informed and aware of these problems. Children are seldom anxious regarding those risks; they are confident in their ability to solve the problems by themselves, or within their peer groups, and would ask their parents or other adults only when faced with dramatic problems. When asking the children about risks they confront, they show a strong confidence in their own capacity to cope with and solve these problems.

In the Flash Eurobarometer (2008), parents of children aged 6 to 17 years were asked if their children have asked for help when a problem occurred using the Internet; and if yes, what kind of problem came up. Only 32% of the participating parents in Europe replied that their children have asked for help, and the data differ greatly among the countries. While 48% of the parents in Denmark were asked for help, only 15% of parents in the United Kingdom were approached. Children who asked for help were most likely to have done so because they had a technical problem, for example, a virus (46%) or when they were looking for information on the Internet (40%). Children asked for help in only 4% of the cases when strangers had tried to contact them online, when they found sexually or violently images, or had been harassed. Only in 3% of the cases were parents asked to help their children when bullied online. It does not come as a surprise that the proportion of children who had asked their parents for help when a problem occurred using the Internet was lower for children whose parents did not use the Internet. Thirty-eight percent of the children of frequent Internet users requested parental assistance, 30% of the children of occasional users asked for help, but only 11% asked for help when their parents were nonusers of the Internet.

In the Flash Eurobarometer (2008), the parents were asked what kind of measures would contribute to safer and more effective use of the Internet for their child. Eighty-eight percent of the parents considered more or improved teaching and guidance on Internet use in schools as important; 87% see a need for more awareness raising campaigns of online risks, with better information and advice for parents on websites. This shows the increasing awareness of parents compared to the situation in 2006 when the Special Eurobarometer 250 document revealed that only 38% of parents in Europe had set rules regarding the Internet use of their children. Rules were mostly applied when children are aged between 10-13 years old (48%), and the number decreases with older children (28%). This can be taken as an indicator of the lack of confidence and knowledge of parents about how to set adequate rules.

Returning to risks, the underestimation of certain risks was confirmed in the Eurobarometer by the children's answers when they were asked to express themselves on the following six types of problems: potentially incorrect or shocking content, potentially dangerous contacts, harassment, falseness of services or goods and illegal downloads. Children minimize these risks and display confidence in their ability to solve the problems alone, which was confirmed also by the young people at the Youth Protection Roundtable meeting. The results of the Eurobarometer studies (2007, 2008) led to the conclusion that activities to be undertaken should not only focus on information material regarding risks on the Internet, but rather make children aware and conscious of the consequences of their own online conduct and the risks occurring from the conduct of others, which most of the questioned children tend to deny or to minimize.

JOINT EFFORTS OF ALL STAKEHOLDERS ARE NEEDED TO ACHIEVE THE GOAL OF A SAFER ONLINE ENVIRONMENT FOR CHILDREN AND YOUTHS

Considering the responses from the young people participating in the Youth Protection Roundtable and the Eurobarometer findings, a generational divide has to be acknowledged in regard to risk perception and digital literacy. Technical tools can address many of the risks and threats mentioned in the Matrix. But one must acknowledge that presently these tools do not reach their full potential. Their effectiveness can be improved by further development of the tools themselves, by improvement of their usability, and by improvement of the users' skills in using the tools. However good the tools might become, it is never recommended to rely on technical tools completely. The best way to help children stay safe is to empower and educate them to avoid and to deal with the risks. In delivering this objective, technologies can play a useful or supportive role, especially where younger children are concerned.

As previously shown, the younger generation is technically better skilled than adults. This might enable them to overrule the technical safety measures their caregivers install, if such measures have been taken. But, it does not empower them and provide them with guidance for digital life. Eventually a combination of effective technical tools and educational measures can lead to a safer online environment. In the light of new Internet appliances—the so-called Web 2.0—not only is there a need for the development of new technical tools, but also a new approach to teaching digital literacy and raising awareness for new challenges, as well as new benefits for youth. This approach can be called education for digital citizenship, that is, to make use of the technology in an autonomous and responsible way. Not only do young people, but also parents and caregivers, need to learn how to be a responsible digital citizen. And they need to understand the habits of young people as digital natives. They need to acknowledge the weight and the impact the Internet has for their children's everyday life. Bans and rules are no adequate means; indeed, banning would make Internet, especially Web 2.0, more interesting than before. Notwithstanding that many parents seem to be unable to set the appropriate rules even if they try (Croll, 2007). In the view of the experts questioned in the survey, parents and pedagogues are the preferred caregivers with regard to youth protection, more so than other stakeholders like companies, policy makers and the police.

In light of the findings from the Youth Protection Roundtable and the Eurobarometer studies, adult carers should get acquainted with the Internet itself by digital literacy training, but first and foremost they should learn about children's and young people's Internet habits. Children's welfare organizations can play an important role in training for parents and pedagogues because the target group is more likely to trust in advice given by well established counselors (Croll & Brüggemann, 2007). As described before, the risks occurring in the virtual world are very similar to those in real life—like abuse, violence, and so forth. Internet safety must therefore be seen as an important task for youth protection in general and implemented in an overall educational approach. The task of setting the stage and providing the funds for this approach should be assigned to policy makers, and higher priority should be given to these points on the political agenda. Companies are liable for the improvement of their products. They should ensure that effective tools for youth protection are at hand of those in need; in case of newly developed end-user based technologies, the possible effects on children and youths should be pre-estimated to avoid endangerment. This gains relevance especially in the light of children's likeliness to obtain new technologies and digital services at an increasingly younger age and definitely faster than their adult caregivers.

To ensure the most effective impact of the measures described, joint efforts of all stakeholders such as policy makers, industry, parents and children's welfare organizations, are needed. Nonetheless, attention has to be paid to diverse and struggling interests of the different groups involved. Therefore, neutral instances for the monitoring and the steering of the development process are necessary.

NOTES

1. For an overview visit the repository at www.eukids-online.net
2. Austria, Belgium, France, Germany, Ireland, Luxembourg, Netherlands, United Kingddom, Israel
3. Denmark, Finland, Norway, Sweden
4. Cyprus, Greece, Italy, Malta, Spain, Turkey
5. Bulgaria, Czech Republic, Hungary, Latvia, Lithuania, Poland, Slovenia
6. Inadequate means here Inappropriate. Due to a mistake in the translation of the questionnaire from German to English language the wrong term was used.
7. PIN—Personal Identification Number
8. TAN—Transaction Number
9. Multimedia Message
10. SMS—Short Message Service

REFERENCES

Anonymous (2007, October 15). BE: Belgium trials eID for kids. *epractice.eu*. Retrieved from http://www.epractice.eu/document/3976

Baacke, D. (1999). Medienkompetenz: Modelle und Projekte [Media Literacy: Models and Projects]. In D. Baacke, S. Kornblum, J. Lauffer, L. Mikos, & G. A. Thiele (Eds.), *Handbuch Medien* (pp. 31-35). Bonn: Bundeszentrale für Politische Bildung.

Crisp Thinking Group Ltd. (2005). *Anti-Grooming Engine*. Retrieved from http://www.crispthinking.com/anti-grooming-engine.htm

Croll, J. (2007). Salto Mortale im Netz: Welche Werte gelten in der digitalen Welt? [Salto Mortale on the Net: Which Values apply to the Virtual World?]. *Leben im Cyberspace. Club of Rome 2007*, 14-23.

Croll, J., & Brüggemann, M. (2007). Förderung der Medienkompetenz sozial benachteiligter Kinder und Jugendlicher [Cultivation of Media Literacy for Socially Disadvantaged Youth]. Beratung, Begleitung und Evaluation von vier Modellprojekten. Im Auftrag des Landesanstalt für Medien Nordrhein-Westfalen (LfM). LfM-Dokumentation 32.

Croll, J., & Kubicek, H. (2007). Wer vertraut wem beim Jugendmedienschutz? [Who trusts Whom in Youth Media Protection?] In D. Klumpp, H. Kubicek, A. Roßnagel, & W. Schulz (Eds.), *Informationelles Vertrauen für die Informationsgesellschaft* (pp. 247-266). Springer Verlag Heidelberg 2008.

Croll, J., Kunze, K., & Bernsmann, S. (2008). Zu Hause in der virtuellen Welt? [At Home in the Virtual World]. Über den Einfluss von Herkunft und kulturellem Hintergrund auf die Nutzung des Mediums Internet durch Jugendliche. *Interkulturell mit Medien. München kopaed 2008*, 163-182.

Croll, J., & Lippa, B. (2008). Digitale Integration durch Medienkompetenz [Digital Inclusion through Media Literacy]. *Merz – medien + erziehung 2008*, 4, 23-30.

Deloitte (2007). *Synthesis Report 2007 Edition. Test and benchmark of products and services to filter Internet content for childref between 6 and 16 years. Tailoring the filtering*. Retrieved from http://www.sip-bench.eu/Reports2007/SIP%20Bench%202007%20-%20Synthesis%20Report.pdf

Eurobarometer (2006). *Eurobarometer on safer Internet: Quantitative surveys 2005-2006*. Retrieved from http://ec.europa.eu/information_society/activities/sip/eurobarometer/index_en.htm

Eurobarometer (2007). *Eurobarometer on safer Internet for children: Qualitative study 2007*. Retrieved from http://ec.europa.eu/information_society/activities/sip/eurobarometer/index_en.htm

Flash Eurobarometer survey (2008). *Towards a safer use of the Internet for children in the EU-a parents' perspective*. Retrieved from http://ec.europa.eu/information_society/activities/sip/eurobarometer/index_en.htm

Luxembourg Safer Internet Helpline Project. (2006). *Definition von Filtersoftware* [Electronic version]. Retrieved from http://www.lusi.lu/index.php?id=16&L=1

Medienpädagogischer Forschungsverbund Südwest (2008). KIM Studie 2008—Kinder und Medien, *Computer und Internet*. Retrieved from http://www.mpfs.de/index.php?id=144

Mercury Interactive Corporation. (2004). SiteScope User's Guide (Version 7.9.5.0). *Monitoring*. Retrieved from http://mon15ny450.doubleclick.net/SiteScope/docs/SiteScopeTerms.htm

Palfrey, J., & Gasser, U. (2008). *Born digital: Understanding the first generation of digital natives*. New York, NY: Basic Books.

Photopatrol (2007). *Mehr Schutz und Erfolg für Ihre Bilder durch digitale Signaturen*. Retrieved from http://www.photopatrol.eu/fileadmin/templates/Hilfe_Texte/Informationen_ueber_Photopatrol_Download_-_V.1.pdf

Wikipedia Encyclopedia (2009). *Webmonitoring*. Retrieved from http://de.wikipedia.org/wiki/Webmonitoring

CHAPTER 9

CHILDREN AND THE JANUS-FACED INTERNET

Social Policy Implications for Mauritius as a Developing Country Case Study

Komalsingh Rambaree

INTRODUCTION

During the past few decades, many developing countries have been shifting towards a technology-based society with a firm belief that investment in the latest technology offers the opportunity for a giant leap forward in the world development ranking (Hilliard, 2002). Heeks (as cited in Ackbarally, 2002, p. 2) argued: "IT (Information Technology) will be a cornerstone of every national economy in the 21st century, and the sooner developing countries recognize this, the better." From this perspective, governments and international donor agencies have aggressively pushed the notion of ICT (Information and Communication Technology), especially access to the Internet, to the forefront of the development agenda in developing countries (Hanna & Schware, 1990). Just as industrial technology has transformed many societies in the nineteenth century, many

High-Tech Tots: Childhood in a Digital World, pp. 185–209
Copyright © 2010 by Information Age Publishing
All rights of reproduction in any form reserved.

contemporary academics argue that the Internet technologies are about to inflict far-reaching socioeconomic changes upon the twenty-first century (Ben-Ze'ev, 2004; Cooper, Mcloughlin, & Campbell, 2000; Hilliard, 2002; Holloway & Valentine, 2003; Kitchin, 1998; Turkle, 1995).

It is a common belief that today's children are the human capital for tomorrow. In particular, ICT education to produce ICT-literate children is consistent with the human capital theory, which emphasizes present investment for a versatile and adaptable workforce for the future (Wims & Lawler, 2007). Within this theoretical perspective, it is expected that the State make efficient investment in children through the promotion of ICT, so as to reap the benefits in the future (Becker, 1993; Yueh, 2001).

In principle, a wise strategy for sustainable development must also take into account the negative impact of technological investment on the human population, especially on children (Rambaree, 2009). Generally, sustainable development is defined as, "development that meets the needs of the present without compromising the ability of future generations to meet their own needs" (World Commission on Environment and Development, 1987, p. 43). From this stance, it is also commonly argued that a country, which is not securing a healthy and sound growth for its population of children, is surely jeopardizing its sustainability within the development process (Rambaree, 2009). Thus, investment in the promotion of modern technologies for socioeconomic change needs to go hand in hand with sound and healthy development of children.

Historically, there has been a continuing wave of public concern and controversy over the significance of the media and new technologies as enablers of social change, and their respective impact on the social life of children (Williams & Frith, 1993). It is argued that the Internet is Janus-faced with regards to children. The Internet is fun, educational and entertaining, as well as scary, confusing and unsafe; children, therefore, need direction to navigate this rapidly emerging and expanding technology safely (Rambaree, 2007). The Internet can open several doors for opportunities, but it also has a number of dangers from which children need to be protected.

At global level, there is a growing concern for child safety and protection (Hetherington, 1999; Mushunje, 2006). Children are at the center of many current debates concerning potential dangers and risks of the Internet (Chase & Statham, 2005; Childnet International, 2003; Holloway & Valentine, 2001, 2003). For some researchers (Barak & King, 2000; Durkin, 1997), the Internet provides a convenient environment for child abuse and sexual harassment by cyber-stalkers. In particular, developing countries are found to be more at risk with regards to online child exploitation and victimization (United Nations Children's Fund [UNICEF], 2004).

Taking Mauritius as a case study, the main aim of this chapter is to make a critical reflection on the social policy implications for online child safety and protection within a developing country context. After this introductory section, the chapter starts by considering the specific forces that are driving Mauritius towards a technology-based society. Then, the chapter presents a section on the situation of children's access to and use of the Internet in Mauritius. Following this, the focus of this chapter is on the potential benefits and challenges of promoting access to the Internet for children in developing countries. Before the conclusion, the social policy implications regarding online child safety and protection in Mauritius are considered.

THE OPPORTUNITY FOR A LEAP FORWARD: MAURITIUS AS A CASE STUDY

Mauritius is a small island situated in the Indian Ocean. It has a population of about 1.2 million with a land surface area of 1,865 sq km. Mauritius has been colonized by different European powers, including the Dutch (1638-1710), French (1710-1810), and British (1810-1968). After 150 years of British rule, Mauritius became an independent democracy within the Commonwealth in 1968. Since its independence, Mauritius has often been referred to as a politically stable country (Eriksen, 1998). Mauritius became a Republic State in 1992. Currently, the ethnic composition of the country is divided in the following way: 52% Hindus, 16% Muslims (both of Indian origin), 27% Creoles (Mauritians of African descent), 3% Chinese and 2% European decedents, mostly of French origin (Bunwaree, 2001). The official language of Mauritius is English, but French is the most common spoken language and is also dominant in the local media. Local people in Mauritius interact in Creole (lingua franca) and one or several other oriental languages, such as Hindi, Urdu, and Mandarin.

During the early 1970s, Mauritius was very much an agriculture-based society, with sugarcane as the main pillar of its economy. The agriculture-based Mauritian society had experienced a rapidly expanding population, huge balance of deficit, soaring prices, massive unemployment and a stagnating mono-crop economy (Bunwaree, 2002). To address these socioeconomic issues the *1971-75 Plan for Social and Economic Development* was prepared by the then government. The government of the day was mainly influenced by the Fabians' ideologies. The Fabians' ideologies were based on the philosophical grounds that the state is more efficient than the market, and therefore, welfare state is the vehicle to provide altruism, solidarity, and community by providing universal social services for all (Parrott, 2002). The then government therefore started the provision of a comprehensive universal welfare program with free education, free health, and universal old age pension for its citizens (Bunwaree, 2005), which is still maintained, despite a difficult economic situation.

During the 1970s, the first "post independence" government also embarked on a radical population control program. The 1971-1975 development strategy managed to incorporate population policy through the promotion of the use and distribution of contraceptives without controversy (Jones, 1989). Such policy resulted in high levels of male and female education, high life expectancy, and low infant mortality and fertility rates (Schensul,, Schensul, Oodit, Bhowan, & Ragobur, 1994). After becoming a successful case in the world on population control, Mauritius then started its second phase of development through industrialization. During the early 1980s, Mauritius was referred to as one of the world's fastest-growing economies, and continued to attract many foreign investors for the development of textile and tourism. During the 1990s, Mauritius diversified its economic structure and created a more vibrant export-processing zone (textile) and developed a strong tourism industry. Mauritius, therefore, became a model of a diversified economy (three pillars—sugar, textile and tourism) in the African context.

Since the beginning of the 1980s, Mauritius has continuously made an effort to diversify its economy, in order to be on the safe side. Although since the early 1980s Mauritius had has an average annual economic growth of around 5% (Shillington, 1991), the economic future of the country is currently considered to be vulnerable. In particular, the global liberal market currently poses several serious challenges to the Mauritian economy. According to The World Bank (2006), the Mauritian sugar production, clothing and textiles are suffering from global completion and the relatively high costs production. In addition, the fear of terrorism and the current global financial crisis is causing concern to the Mauritian tourism sector.

Thus, the setting up of an information technology industry has been earmarked as a new and promising economic pillar for the country in order to support other vulnerable sectors (Goburdhun, 2007). As the *Mauritian National ICT Strategic Plan 2006-2010* puts it: "With the globalization process and the gradual depletion of our competitive advantages in our major income sectors, ICT has been identified as a potential sector for sustaining economic development" (United Nations [UN], 2007, p. 6). From the year 2000, Mauritius has therefore invested in a new phase of development, one that could be described as leading towards a technology-based society (Rambaree, 2007). This is the type of society that the policy makers are projecting for the future of Mauritius. At the beginning of the new millennium, the then government of Mauritius embarked on a mammoth project for a Mauritian cyber city. Part of the construction work has been completed and people of all ages from all around the island are being actively trained in ICT. In this connection, Leithead (2003) states: "the expansion into the high-tech sector doesn't end with just infrastructure. Huge investment is being put into education ... even for those who haven't even seen a computer before" (¶ 12).

As part of the effort to turn Mauritius into a cyber island, the current government is also continuing to liberalize the use of the Internet among its population. In 2001, the then Mauritian government had outlined a policy for supplying Internet access to almost all households, like water and electricity (Leithead, 2003). With such a policy in Mauritius, there has been an increase in the number of households having an Internet connection. With the installation of SAFE (South Africa Far East) fiber optic submarine cable in June 2002, a number of households in Mauritius are connected via broadband (International Telecommunications Union [ITU], 2004). For many families, the Internet has become essential at home (Jackson, Eye, Biocca, Barbatsis, Zhao, & Fitzgerald, 2006).

In fact, Mauritius has already become a reference point in terms of investment and promotion of ICT in Africa. The African Development Bank/Organisation for Economic Co-operation and Development (2008) reports that, in Mauritius the communication infrastructure is among the best in the African region, the number of Internet users has grown rapidly, and Internet access is readily available to residential and business users. The ITU (2008) indicators also confirm Mauritius as a model, in terms of Internet use among its population, in Africa. In fact, the Mauritian ICT industry has been growing by 25% from October 2006 to March 2007, with 41 new companies starting operations during this period (Board of Investment, 2007).

Compared to many African countries, Mauritius already has better access to the Internet (Oyelaram-Oyeyinka & Adeya, 2002). However, with the vision of making ICT the fifth pillar of the national economy,[1] the current government is continuing its effort to boost up this particular sector. One of the measures proposed by the Government of Mauritius (2007) in the *Mauritian National ICT Policy 2007-2011* reads:

> Action will be taken to increase ICT integration in society, by providing access to ICTs to all communities including those who are isolated geographically or economically. In order to increase household PC penetration, financing options will be provided for low-income individuals to purchase a computer with broadband Internet access. The primary school PC penetration will also be increased. (p. 14)

The threat to the already established sectors and the potentials of a promising ICT sector have therefore led Mauritius no other choice than to invest towards a technology-based society. In particular, the investment in technology is expected to provide a new opportunity for Mauritius to leap forward and position itself within the digital world together with developed nations. Within this context, Mauritius is trying to liberalize the use of Internet among its population (including children) with the view to achieve a sustainable economic development. Mauritius has already domesticated the Internet, and the country's children are plugged into the digital world too.

Before embarking on further details, now it would be interesting to look at the case of Mauritius and consider where, why, and how the children are using the Internet. The consideration of the situation of children's access and use of the Internet in Mauritius would allow for a more grounded reflection on the potential benefits and risks associated with this new technology and a more focused approach in the examination of the social policy implications.

THE SITUATION OF CHILDREN'S ACCESS AND USE OF THE INTERNET IN MAURITIUS

Children (below the age of 14 years old) represent about 30% of the total Mauritian population (Central Statistics Office, 2007). In Mauritius, the Ministry of Women's Rights, Child Development and Family Welfare is mandated to support children ages 0-18 years (MWRCDFW, 2006). The Ministry has expanded children's policies much beyond child survival and basic education. Policies now encompass other aspects of child development, including children's rights and protection. In addition, following the enactment of the *Ombudsperson for Children Act No. 41 of 2003*, the office of the Ombudsperson for children has been set up for ensuring children's rights and protection in Mauritius (MWRCDFW, 2008). According to the composite child-friendliness index, Mauritius has emerged first among the most child-friendly governments in Africa (African Child Policy Forum, 2008). However, with regards to online child safety and protection, Mauritius is still lagging behind in comparison to many other countries, like Singapore, Canada, Australia and the United States (Childnet International, 2003; Rambaree, 2008).

More and more people are having access to the Internet in Mauritius. Mobile phones, computers, and computer-based technologies have become the new craze for children in Mauritius (National Computer Board [NCB], 2004). In fact, the NCB (2003) reports that about 11% of the computer users were children below the age of 12 years, and 5% of the population below 12 years old had access to the Internet at home (p. 8). With both the previous and current government's initiatives and policies, children's access to the Internet has dramatically increased in Mauritius. Currently, it is estimated that more than 30% of children (below the age of 14 years) have access to the Internet at home (Rambaree, 2007). In Mauritius, just like in the United Kingdom Singapore, Australia and Canada, children are very much attracted by the interactive areas of the Internet (Childnet International, 2003).

Mauritian children access the Internet from five main locations: their homes, schools, cyber cafés, public libraries, and other people's homes (cousins, friends and neighbors, etc.). Given that living with an extended family is still rather common in Mauritius, a number of children share facilities with their cousins. A small minority of children have also reported accessing the Internet from their neighbors' place (Rambaree, 2007). In addition, in both rural and urban areas of Mauritius, there has been a noticeable increase in cyber cafés (Childnet International, 2003). Cyber-cafés are expensive, but they have the advantage of offering a rapid connection service (ITU, 2004) and therefore attract many children who want to play games. Usually, children go to cyber cafés with their elder friends and/or relatives (Rambaree, 2007).

Home and school remain the two most common places from where children have access to the Internet (ITU, 2004). In particular, home is the most easily accessible place for many children to make use (or abuse) of the Internet. In fact, the majority of the Mauritian children access the Internet for educational purposes (Rambaree, 2007). Schools and even parents are encouraging children to go online for undertaking search and research for academic purposes. In Mauritius, primary school children are having training on the Internet (Ministry of Education and Human Resources, 2006). In particular, ITU (2004) reports that, in order to encourage students to use and apply ICT, the NCB organizes annual software competitions with cash prizes for various levels of students in Mauritius. The Internet is indeed the virtual library, open and available to all on a 24/7 basis.

Communication and entertainment activities dominate the use of the Internet, primarily through the use of e-mail, instant messaging, Internet Chat, and games. In fact, Internet-mediated entertainment and communication has been gaining enormous popularity among Mauritian children (NCB, 2003). Mesch and Talmud (2003) write that, through its use for communication, the Internet can have an important positive social effect on individuals as it permits social contact and connection with distant, as well as local, individuals who share interests and experiences. Thus, for a number of children the Internet provides a well-needed medium to maintain contacts with their close friends and siblings who are physically at a distance from them. With new software, young people can also download and share music, songs, and videos. Therefore, the Internet has become the vital medium for communication and entertainment for a number of children in Mauritius (Rambaree, 2007)

Given that the majority of Mauritian children have easy access to the Internet for academic related work, Rambaree (2007) found that a small number of children also unintentionally (or sometimes by curiosity) access sexually explicit online materials. In his study on Mauritian children, Rambaree (2007) also mentioned about a minority number of research participants who reported having regular access to sexually explicit online materials. Thus, over the last few years there has been a growing concern over children using the Internet to access pornographic materials (Griffiths, 1997, 1998).

Particularly, the Internet is dramatically impacting human social and sexual behavior (Cooper et al., 2000). Peter and Valkenburg (2006) believe that, "more than any other medium, the Internet is a sexual medium" (p. 178). In fact, millions of people interact in a sexual way on the Internet (Golberg, as cited in Putnam, 2000). Being part of the same digital world as adults, many children do get involved (intentionally or unintentionally) with Internet-mediated sexual interactions (Boies, Knudson, & Young, 2004; Cho & Choen, 2005; Lo & Wei, 2005; Mitchell, Finkelhor & Wolak, 2001, 2005; Ong, 2006; Quinn & Forsyth, 2005; Subrahmanyam, Kraut, Greenfield, & Gross, 2000; Turkle, 1999; Wolak, Finkelhor, & Mitchell, 2004).

ICT development and its relationship with children have been viewed from two different perspectives: the pessimistic view is that children become victims of the pervasive and powerful multi-media; the optimistic view is that ICT advancement contributes immensely towards empowering children, making them more creative and knowledgeable than ever before (UN, 2003). Within the same context, Holloway and Valentine (2003) state:

> ICT are regarded by some as a potential threat, not only to individual children, but also to childhood as an institution because of its potential to threaten childhood "innocence" and blur the differentiation which is commonly made between the states of childhood and adulthood. (p. 2)

In particular, Internet is considered as being Janus-faced with regards to children. It presents a number of potential benefits as well challenges for developing countries. The following section therefore considers potential benefits and challenges of the promotion of Internet access for children in developing countries.

THE POTENTIAL BENEFITS AND CHALLENGES OF PROMOTING INTERNET ACCESS FOR CHILDREN IN DEVELOPING COUNTRIES

Potential Benefits

There is high hope that the latest technology, like the Internet, will help to close the socioeconomic and political gaps between developed and developing countries (Mbambo & Cronjé, 2002; Vetter, 2008). In particular, there is a general belief that the Internet can stimulate economic growth in developing countries by making the national economic sector more efficient through e-commerce and by attracting foreign investors. It is commonly known that the Internet capabilities offer the potential of benefiting personal and corporate users by saving time and money for transactions, research, and correspondence (Clarke & Wallsten, 2004; Ebrahimian, 2003). Clarke and Wallsten (2004) report that Internet can play a vital part in the economic growth of poorer nations as it may help to stimulate exports from poor countries to rich.

In addition, Internet as a powerful technological tool is also gradually pervading all aspects of the health, educational, business, and economic sectors in developing countries (Singhal, 1997). For instance, it is expected that developing countries will have better access to health information and services though telemedicine and the Internet (Edejer, 2000; Edworthy, 2001), as well as better access to education through online learning and courses (Ebrahimian, 2003). In addition, the hope is widespread that the Internet will provide a powerful new tool in the battle against poverty in developing countries (Kenny, 2003). Moreover, the Internet is also referred to as an essential tool for promoting good governance through democratic participation and transparency (Vetter, 2008). Thus, the Internet is being considered as an essential element in the development of human capital.

Mutula and Brakel (2007) write: "investment in human capital ... is becoming increasingly recognized as a critical factor in preparing citizens to participate in the digital age" (p. 232). By promoting access to the Internet, developing countries are therefore expecting to be well-prepared for the future economic requirements. For instance, the promotion of Internet use in primary schools is mainly carried out by developing nations in order to cultivate information literacy and to improve their future global competitiveness through ICT training (Yang & Tung, 2007). It is expected that with the Internet, children of the developing countries might have a brighter and better future in the globalized digital world. However, developing countries should not ignore the challenges in promoting Internet access for children.

Challenges

Some conservative societies invest in technology mainly for economic reasons, but then face cultural shocks from the contents that can be accessed through this medium (Hilliard, 2002). For instance, in Mauritius the Internet is breaking down cultural barriers on sexuality (Rambaree, 2005, 2007, 2008). In fact, Mauritius is considered to be a conservative society where sex is still taboo and sexuality education is absent both at school and at home (Hillcoat-Nalletamby & Ragobur, 2005; Mauritius Family Planning Association, 1993; Mauritius Institute of Health, 1996). With the advent of the Internet, there is a breakdown of cultural barriers through online sexuality information, communication, and interaction opportunities (Rambaree, 2005, 2007, 2008, 2009). The Internet presents sexuality information, communication, interaction and educational opportunities to its users without distinguishing between their sociocultural contexts, geographical location, age, and so forth (Cooper et al., 2000; Peter & Valkenburg, 2006; Valkenburg, Schouten, & Peter, 2005).

The current challenge for Mauritius is that the population and even policy makers are left with a dilemma of how to deal with the issue of technology and sexuality with regards to children's safety (Childnet International, 2003), and the prevailing moral panic is perhaps heightened as a result of a lack of empirical evidence on this particular issue. Nevertheless, most researchers and policymakers have long realized that the Internet is Janus-faceted when it concerns children. Within this context, a number of developing countries are facing the challenge of finding the right balance between the promotion of Internet access for children and online child safety and protection. For instance, Shukor (2006) writes: "In the emerging information focused society and the widespread use of … ICT most governments have been facing the dilemma of regulating the borderless domain known as cyberspace" (p. 1). In fact, a number of developing countries are unable to scientifically monitor for the "right kind of investment," as they have limited resources for research. For example, a country like Mauritius spends only 0.3% of its GDP in research and development (Gokhool, 2007b).

In particular, there is a growing concern for child safety and protection, especially in developing countries (Hetherington, 1999; Mushunje, 2006). Various reports have for long been pointing out that pedophiles are using the Internet to travel for child sexual tourism to developing countries, where there are limited or almost nonexistent online child safety and protection structures, mechanisms, and legislation (The Guardian, 2008; UNICEF, 2004). For instance, in Mauritius investment for a technology based society started in 2000, and a decade later policy makers of the country are still reflecting on what and how to do with regards to online child safety and protection. In Mauritius, just like in a number of developing countries (and even in some developed countries) resolutions on ethical, legal, and regulatory issues regarding the Internet are lagging behind current realities (Cooper et al., 2000). For example in Mauritius, the current Child Protection Act urgently needs to be amended to cater for offences such as luring children online and grooming (NCB, 2007).

The major challenge of developing countries is therefore to have adequate trained ICT experts for making ethical, legal and regulatory frameworks. But, developing countries also face the challenge to attract and retain qualified ICT experts because of brain drain. Brain drain, that is the migration of skilled workers from the developing countries to the developed ones mainly because of better wages and conditions, represents a major setback for developing nations, in terms of lost of vital human capital. In a similar manner, Pichappan (2004) argued: "Many developing nations are experiencing a significant and a protracted period of brain drain of professional, semi-professional, and technical personnel" (p. 105). For the case of Mauritius, Gokhool (2007a) opines: "There is an urgent need ...to prevent such a drain of resources as it jeopardizes the future of the emerging economies. Rather we should encourage a process of brain circulation and attract highly qualified human resources to Mauritius" (p. 2). But, does a small developing state, like Mauritius have the capacity and resources to control this liberal and highly competitive global market?

In fact, the available human resources should be optimally used in developing countries for achieving the best possible child safety and protection. For instance, human resources for the supervision and ethical use of the Internet are crucial for online child safety and protection. In a number of developing countries, like Mauritius, there is an urgent need for capacity building in terms of training and awareness raising for a range of professionals, such as teachers, social workers, the police, and other professionals providing both direct and indirect services and support to children (Chase & Statham, 2005). However, it is also important that such tasks be carried out in a systematic way without causing moral panic in society (Shade, 2002). Otherwise, children might have all Internet access revoked and have difficulties in using this necessary tool for improving their futures (Holloway & Valentine, 2003).

In Mauritius several places from where children are accessing the Internet have been found to be unsafe and unsecured (Rambaree, 2007). In a similar line, NCB (2007) reports that, "at the level of cyber cafés and public libraries there is limited filtering mechanism in place and children using the facilities there can be at risk" (p. 1). Therefore another important challenge is to study the type of adult supervision provided and the child protection issues in the cyber cafés. It is commonly argued that the terms appropriate or responsible supervision are still ambiguous in child protection discourses (Pierpoint, 2004). Just having an adult supervising in the cyber cafés does not necessarily imply a safe and secure place for children. Child protectionists should also question and consider the types and form of supervision given to children, including that provided by parents at home.

Particularly, parents' roles and responsibilities are vital in guiding children towards appropriate use and protection from potential risks of the Internet. However, in a number of developing countries the common communication gap between parents and adolescents has widened with the advent of the Internet (i-Safe, 2003). In many developing countries parents are unable to direct, support, and assist their children in accessing and using the Internet. This is a direct result of some parents not having sufficient information, knowledge, and understanding of the Internet; and not having sufficient skills in communicating with their children on this issue. Thornburgh and Lin (2002) argued: "Perhaps for the first time, children (as a group) are more knowledgeable than their parents about an increasingly pervasive technology" (p. 163). This argument applies to the case of Mauritian children whose parents had the opportunity to have only 3 to 5 years of primary education (Rambaree, 2007). Thus, another major challenge in developing countries is to deal with the *Generational Digital Divide,* that is how to have an inclusive society where the young and the old generation can have a proper understanding of the Internet.

Policymakers should treat the issue of children's online protection with great care and consideration (Nair, 2006). Children should be protected, and at the same time they should not be denied access to the Internet, as the medium is an indispensable tool for the modern digital world (Ong, 2006; Oswell, 1999). In a similar vein, Berson (2003) states: "like the fire, the potential brilliance of the Internet may only be obscured by the hidden dangers which lurk beneath a mesmerizing façade" (p. 5). Therefore, developing countries like Mauritius should have clear social policies with regards to the promotion of Internet access for all, including that for children. As Thornburg and Lin (2002) write:

> The Internet is both a source of promise for our children and a source of concern. The promise is of Internet-based access to the information age and the concern is over the possibility that harm might befall our children as they use the Internet. (p. 17)

KEY SOCIAL POLICY IMPLICATIONS REGARDING ONLINE CHILD SAFETY AND PROTECTION IN DEVELOPING COUNTRIES

Online Child Safety and Protection

According to Childnet International (2003), the importance of an Internet safety policy is reflected in the potential dangers facing children online. Protecting children and looking after their welfare is a moral and legal responsibility of everybody and importantly the State (Hetherington, 1999; World Health Organization [WHO], 2003). Indeed many countries, including Mauritius, have signed the UN Convention on the Rights of the Child (CRC), which clearly stipulates the responsibilities of all stakeholders towards child safety and protection (UN, 1989). For example, WHO (2003) states that under the CRC, Governments have a duty to ensure that young people can express themselves and that their views are given weight according to their age and maturity. In addition, the *Mauritian National Children's Policy* clearly establishes, amongst the aims of child protection measures, the protection of children from inappropriate and harmful content (Childnet International, 2003). However, this particular policy paper needs to be updated with regards to the digital era where the Internet is playing an important role in causing harm to a number of children from all around the world.

Moreover, the plans and policies should also be translated into practical realities. In a number of developing countries, it has been found that plans and policies remain on paper only, and never get translated into practice. In fact, there are a number of other considerations such as financial, economic and strategic factors, political ideologies, and public participation/pressure, which impact on the process of turning plan and policy into reality (Nutley, Davies, & Walter, 2003; Packwood, 2002). It is generally known that developing countries face several challenges in terms of financial and political stability, and in the meantime thousands of children from the developing nations are becoming cyber victims of online sexual exploitation, harassment, and pornography.

Internet-Based Pornography

Thornburg and Lin (2002) write: "The term 'pornography' has no well-defined meaning. Despite the fact that individuals use the term as though it does and behave as though there is a universal understanding of what is and is not covered by the term" (p. 20). In particular, the definition of pornography has varied over time, and it varies between different social and cultural contexts (Traeen, Nilsen, & Stigum, 2006). According to Williams (2005), protecting children from legal pornographic images is controversial, as there is little agreement about what constitutes pornography. Nevertheless, it is generally agreed that pornographic materials are inappropriate for children, for a variety of reasons. Russell (1998) refers to pornography as "materials that combines sex and/or the exposure of genitals with abuse or degradation in a manner that appear to endorse, condone, or encourage such behavior" (p. 3). Pornography is usually negatively loaded, and often associated with the socially unacceptable, the deviant, the censured, or the shameful for children (Beggan & Allison, 2003; Traeen et al., 2006; Traeen, Spitznogle, & Beverfjord, 2004). Second-wave feminists argue that pornography is the theory, and that rape is the practice of this theory (Morgan, 1980).

Moreover, several researchers (especially feminists) argue that pornography degrades, dehumanizes, and debases people, especially women (Fisher, 2001; Russell, 1998). In addition, children are easily affected by exposure to extremely shocking and disturbing online pornographic materials, such as pedophilic acts, child molestation, and child sexual torture (Cameron, Salazar, Bernhardt, Burgess-Whitman, Wingood, & DiClemente, 2005; Cooper et al., 2000; Durkin, 1997; Kanuga & Rosenfeld, 2004; Lo & Wei, 2005; Ong, 2006; Wolak, Finkelhor, & Mitchell, 2004). Thus, it is a common view that children should be protected from exposure to these kinds of materials.

While it is important to protect children, identifying and providing support to those who are affected by exposure to online pornography is highly complex and in some cases almost impossible (Chase & Statham, 2005; Downey, 2002; Gillen, 2003). This may indeed be a mammoth and complicated task, but for policymakers it is vital to look at some of the possible policies for minimizing such risks. As Beaver (2000) puts it, "the common sense notion that pornography is not the most appropriate way for children to develop their sexual attitudes and beliefs, suggests that some action is needed" (p. 376). In the digital world, effective means of reining in the Internet—so as to prevent harm (real or potential) to users or others—should therefore be a perennial issue for child protection workers and policymakers (Akdeniz, 2001; Williams, 2005). Therefore policy makers in Mauritius, through scientific research, should consider ways to minimize the risks of children's exposure to online pornographic and other harmful materials. In a similar vein, Wilkinson (1995) writes:

> We are all having to face up to the fact that our children's familiarity with technology is bringing a new set of risks, especially if we want them to take full advantage of computers as tools of empowerment and education. (p. 21)

In relation to this, it is important to have policies on IEC (Information Education and Communication) campaigns in order to raise awareness for parents as to how children can avoid being exposed to online sexually explicit materials. In addition, extensive training and awareness-raising campaigns across a range of sectors, institutions, and agencies might be required in order to set up multiagency, multisectoral, multidisciplinary protocols and to explain to parents, teachers, and other professionals how children can be vulnerable to and protected from online pornographic materials (Chase & Statham, 2005). For example, an IEC campaign could focus on making the general public aware about the various brands of filtering software (Beaver, 2000). In addition, parents should also be made aware that filtering software is limited in its ability to avoid user exposure to online sexually explicit materials. Nevertheless, as Armagh (1998) explains: "Filtering options are not foolproof—they may not block all objectionable materials and may prevent access to sites approved by parents" (p. 8).

Thus, an IEC campaign might bring some beneficial outcomes. In particular, Williams (2005) argues that for parents, carers, and teachers to protect children from undesirable materials, some information, knowledge, and understanding of the means and applications of child online protection methods is needed. At the very least parents should be informed and made to understand the potential and real risks of allowing children to have the Internet in their bedrooms. Nair (2006) argues that it is important to educate parents and teachers, recognizing their roles in controlling access to the Internet for children.

Internet Grooming

Internet grooming refers to the activity of a potential offender in setting up opportunities for child abuse by gaining the trust of the child in order to prepare him or her for abuse through the Internet (Chase & Statham 2005; Gillespie, 2000, 2002, 2004; McAlinden, 2006). It is perhaps worth pointing out that grooming is not restricted to online behavior; it is part of the complex "cycle of abuse" through which a perpetrator and victim must travel in order for abuse to occur. (Gillespie, 2002). According to Chase and Statham (2005) the Internet has become a significant mechanism for grooming children for sexual exploitation. In this sense, legal regulation and frameworks have become a vital element in dealing with the Internet use (or abuse). Mauritius is still lagging behind in debating the issue of Internet grooming within the local context (Childnet International, 2003).

In relation to online child safety and protection, a report carried out by Childnet International (2003) strongly advised the Mauritian authorities to consider introducing legislation designed to protect children from abuse stemming from an original contact via the Internet, similar to the grooming offense in the United Kingdom and laws that have been introduced in Canada, United States, and Australia (see Childnet International, 2003). In particular, Childnet International wrote:

> There is no so-called "silver bullet" solution to the problem of keeping children safe online. The shared responsibility of the problem means that the response necessarily needs to be cross-sectoral and also across ministries, which in turn requires a level of cooperation towards this common goal. (p. 32)

Government can prepare regulations regarding supervision and involvement, but it is only with the help of civil society and all relevant stakeholders that real safety and child protection can be achieved. The Government should prepare regulations regarding supervision and involve civil society in facilitating this. For example, the participation of parents, teachers, and professional social service providers is imperative. In Mauritius, there is a need for capacity building, training, and awareness-raising for a range of professionals, such as teachers, social workers, the police, and other professionals providing direct services and support to children and young people (Chase & Statham, 2005). However, it is also important that such tasks be carried out in a systematic way without causing moral panic in society (Shade, 2002). Otherwise, children could be denied access to an important empowering medium (Holloway & Valentine, 2003).

Bridging the Generational "Digital Divide"

Many countries, such as Sweden, Singapore, the United Kingdom, the United States, and others, provide evening courses for parents who want to learn about the Internet (Childnet International, 2003). Perhaps Mauritius could think about taking similar steps. Involving parents through adult education could bring parents closer to their children in terms of supervision and support. At the same time, it is also important that children have some freedom and privacy while they are using the Internet (Holloway & Valentine, 2003). In other words, parents should be trained in how to build trust in their relationship and interaction with their children; and how to empower their children to make responsible use of the Internet. In this context, it is therefore important to consider promoting an ethical use of the Internet among children.

It would perhaps be a wise strategy to start by getting parents involved in making the Internet a safe and enjoyable place for children in Mauritius. Even with improved technology, protecting children will not work if parents do not get involved in making the Internet a safe medium for children (Beaver, 2000). Parents are mainly responsible for the safety and general welfare of their children, especially within the home environment. In fact, parents have a key role to play in creating a safe online environment for their children, through promoting, guiding, and supervising Internet use and overseeing safety issues at home together with their children (Childnet International, 2003).

In this respect, parents should be involved in guiding children towards appropriate use of the Internet. According to Burgess, Dziegielewski, and Green (2005) empowering parents to communicate about Internet safety can reduce the psychosocial barriers that many children often face when having to discuss sensitive issues with their parents. The bridging of the digital gap between the generations is crucial if parents are to be involved in children's use of the Internet. As Thornburg and Lin (2002) write:

> it is often said that the best protection against children being exposed to inappropriate material on the Internet is the presence and guidance of a responsible parent or guardian while the child is using the Internet—the reason is that when such an adult is involved, his or her standards can be trusted as the basis for good judgment for the child's welfare. (p. 184)

Ethical Use of the Internet

Some researchers have argued that the "just say no" strategy does not work with children (American Psychological Association, 2002). In other words, parents and policymakers cannot rely on campaigning purely through a strategy of denying children's access to the Internet, just because the latter can be exposed to inappropriate online materials. Children should be explained and informed about making ethical use of the internet, rather than controlling their use and access.

In addition, legislative and policy reforms alone will not provide adequate protection for children and young people (Chase & Statham, 2005). Internet safety has social education implications where children could be empowered to make informed and responsible judgments. In particular, children need empowerment programs so that they can make informed and ethical decisions on their own on the use of the Internet and help their peers in promoting online child safety and protection. Social education relating to the Internet is essential for children to make wise choices about how they behave on the Internet and to take control of their online experiences (Thornburg & Lin, 2002). Childnet International (2003) recommends that children need to be empowered so that they know how they can be in charge and in control while they are online, and how to stay smart online by keeping safe. Thornburg and Lin (2002) argue:

> A child who faces a free choice—and chooses responsible and ethical options over others—is protecting himself. Thus, the issue at hand is one that relates to the sense of ethics and responsibility and the character underlying a free (and often unaided) choice. (p. 218)

In Mauritius, several courses and training programs are being organized for closing the digital divide among young people from various socioeconomic levels. For example, the NCB uses cyber-bus tours throughout the island. The cyber buses are used for creating computer awareness and teaching basic computer skills to people in Mauritius. According to Childnet International (2003), the numerous awareness initiatives taking place across Mauritius lack a strong Internet safety element. Thus, perhaps Mauritius should start an online child safety and protection campaign by including the ethical use of the Internet and issues related to self-regulation and self-protection.

CONCLUSION

Indeed, the Internet has an enormous potential for contributing towards the development of a society, and children should not be scared of making maximum use of it (Cooper et al., 2000). However, just as the Internet has become a source of significant positive change, it has also created new openings for the abuse or exploitation of children (Stanley, 2001). Within this technological era, child victimization and abuse has taken another dimension. There is now growing evidence that the Internet is a new medium through which some commonly recognized forms of child maltreatment, sexual, and emotional abuse are taking place. Thus, the Internet is Janus-faced with regards to children. In fact, the digital world will continue to expand further, thereby bringing new risks and opportunities for children. Clearly, if we are to have a say in shaping the future of the digital world, we need to first understand the changes that are unfolding around us now and prepare ourselves so that we do not regret what we will leave for the future generation (Cooper et al., 2000). Children, the future and hope of our humanity, need a safer and better place for making a pleasant and sustainable digital world.

NOTE

1. Agriculture, manufacturing, tourism and financial services are considered as the four pillars of the Mauritian economy.

REFERENCES

Ackbarally, N. (2002). Mauritius: A cyber-island in the making. *The Communication Initiative*. Retrieved from http://www.comminit.com

African Child Policy Forum. (2008). *The African Report on Child Wellbeing 2008*. Retrieved from www.africanchildinfo.net/africanreport08/

African Development Bank/Organisation for Economic Co-operation and Development. (2008). *Mauritius*. Retrieved from ww.oecd.org/dataoecd/13/7/40578285.pdf

Akdeniz, Y. (2001). Controlling illegal and harmful content on the Internet. in D.S. Walls (Ed.), *Crime and the Internet: Cybercrimes and Cyberfears* (pp. 113-141). London: Routledge.

American Psychological Association. (2002). *Developing adolescents: A reference for professionals*. Washington DC: Author.

Armagh, D. (1998). A safety net for the Internet: Protecting our children. *Journal of Juvenile Justice*, 5(1), 9–15.

Barak, A., & King, S. (2000). The two faces of the Internet: Introduction to special issue on the Internet and sexuality. *CyberPsychology & Behavior*, 3(4), 517-520.

Beaver, W. (2000). The dilemma of Internet pornography. *Business and Society Review*, 105(3), 373-382.

Becker, G. S. (1993). Nobel lecture: The economic way of looking at behavior. *The Journal of Political Economy*, 101(3), 385-409.

Beggan, J. K., & Allison, S. T. (2003). Reflexivity in the pornographic films of Candida Royalle. *Sexualities*, 6(3-4), 301-324.

Ben-Ze'ev, A. (2004). *Love Online*. Cambridge, England: Cambridge University Press.

Berson, I. R. (2003). Grooming cybervictims: The psychosocial effects of online exploitation for youth. *Journal of School Violence*, 2(1), 5-18.

Board of Investment. (2007). *BPO Flash Semi Annual Review March 2007*. Retrieved from http://www.boimauritius.com/download/BPO%20flashMarch2007.pdf

Boies, S. C., Knudson, G., & Young, J. (2004). The Internet, sex, and youths: Implications for sexual development. *Sexual Addiction and Compulsivity*, 11(1), 343-363.

Bunwaree, S. (2001). The marginal in the miracle: Human capital in Mauritius. *International Journal of Educational Development*, 21(3), 257-271.

Bunwaree, S. (2002). Economics, conflicts and interculturality in a small island state: The case of Mauritius. *Polis/R.C.S.P./C.P.S.R.*, 9(Special Number), 14-21.

Bunwaree, S. (2005, December). *State—Society Relations: Re-engineering the Mauritian Social Contract*. Paper presented at the CODESRIA General Assembly, held in Maputo, Mozambique.

Burgess, V., Dziegielewski, S. F., & Green, C. E. (2005). Improving comfort about sex communication between parents and their adolescents: Practice-based research within a teen sexuality group. *Brief Treatment and Crisis Intervention*, 5(4), 379-390.

Cameron K. A., Salazar L. F., Bernhardt J. M., Burgess-Whitman N., Wingood G. M., & DiClemente, R. J. (2005). Adolescents' experience with sex on the web: Results from online focus groups. *Journal of Adolescence*, 28(4), 535-540.

Central Statistics Office. (2007). *Digest of Demographic Statistics 2007*. Retrieved from http://www.gov.mu/portal/goc/cso/report/natacc/demo06/toc.htm

Chase, E., & Statham, J. (2005). Commercial and sexual exploitation of children and young people in the UK—A review. *Child Abuse Review*, 14, 4-25.

Childnet International. (2003). *Report on child protection on the Internet in Mauritiu*s. A Report for the Ministry of Women' Rights, Child Development and Family Welfare, Mauritius.

Cho, C-H., & Choen, H. J. (2005) Children's exposure to negative Internet content. *Journal of Broadcasting and Electronic Media*, 49(4), 488-509.

Clarke, G. R. G., & Wallsten, S. J. (2004). *Has the internet increased trade? Evidence from industrial and developing countries*. Policy Research Working Paper Series 3215, The World Bank.

Cooper, A., Mcloughlin. I. P., & Campbell, K. M. (2000). Sexuality in Cyberspace: Update for the 21st Century. *CyberPsychology & Behavior*, 13(4), 521-536.

Downey, R. (2002). Victims of wonderland. *Community Care*, 1412(1), 30-31.

Durkin, K. F. (1997). Misuse of the Internet by paedophiles: Implications for law enforcement and probation practice. *Federal Probation*, 61, 14-18.

Ebrahimian, L. D. (2003). Socio-Economic Development in Iran through Information and Communications Technology. *Middle East Journal*, 57(1), 93-111.

Edejer T. T. (2000). Disseminating health information in developing countries: The role of the Internet. *British Medical Journal*, 321(7264), 797–800.

Edworthy S. M. (2001). Telemedicine in developing countries. *British Medical Journal*, 323(7312), 524–525.

Eriksen, T. H. (1998). *Common denominators: Ethnicity, nation-building and compromise in Mauritius*. Oxford, England: Berg.

Fisher, W. A. (2001). *Internet pornography: A social psychological perspective on Internet sexuality*. Retrieved from http://www.findarticles.com

Gillen A. (2003, November 4). Race to save new victims of child porn. *The Guardian*. Retrieved from http://www.guardian.co.uk/society/2003/nov/04/childrensservices.childprotection

Gillespie, A. (2000). Children, chat rooms and the law. *Childright*, 172, 19-20

Gillespie, A. (2002). Child protection on the Internet: Challenges for criminal law. *Child and Family Law Quarterly*, 14(1), 411-425.

Gillespie, A. (2004). "Grooming": Definitions and the law. *New Law Journal*, 154(1), 586-587.

Goburdhun, K. (2007). Enforcement of intellectual property rights—Blessing or curse? A perspective from Mauritius. *Africa Development*, 32(3), 131-142.

Gokhool, D. (2007a). *Address by Hon D. Gokhool, Minister of Education and Human Resources on the occasion of the ACM Regional Programming Contest at IIT Kanpur.* Retrieved from http://www.gov.mu/portal/goc/educationsite/file/sp24oct07.doc

Gokhool, D. (2007b). *Address by Hon D. Gokhool, Minister of Education and Human Resources on the occasion of the launching of research week.* Retrieved from http://www.gov.mu/portal/goc/educationsite/file/j16jan07.doc

Government of Mauritius. (2007). *National ICT Policy 2007-11.* Retrieved from http://www.gov.mu/portal/goc/telecomit/file/ICT%20Policy%202007-2011.pdf

Griffiths, M. D. (1997). Children and the Internet. *Media Education Journal, 21*(1), 31-33.

Griffiths, M. D. (1998). Children and the Internet: Issues for parents and teachers. *Education and Health, 16*(1), 9-10.

Hanna, N., & Schware, R. (1990). Information technology in World Bank financed projects. *Information Technology for Development, 5*(3), 253-275.

Hetherington, T. (1999). Child protection: A new approach in South Australia. *Child Abuse Review, 8,* 120-132.

Hillcoat-Nalletamby, S., & Ragobur, S. (2005). The need for information on family planning among young, unmarried women in Mauritius. *Journal of Social Development in Africa, 20*(2), 39-63.

Hilliard, R. L. (2002). Getting ready for cyberspace. In M. B. Robins & R. L. Hilliard (Eds.), *Beyond Boundaries: Cyberspace in Africa* (pp. 1-17). Portsmouth, OR: Heinemann.

Holloway, S. L., & Valentine, G. (2001). Children at home in the wired world: Reshaping and rethinking home in urban geography. *Urban Geography, 22*(6), 562-583.

Holloway, S. L., & Valentine, G. (2003). *Cyberkids: Children in the information age.* London: RoutedgeFalmer.

International Telecommunications Union. (2004). *The Fifth Pillar: Republic Of Mauritius ICT Case Study.* Geneva, Switzerland: Author.

International Telecommunications Union. (2008). *African telecommunication ICT indicators 2008.* Retrieved from www.itu.int/ITU-D/ict/publications/africa/2008/index.html

i-Safe. (2003). *The parent-child gap: Bridging the digital divide.* Retrieved from http://www.i-safe.com/channels/sub.php?ch=op&sub_id=media_digital_divide

Jackson, L. A., Eye, A. V., Biocca, F. A, Barbatsis, G., Zhao, Y., & Fitzgerald, H. E. (2006). Does home Internet use influence the academic performance of low-income children? *Developmental Psychology, 42*(3), 429–435.

Jones, H. (1989). Fertility decline in Mauritius: The role of Malthusian population pressure. *Geoforum, 30*(3), 315-327.

Kanuga, M., & Rosenfeld, W. D. (2004). Adolescent sexuality and the Internet: The good, the bad, and the URL. *Journal of Paediatric and Adolescent Gynaecology, 17,* 117-124.

Kenny, C. (2003). The Internet and economic growth in less-developed countries: A case of managing expectations? *Oxford Development Studies, 31*(1), 99-113

Kitchin, R. (1998). *Cyberspace: The world in the wires.* Chichester, England: Wiley.

Leithead, A. (2003). *Ciber-city in Mauritius.* Retrieved from http://news.bbc.co.uk/1/hi/business/2710319.stm

Lo, V.-H., & Wei, R. (2005). Exposure to Internet pornography and Taiwanese adolescents' sexual attitudes and behavior. *Journal of Broadcasting and Electronic Media*, *49*(1), 221-237.

Mauritius Family Planning Association. (1993). *Research report on young women, work and AIDS-related risk behaviour in Mauritius*. Port Louis, Mauritius: Mauritius Family Planning Association.

Mauritius Institute of Health. (1996). *National survey on youth profile*. Pamplemousses, Mauritius: Author.

Mbambo, B., & Cronjé, J. C. (2002). The Internet as information conduit for small business development in Botswana. *Aslib Proceedings*, *54*(4), 251-259.

McAlinden, A. M. (2006). Familial and institutional grooming in the sexual abuse of children. *Social & Legal Studies*, *15*(3), 339–362.

Mesch, G. S., & Talmud, I. (2003). *Making friends online: Personal needs and social compensation*. Retrieved from http://www.hevra.haifa.ac.il/~soc/events/cn/abstracts/mesch_talmud_5_fp.pdf

Ministry of Women's Rights, Child Development and Family Welfare. (2006). *Mauritius national progress report of the special session of the general assembly on children: A world fit for children*. Retrieved from http://www.unicef.org/worldfitforchildren/files/Mauritius_WFFC5_Report.pdf

Ministry of Women's Rights, Child Development and Family Welfare. (2008). *Ombudsperson for children*. Retrieved from http://www.gov.mu/portal

Mitchell, K. J., Finkelhor, D., & Wolak, J. (2001). Risk factors for and impact of online sexual solicitation of youth. *Journal of the American Medical Association*, *285*, 3011-3014.

Mitchell, K. J., Finkelhor, D., & Wolak, J. (2005). The Internet and family and acquaintance sexual abuse. *Child Maltreatment*, *10*(1), 49-60.

Morgan, R. (1980). Theory and practice: Pornography and rape. In L. Lederer (Ed.), *Take back the night: Women on pornography* (pp. 134-140). New York, NY: William Morrow.

Mushunje, M.T. (2006). Child protection in Zimbabwe: Yesterday, today and tomorrow. *Journal of Social Development in Africa*, *21*(1), 1-12

Mutula, S. M., & Brakel, P. V. (2007). ICT skills readiness for the emerging global digital economy among small businesses in developing countries: Case study of Botswana. *Library Hi Tech*, *25*(2), 231-245.

Nair, A. (2006). Mobile phones and the Internet: Legal issues in the protection of children. *International Review of Law Computers & Technology*, *20*(1&2), 177-185.

National Computer Board. (2003). *ICT Outlook 2002: ICT Penetration within the Mauritian Society*. Port Louis, Mauritius: Author.

National Computer Board. (2004). *ICT Outlook 2000-2004*. Port Louis, Mauritius: Author.

National Computer Board. (2007). *News & events*. Retrieved from http://www.gov.mu/portal/site/ncbnew?content_id=186eb85183248110VgnVCM1000000a04a8c0RCRD

Nutley, S., Davies, H., & Walter, I. (2003, April). *Evidence-based policy and practice: Cross sector lessons from the UK*. Paper presented at The Social Policy Research and Evaluation Conference held at the Wellington Convention Centre, New Zealand.

Ong, R. (2006). Internet sex crimes against children: Hong Kong's response. *International Review of Law Computers and Technology, 20*(1&2), 187–200.

Oswell, D. (1999). The dark side of cyberspace: Internet content regulation and child protection. *Convergence, 5*(4), 42-62.

Oyelaram-Oyeyinka, B., & Adeya, C. N. (2002). *Internet access in Africa: An empirical exploration.* Maastricht, The Netherlands: United Nations University Press.

Packwood, A. (2002), Evidence-based policy: Rhetoric or reality. *Social Policy and Society, 1*(3), 267-272.

Parrott, L. (2002). *Social work and social care.* Oxon, England: Routledge

Peter, J., & Valkenburg, P. M. (2006). Adolescents' Exposure to sexually explicit material on the Internet. *Communication Research, 33*(2), 178-204.

Pichappan, P. (2004). Mapping human potential in developing countries: Can the ICT pave the way? *Journal of Digital Information Management, 2*(2), 105-108.

Pierpoint, H. (2004). A survey of volunteer appropriate adult services. *Youth Justice, 4*(1), 32-45.

Putnam, D. E. (2000). Initiation and maintenance of online sexual compulsivity: Implications for assessment and treatment. *CyberPsychology & Behaviour, 3*(4).

Quinn, J. F., & Forsyth, C. J. (2005). Describing sexual behavior in the era of the internet: a typology for empirical research. *Deviant Behavior, 26*(1), 191-207.

Rambaree, K. (2005, January). *The ecology of sexuality in a Mauritian Internet chat room (MICR): An Internet mediated research (IMR).* Paper presented for the SIDS Conference at the University of Mauritius.

Rambaree, K. (2007). *The ecology of the internet and early adolescent sexuality in a technology-driven Mauritian society.* PhD thesis at the University of Manchester, England.

Rambaree, K. (2008). Internet-mediated dating/romance of Mauritian Early adolescents: A grounded theory analysis. *International Journal of Emerging Technologies and Society, 6*(1), 34-59.

Rambaree, K. (2009, January). *Internet, sexuality and development: Putting early adolescents first.* Paper presented at the Fifth International Conference on Environmental, Cultural, Economic and Social Sustainability, held in Mauritius.

Russell, D. (1998). *Dangerous relationships: Pornography, misogyny, and rape.* Thousand Oaks, CA: SAGE.

Schensul, L. S., Schensul, J. J., Oodit, G., Bhowan, U., & Ragobur, S. (1994). Sexual intimacy and changing lifestyles in an era of AIDS: Young women workers in Mauritius. *Reproductive Health Matters, 3*, 83-93.

Shade, L.R. (2002). Protecting the kids? Debates over Internet content. In S. Ferguson & L. R. Shade (Eds.), *Civic discourse and cultural politics in Canada: A cacophony of voices* (pp. 76-87). Westport, CT: Ablex.

Shillington, K. (1991). *Jugnauth: The Prime Minister of Mauritius.* London: McMillan.

Shukor, S. A. (2006, April). *Protecting children's rights in the Internet: Challenges.* Paper presented at the 21st Annual BILETA Conference on "Globalisation and Harmonisation in Technology Law, held in Malta.

Singhal, M. (1997). The Internet and foreign language education: Benefits and challenges. *The Internet TESL Journal, 3*(6), 1-5.

Stanley, J. (2001). *Child abuse and the Internet. Child Abuse Prevention Issues, 15.* Melbourne: Australian Institute of Family Studies.

Subrahmanyam, K., Kraut, R. E., Greenfield, P. M., & Gross, E. F. (2000). The impact of home computer use on children's activities and development. *Future of Children, 10*(2), 123–144.

The Guardian. (2008). *Interpol makes public appeal in hunt for web paedophile.* Retrieved from http://www.guardian.co.uk/world/2008/may/07/internationalcrime

Thornburgh, D., & Lin, H. S. (Eds.). (2002). *Youth, pornography, and the Internet.* Washington, DC: National Academic Press.

Traeen, B., Spitznogle, K., & Beverfjord, A. (2004). Attitudes and use of pornography in the Norwegian population 2002. *The Journal of Sex Research, 41*(2), 193-200.

Traeen, B., Nilsen, T. S., & Stigum, H. (2006) Use of pornography in traditional media and on the Internet in Norway. *The Journal of Sex Research, 43*(3), 245-255.

Turkle, S. (1995). *Life on the screen: Identity in the age of the Internet.* New York, NY: Simon & Schuster.

United Nations. (1989). *Convention on the rights of the child.* Retrieved from http://www.ohchr.org/english/law/pdf/crc.pdf

United Nations. (2003). *World youth report,* 2003. New York, NY: United Nations.

United Nations. (2007). *National strategic plan 2006-2010.* Retrieved from http://un.intnet.mu/undp/downloads/info/SOCIAL_DEVELOPMENT/NICTSP/PROJECT%20DOCUMENT/NICTSP(1).pdf

United Nations Children's Fund. (2004). *Child protection: A handbook for parliamentarians, No.3.* New York, NY: Author.

Valkenburg, P. M., Schouten, A. P., & Peter, J. (2005). Adolescents identity experiments on the Internet. *New Media and Society, 17*(3), 383-402.

Vetter, T. (2008). *Internet governance forum: A development perspective.* Winnipeg, Manitoba: International Institute for Sustainable Development.

Wilkinson. H. (1995, December 1). Take care in cyberspace children. *Independent* Retrieved from http://www.independent.co.uk/opinion/take-care-in-cyberspace-children-1523488.html

Williams, J. D., & Frith, K. (1993). Adolescents and the media. In R. M. Lerner (Ed.), *Early adolescence: Perspectives on research, policy, and intervention* (pp. 401-407). London: Erlbaum.

Williams, K. S. (2005). Facilitating safer choices: Use of warnings to dissuade viewing of pornography on the internet. *Child Abuse Review, 14,* 415-429.

Wims, P., & Lawler, M. (2007). Investing in ICTs in educational institutions in developing countries: An evaluation of their impact in Kenya. *International Journal of Education and Development using ICT, 3*(1), 5-22.

Wolak, J., Finkelhor, D., & Mitchell, K. J. (2004). Internet-initiated sex crimes against minors: Implications for prevention based on findings from a national study. *Journal of Adolescent Health, 35*(5), 424.e11-424.e20.

World Bank. (2006, April). *Mauritius from preferences to global competitiveness. A Report of the aid for trade mission.* Retrieved from http://siteresources .worldbank.org/INTEDS14/Resources/AIDFORTRADE.pdf

World Commission on Environment and Development. (1987). *Our common future (The Brundtland Report).* Oxford, England: Oxford University Press.

World Health Organization. (2003). *Adolescent friendly health services: An agenda for change.* Geneva: Author.

Yang, S. C., & Tung, C. (2007). Comparison of internet addicts and non-addicts in taiwanese high school. *Computers in Human Behaviour, 23*(1), 79-96.

Yueh, L. Y. (2001). A model of parental investment in children's human capital. *SKOPE Research Paper, 15,* 1-13.

CHAPTER 10

CHILDHOOD, CELL PHONES, AND HEALTH

Richard Chalfen

It's the wave of the future,... Why, it's only a matter of time before hospitals distribute cell phones to newborns right along with birth certificates

—Clinch (2009, p. 2)

In postindustrialized parts of the world, digital technology and telecommunications are now an accepted, virtually expected part of everyday life, part of the physical baggage we carry with us on a moment-to-moment basis. In turn, attention to childhood and children is noteworthy on two counts. It comes as no surprise that increasing numbers of children are owning and using their own cell phones; what may be surprising is how rapidly this diffusion of innovation has occurred or how intimately embedded mobile technology has become in everyday life. Clearly cell phone technology is not the sole domain of an adult population. Possession and use of these phones has become more a part of children's lives every day (Chmielewski, 2005).

Cell phones[1] are frequently cited as one of the most preferred and important electronic devices on the market: "Cellphones, laptops, digital cameras and MP3 music players are among the hottest gift items this year for preschoolers" (Richtel & Stone, 2007, p. 1). Reports indicate the targeted age range is becoming lower; niche marketing is abundant in conjunction with anticipated and unanticipated consequences for children, their parents and caregivers. Several commentators have noticed that marketing agencies are aiming their campaigns at increasingly younger sectors of the population (Holleran, 2007). One salesman for Disney phones reported: "Most of the families are looking for phones for 7- or 8-year-olds" though he said he recently "sold a plan to a divorced mother looking for a phone with a GPS system to keep track of her 5-year-old" (Heyboer, 2006, p. 3). In another commentary we read:

> Still, the indispensable cell phone is making its way into younger and younger hands every day.... Growing minds can become addicted to the attention that a cell phone provides. [This] may actually prevent teenagers from growing mentally, ... Youths often call a select few to deal with problems. The result is that a cell phone actually prevents them from seeking new sources for help, or considering new solutions, which is a necessary learning experience. (Dinkins, 2006, p. 1)

As early as November 30, 2005 we read that "a mobile phone firm launches handset for four-year-olds" (Butt, 2005), and a cell phone company called Kajeet, based in Bethesda, Md., introduced a cellphone this year for children ages 8 and up (Richtel & Stone, 2007).

Updating to 2008, we read that numbers continue to rise for cell phone use by younger and younger children. One report from Norway stated:

> According to a survey conducted by Opinion on behalf of Telenor, 85% of ten-year-olds have cell phones. Six in ten parents state their ten-year-old got a cell phone because their parents wanted it.... Today 27% of parents would allow nine-year-olds to have cell phones, 16% would allow eight-year-olds while 6 percent would allow seven-year-olds to have cell phones. ("Nine in ten," n.d., paras. 1, 6)

One marketing research firm based in Boca Raton, Florida reported that of

> the 1,100 parents surveyed with school age children, about a quarter allow their elementary school children to have a cell phone, 53% allow their middle school children to have a cell phone, and 72% allow their high school children to have a cell phone, according to the survey. (Holleran, 2007, p. 1)

Direction and trends are clear.

Technological development and human creative adoptions of cell phones are moving so quickly that we have difficulty taking account of current conditions and circumstances. This is especially true for mobile telephony. Part of this rapid change is due to the diffusion of this technology through a broad spectrum of the population, across sociocultural variation as well as age levels. Part of the observed increase in sales and use is due to the fact the age of cell phone owners has become increasingly younger. Mobile telephony has already become well integrated into childhood, yet there are few attempts to examine the range of cell-related behaviors or to construct a balance sheet of attributes for children. The need arises to step back and examine the range of applications of pro-social and antisocial uses and effects of evolving technology. On occasion, social and psychological concerns lose pace to technological ones as we see the appearance of unanticipated dangers threatening, and sometimes reversing, the hopes and dreams of innovative technology.

THE HEALTH AND SAFETY CONTEXT

We regularly read about the seemingly uninterrupted growth of health and safety-related concerns associated with cell phones and youth. We are learning more and more about *both* the benefits and dangers of cell phone technology; clearly, many notices make direct reference to the physical, mental and social health of children. Within this problematic context, it is necessary to ask: What do we know of the emerging relationship between health issues, mobile technology and children? What have emerged as anticipated and unanticipated risks to children's physical and mental health? How do the risks articulate with observed benefits to children's health, and what connections are we finding related to issues of child safety that impinge on safeguarding a healthy life style?

For the purposes of this overview, I will examine these questions along two dimensions: medically-centered issues followed by questions of health-related safety and even survival. We will quickly see the need to include both physical and mental health as well as matters of private, public and preventive health. One of my objectives is to give readers a more comprehensive and informed view of cell phones as a medium of communication, with its own set of beneficial and detrimental attributes for both the health and well being of children born into a digital world.

Relationships of health, safety and technology need continual review, often provoking a central question: Why is it important to give priority attention to youngest children, teenagers and young people? This question elicits at least three responses, each of which stresses attention to current trends.

First we know that there are more cell phones in the world every day. A report dated December 14, 2008, notes:

> Wireless Intelligence, a market database, reports that it took 20 years for the first billion mobile phones to sell, just four years for the second billion, and two years for the third billion. The firm projects there will be 4 billion cell phones in the world by the end of 2008. (Anderson & Rainie, 2008, p. 1)

Second we may want to reassess what is meant when some people classify the cell phone as "just a toy," perhaps with a little denial of other possibilities. The toy classification remains strong as was seen in the 2007 Christmas season when I came across the following note titled: "Cell phone tops preschoolers wish lists this Christmas": Toy makers and retailers are filling shelves with new tech devices for children ages 3 and up, and sometimes even younger. They say they are catering to junior consumers who want to emulate their parents and are not satisfied with fake gadgets. ("Cell Phone Tops," 2007, Trisha post). But cultural categories can be hard to change,[2] and some labels such as "toy" can discourage critical assessment. Readers will recall the classification of a television as an entertainment toy and a subsequent reevaluation that now includes critical attention by public health practitioners (Parker-Pope, 2008). We have seen a growing vigilance and warning signs for certain toys. In short any piece of a material culture allows for multiple meanings and functions serving various personal needs and gratifications. We now see that threats and dangers to young people's personal health and safety must also be considered in critical ways.

This discussion leads us directly to a third consideration, namely an important and pragmatic concern that parents are now forced to face: "Should I buy a cell phone for my kid?"[3] and "Does my child need a cell phone?" "Should I allow my child to communicate via mobile, wireless technology?" In turn, the question turns to: "How young is too young for a cell phone?" and the general inquiry, "Do the benefits balance and possibly outweigh the newly recognized threats?" Is the answer, "Just for safety purposes" sufficient? Parents have been pressed into new models of control and justifications for such technology. But as of late 2006, the American Academy of Pediatrics offered no clear answer. For most there will not be one satisfactory answer since personal circumstances can differ in many ways.

PART OF THE PROBLEM

How have the medical profession and health care personnel reacted to these circumstances? I use a lengthy quotation to set the stage for the following discussion.

> As the adult and teenage cell phone market becomes saturated, cell phone companies are targeting younger and younger users.... [Several companies] are pushing brightly colored cell phones specially designed for children as young as kindergartners.... But with the number of children carrying pint-sized mobile phones expected to double to 10.5 million by the end of the decade, education and health experts say the trend raises an important

question: "How young is too young for a cell phone?" *The American Academy of Pediatrics says there is no clear answer* [emphasis added].

Models that come equipped with video games, text messaging and other features can drastically increase a child's media exposure and cut into their physical exercise and social interaction, said Regina Milteer, a Virginia pediatrician and member of the American Academy of Pediatrics Committee on Communications. "They can sit there endlessly—almost unsupervised," Milteer said.... "The study predicts that number [of 8-12 year-old cell users] will double by 2010, when nearly 54% of the nation's 8- to 12-year-olds will be carrying cell phones. Many of those phones will be powerful pieces of technology with video, music and e-learning tools, said Marina Amoroso, the analyst who wrote the Yankee Group study. (Heyboer, 2006, pp. 1-2)

My review suggests that the medical community has been very slow to distribute any sense of formal ruling on children's use of mobile technology. Second, authorities and credible sources have been very divided on the counsel they are willing to offer the public. One key reason is that the number of biological studies relevant to children is far less than what is found for adults (Martens, 2005).[4]

TOPICS OF INTEREST

While keeping children's health in the foreground, relevant topics cannot be addressed without referencing broader contexts; health threats and risks that potentially affect all life stages with the implication that adult issues will trickle down to young people as children become long-term users of cell phones. The territory is deceivingly broad. For the sake of coherent organization, I will start with the most frequently mentioned health threats and move towards more speculative claims.[5] These topics will be followed by a range of issues central to relationships of cell phone use and child safety.

Cancer Scares

To no one's surprise, the most contentious and frequently cited health risk has been the threat of cancer from exposure to electromagnet radiation (EMR) from handheld receivers or cell phone towers ("masts"), ("Phone Mast Allergy," n.d.; Thomson, 2004) especially when situated near areas where children congregated, namely schools and playgrounds (Goggin, 2006, pp. 110-111). Similar to smoking studies, representatives of the medical community are often pitted against spokespersons for the telecommunication industry. Given that mobile manufacturers acknowledge their cell and wireless phones emit EMR, the major fear is that electromagnetic fields are likely to penetrate the brain more deeply for young children than for mature adults. The speculation is that young children are more susceptible to EM fields due to thinner skulls, smaller sized brains, softer brain tissue and developing nervous system.

Findings are mixed, even in studies coming from the same region of the world, specifically Scandinavia where cell phones have been used longer than most places, there are many early adopters, and they share a high rate of phones per capita and high user rates. For instance, some Swedish researchers found links between cell phones and brain tumors, especially on the side of the head they use most often and for rural areas more than urban ones (Hardell, Carlberg, Söderqvist, Mild, & Morgan, 2005). In comparison, one large-scale study conducted by researchers from the Danish Institute of Cancer Epidemiology in Copenhagen found the opposite, stating that neither short- nor long-term cell phone use boosted the risk of brain or face cancer (Anonymous, 2006; Niccolai, 2005).

Especially relevant to young people are the immediate and long-term effects of relatively new cellular technology, since over time they will be exposed to health hazards for longer than their seniors. If various malignant tumors are discovered in the brains, jaws, salivary glands, eyes of adult long-term heavy users of cell phones, early EMR exposure from cell phones will be blamed. Early adopters are valuable to these studies, necessitating the need to locate children at the youngest possible ages using cell phones and following them through developmental stages of their lives. Readers will sense a connection to studies of cigarette smoking, and some researchers are explicit in making this comparison, that life-threatening smoking-related cancers take time to become manifest (Lean, 2008). Studies of cigarette smoking are frequently cited for comparisons. Noting that there was no link to any lung cancer until after 10 years of smoking, researchers have acknowledged a scarcity of people who have been using mobile phones for over 10 years.[6] Some observers have speculated that radiation coming from cell phones is more permeating and more dangerous than smoking or industrial pollution. We see that longitudinal studies continue to gain interest for gaining a clearer understanding of short term versus long term effects.

Contagion

Young people, perhaps more than adults, have been observed to share the use of their mobiles. But these phones have been cited as a health hazard in that sharing has been identified as a source of passing on various illnesses (Childs, 2009; Neisteadt, 2009). The concern here is that colds and flus are easily transmitted via handsets that have been subjected to coughing, sneezing and wheezing.

> With tens of thousands of microbes living on each square inch, cell phones harbor more bacteria than a toilet seat, the sole of a shoe, or a door handle. Microbiologists say the combination of constant handling and the heat generated by the phones creates a prime breeding ground for all sorts of bugs that are normally found on our skin. (Farby, 2006, p. 1; Kwan, 2006, p. 1)

In addition to the finding that cold and flu viruses are commonly found on cell phones, a related report comments on how some skin infections can be caused by sharing phones "infected" with a range of germs and bacteria (Stevens, 2007, p. 1). Researchers from the British Association of Dermatologists have even identified a face and ears skin rash. If you are allergic to nickel and use your cell phone for an extended time, you can get an irritating rash now called "mobile phone dermatitis," an allergic reaction to the metal in the cell phone's exterior casing (Low, 2008).

Mental Health Issues

In addition to the threats to physical health cited above, observers have speculated on the mental and emotional consequences of children's cell phone use. While more studies have been done with teenagers and adolescents than younger children, there are important implications for young children as more and more have their own cell phones and their frequency of use increases. For example, cognitive functioning and memory have also been studied, including auditory memory task (encoding and recognition) and brain oscillatory responses during cognitive processing in children (Haarala et al. 2005; Krause et al., 2006). Again we see how relationships of developing brains and EMR are continually being questioned and reevaluated.

Another set of concerns involves frequency of cell phone use. Children have little or no sense of what might be classified as "too much" or excessive use, and parents may not have standards to draw upon. The term "addiction" is easily invoked to hasten attention to emotional danger points; again, problems noted for teenagers, e.g. becoming irritable, withdrawn and antisocial ("Spain Treats Child," 2008)—may be applicable to young children as frequency of ownership and use increase.

Other researchers are attending to an area that spans both mental and physical health, namely sleep patterns. Relationships of cell use, sleep, electromagnetic radiation and young people are gaining attention (Punamaki, Wallenius, Nygard, Saarni, & Rimpela, 2007; Nally, 2008; United Press International, 2008; van den Bulck, 2003). Other researchers have been studying children and teens who tend to use their phones late at night, resulting in sleep disturbances possibly caused by the radiation. Still others have been examining potential harmful effects of excessive phone habits that might be responsible for childhood depression, mood swings, ADHD-like symptoms and personality changes. As cell phone users are younger and frequency increases, there is ample reason for us to consider potential harm to younger children.

In summary, the breadth of current concern for harmful effects is quite broad and appears to be growing. I will refrain from reviewing some of the more speculative claims and areas of concern. These include damage to hearing, eyesight and even one extending into the pre-tot age category. There is speculation that pregnant woman's excessive use of her cell phone might be causing problems for her unborn child (Elgan, 2008; Timmer, 2008). The science behind some claims is highly questionable, and too many sociocultural variables are ignored. Correlations of harmful danger and excessive phone use must not be confused with claims of causation. Debate continues over the validity of evidence of direct causal effects for how EMR affects living organisms. In most cases we find a cautionary tale along the lines of: We have no known biologic mechanisms to explain these associations, and confounding by unmeasured causes of behavioral problems could have produced the results.

MEDICAL SETTINGS AND IN MEDICAL CARE

In previous pages, I reviewed several physical and mental threats to child health that are frequently ignored in everyday life. Any consideration of relationships of cell phones and children's health also requires attention to activities that involve medical clinics, hospital settings, ambulances and even areas where medical facilities are rare and only at a remote location. This takes us into the growing fields of mobile medicine and telemedicine. Health care facilities have had to face potential risks in explicit and visible ways, to avoid unfavorable outcomes in both medical and legal terms. The majority of hospital related studies of cell phone use are relevant to the pros and cons of patient care, whether adult or child. But relevant reports have much less to do with children using mobiles than with medical personnel using cell phones in medical facilities dedicated to children's health.

When children are admitted to hospitals, they are subjected to the same health and safety conditions as older patients. One primary concern has been cell phone use within hospitals, including interference and potential malfunction of life support devices such as ventilators, intravenous infusion pumps, and monitoring equipment, perhaps being most significant in intensive care units and surgical suites.[7] There is less concern in hospital lobbies, cafeterias, elevators, waiting rooms and lounges ("Cell Phones in the Hospital," 2007; Freehling, 2006). There has also been the potential loss of patient privacy when cameras in cell phones are used by visitors. In general, early fears and problems have dissipated as equipment has become better protected from EMR, and child-patient use of mobiles as well as visitor regulations have been codified and institutionalized.

Applied Cell Phone Use: Health Management

It is equally important to acknowledge ways cell phones can be beneficial to children's health. For instance, on the positive side of the wellness ledger, there's a proliferation of new health applications that run over wireless networks to mobile phones. We find several important pro-health applications when cell phones are incorporated into new models of telemedicine, helping make effective diagnoses and offering patient care at-a-distance.

Applied uses of cell phones have become particularly useful for young children who might be more forgetful of their health needs than their adult counterparts. I will shortly acknowledge how GPS-enabled cell phones are meeting the need some parents have developed for monitoring their child's location in the interests of keeping them out of danger. Less known perhaps are new health management services whereby cell phones can be used to monitor health symptoms or drug reactions and collect illness-related data. Cell phones are also being used to send health warning signals (including sexual health services [Levine, McCright, Dobkin, Woodruff, & Klausner, 2008]) and personal reminders to take prescribed medicines on time (Neergaard, 2008; Singh, 2008). Mobile phones can even help count infected blood cells (Camera Phone Counts," 2008) as well as monitor blood glucose for diabetes patients (Gray, 2007), and blood pressure numbers can then be transmitted as health data to caregivers (Sarasohn-Kahn, 2008).

PERSONAL SAFETY:
THREATS TO CHILDREN'S HEALTH AND WELL-BEING

As previously suggested, relationships between cell phone use and health are naturally extended to questions of personal safety involving both immediate and long-term results on health. We know that one key motive and justification for parents buying their children cell phones is for the general sense of security, keeping them safe[8] while away from home, and reducing their own parental anxiety (Pogue, 2006; Withers, 2006). Indeed, searching for and locating temporarily lost or missing very young children or very old people has been emphasized and has recently been aided by new models of mobiles now equipped with GPS technology. The allure of GPS tracking capability has parents of children as young as three considering a cell phone a worthwhile investment in safety (Felton, 2008). This has not been lost on promoters of the cellular phone industry: "Wireless phones are an incredible safety tool,... They are the most valuable tool invented for some time. They save scores of lives. And they will continue to get better."[9] This sense of safety is often cited and "used" by children. According to one late-2006 report, a sample of children was asked to respond to the topic, "I need a cell phone because ..." The reason listed most often was emergencies for 10 of the 12 4th and 5th graders (Dinkins, 2006). "Emergency" is a poorly defined category, one that can range from requests for important information about being lost, late or in trouble to being sick or hurt, among other reasons. Importantly, we find a mixture of aids and threats to safety, some predictable but many unanticipated, as mentioned below.

Related concerns focus on the ways young people and adults can become distracted when using a cell phone, putting young people (as well as adults) in danger. For older teenagers and adults, these include safety concerns surrounding driving a motor scooter or motor cycle, and driving a car; drivers have been frequently observed talking on a cell phone or using a mobile's texting capabilities. Young children using cell phones can lose attention to danger signs while being a pedestrian or riding a bicycle. We find articles with such bylines as: "Family of Girl Killed Riding Bike Wants Cell Phone Law" (Ayers, 2008), describing how a 9-year old girl died swaying from the bike lane.[10]

School Settings

Perhaps schools have been the liveliest setting for debate about problems most central to mobile use, health and safety. According to "The Mobile Life Youth Report" conducted in the United Kingdom in 2006, mobile phone ownership rises sharply as children prepare to leave primary school—"up from 24% of nine-year olds to 51% of 10-year-olds. By the time they are at secondary school at the age of 12, 91% of youngsters have a mobile phone" (Smithers, 2006, p. 1). Other reports indicate that the average age of mobile-equipped students is getting lower each year.

But some school officials have said that cellphones were becoming a "chronic cause of conflict."[11]

Large and busy cities have become laboratories for experimentation with bans, restrictions and countermeasures, all determining the place, if any, that cell phones have in school. Or, as one account asked: Who says a 6-year old can take a cell phone to kindergarten? For instance, would students adhere to an honor system to turn off their phones during the school day?[12] Would students be required to keep their phones in their lockers or stored in lockers located outside of school buildings (de Meglio, 2007)?

Parents commonly say they want to know immediately if their children experience any kind of health or safety problem or have transportation problems. However, teachers and administrators are continually disturbed by ringtones being heard during their classes or students using their mobiles during class time. Parents insist on being able to check on the safety of their kids as they travel long distances to and from school and possibly travel to after-school sports events, tutoring, friendship gatherings and the like. Teachers do not appreciate the threat of classroom disruption and distractions or even the chance of cheating as students might text message one another for best answers during a test (Campbell, 2006). In comparison, some innovative educators are developing creative use of cell telephony, when cell phones can be embraced as learning tools rather than just disruptive distractions. Work is being done to enhance instruction, both in classrooms and after the school day (Levine & Shuler, 2009; Shuler, 2009).

Again, the relationship of cell use, health and safety problems have become especially important to debates with complex and significant variables. Parents of students with medical problems may insist their children be allowed to keep their phones; the school may counter with a requirement to store the phone with the school nurse or seek a waiver from the school's principal ("City Amends Cell Phones," 2006). We see now that there is no one school policy and practice regarding cell phone use by teachers and students with various health problems.

Other School-Related Threats—Cyberbullying and Sexting

Just as the age of cell phone use has been getting lower, the spread of potentially harmful habits has been appearing earlier in children's lives. The young children referenced in this paper may be heading into a series of harmful school-related activities, possibly inspired by their older counterparts. Some teenagers are using the texting capabilities of their cell phones for purposes of bullying and sexting (Campbell, 2005). Student bullying is certainly not a new activity and varies cross-culturally, but now we see the incorporation of electronic media (for an active overview of this topic see, Cyberbullying Research Center, n.d.). According to some reports, cell phone bullying may have more tragic consequences than the Internet and traditional playground methods (Raskauskas, 2006).

Problems associated with cameras in cell phones are new and on the rise. Camera functions are available in most contemporary cell phones. As just one of a rapidly growing number of reports:

> Boulder investigators were notified this week about an incident involving two elementary-school children [6-year old boy and 11-year old girl] snapping inappropriate pictures of each other with a cell phone,... It was reported to police as a potential "sexual assault," but detectives are considering it an "incident" at this time. (Miller 2008, p. 1)

Both children were partially or totally naked while playing. Parents and officials worried if the play led to inappropriate physical activities.

Though such photographic incidents are a minority, we see a general slippage of phone-related activities from adolescent and teenage years on into early childhood. Not all phones have cameras, but buyers now have to seek this option or make certain their service contracts do not allow photograph transmission. The obvious extension of this camera activity into sexting is the latest example of a harmful cell phone-related threat to child safety.

DISCUSSION

The need for undertaking this overview has been predicated on several points. First is the importance of recognizing the problematic place of cell phones in young children's lives, especially in the particular interface of home and medical cultures. Second the recognition that human-technology relationships are changing rapidly, demonstrating the fast-paced development of mediated life associated with the potential for benefit and harm that accompanies any innovation. We continue to read reports that suggest and document a series of unanticipated threats and results of children's cell phone use. The "human interest" category of the news industry is prone to publicize the bizarre, especially when some negative surprise is the centerpiece of a news item. Again, the problem is to separate the anecdotal, the speculative and the scientifically sound. Such an overview has yet to be written.

In a broad perspective, the fact remains that carrying a cell phone has become as common as wearing clothes. Mobile telephonic communication has produced new expectations and even demands of human interaction, of states of information, identity, knowledge and competence. Cell phones allow us to live life in different ways, ways that many consider improvements and beneficial, but others find intrusive, harmful and unnecessary. But what do we know about the subject close at hand, namely that by wanting to help children by keeping them safe, we might be harming them in irreparable manners?

Many people consulted for this review cited the cell phone as an innovation that has taken hold faster than ever anticipated, that mobiles have become a significant part of children's lives much more than ever expected, and, in turn, much more than is currently even realized. One purpose of this paper has been to raise awareness of the questions and problems that are now associated with just one sector of this involvement, namely relationships of mobile use, medicine and young children.

To accomplish the goals of this paper, I have had to veer into areas that seemingly had little to do with children. One point is that most of the adult-related issues are applicable to young people—perhaps even more because young people will have more life-long experience with cellular technology than their parental counterparts. In short, kids will have been using cell phones for longer and will have conceptualized them quite differently (needs, gratifications, requirements, senses of gain and loss, etc.) compared to their parents. Cell phones may have been built into their lives in different and more multi-dimensional ways, far more complex than those of their parents or the older generation in general. Importantly, they will become the subjects for important longitudinal test cases and studies. The need arises to acknowledge potential difference in attitude and values that kids will bring to mobile technology and, second, to relating cell technology to their medical care that adults might not have developed.

My review indicates as of early 2009, few studies of the appropriation and use of cell phones by our youngest "digital natives" (Gasser & Palfrey, 2008) have been published. My frequent reference of internet reports has been an attempt to know the most recent developments and thinking on this and closely related topics. Trends cited above point in the direction of increased debate regarding the wisdom of cell phone use, especially in relation to uncertain health and safety issues. It would be a tragedy if by getting their young children cell phones primarily for their safety, parents could be causing them harm.

NOTES

1. Cell phones are also referred to as mobile phones or mobiles, cellular phone, cell, wireless phone, cellular telephone, mobile telephone or cell

telephone. For purposes of this paper, I will use "cell phone" most of the time, but cited references may use one or more of these alternative terms.

2. Indeed the toy industry is in the midst of redefining the meaning of "toy." Jim Silver, editor of *Toy Wishes* magazine and an industry analyst for 24 years, said—"The bigger toy companies don't even call it the toy business anymore,... They're in the family entertainment business and the leisure business. What they're saying is, 'We're vying for kids' leisure time" (Richtel & Stone, 2007)

3. Several pros and cons mentioned by advocacy groups include: As Cons:

    (1) Children's safety, privacy, education and health.
    (2) Privacy advocates worry that pedophiles may use cell phones to contact children.
    (3) Cell phones could become a vehicle for showing advertisements to children, ultimately reaching their parents' wallets.
    (4) Advocates also worry about potential health risks: radiation, brain tumors.

    As Pros:

    (1) Cell phones let you stay in touch with your child almost all the time.
    (2) Having a cell phone can help you easily get in touch with your kids in case of an emergency.
    (3) In the event of a real tragedy, like a school shooting or terrorist attack, a cell phone can be your only lifeline to your kids.
    (4) A cell phone can also be a way to stay in touch with your teen who might be driving ... the GPS feature can help you figure out where your teen is at all times (Barnett, 2008).

4. Equally as rare are studies devoted to comparing adult and child reactions (de Salles, Bulla, & Rodriguez, 2006) or to documenting the medical relevance of what children are actually doing with their mobiles as part of everyday life. One rare example is: "Ownership and use of wireless telephones: a population-based study of Swedish children aged 7-14 years" (Soderqvist, Hardell, Carlberg, & Mild, 2007).

5. A note about the following statements. I am not seeking the definitive word on certain problematic relationships of cell phone use and health. Nor am I qualified to reach a professional judgment regarding the scientific validity of the reports included in this overview. Rather I feel the need to create a summary of what has been suggested, claimed and studied.

6. "However, in 2005 Sir William (Sir William Stewart, who directed a 2000 study group) warned that mobile phone use by children should be limited as a precaution—and that under-eights should not use them at all."

7. An interesting and rare exception occurred in July, 2007, when "a blackout hit the city of Villa Mercedes in the San Luis province of Argentina. Leonardo Molina was on the operating table when the lights went out, undergoing an emergency appendix surgery." The backup generators failed and that's "when one of Leonardo's family members got crafty and started col-

lecting cell phones from others in the halls outside the operating room. The surgeons used the cell phones to provide the illumination they needed to complete the surgery.... This is just a few short months after Vietnamese doctors used cell phones during a black out to finish delivering a child" (O'Brien, 2007).

8. In one survey of 339 parents, 78% of them considered being able to contact their children in the event of an emergency to be the top reason for buying a cell phone (see TechnologyExpert, 2007).

9. Said by Joe Farren, director of public affairs for CTIA-The Wireless Association, a trade organization representing mobile operators (Reardon, 2006).

10. New Jersey Assemblyman Jon Bramnick sponsored a bill meant to protect bicyclists and the people they may strike—a bill that that would make it illegal for people to use a cell phone while riding a bicycle on a public road. Retrieved from Web site: http://www.cn.com/apps/pbcs.dll/article?AID=/20070119/FRONT01/70119028 but no longer accessible.

11. A good summary of problems appeared as follows: "the incidents range from the cell phone going off in class, text messaging during class, taking pictures of tests, storing test information and text messaging friends with answers to test questions, to reports of cell phones being stolen. Some of the more worrisome misuses of cell phones included making false 9-1-1 calls, taking and sending inappropriate pictures, and using the cell phone to set up drug deals. Shuman said cell phones have also been used to instigate fights off of school property, and to harass or bully other students" (Schehl, 2008).

12. Changes are being made; in one Louisiana public school as of December, 2007, we read: "Instead of saying, "No student shall possess, use or operate any electronic telecommunication device," the policy the board approved Tuesday says, "No student shall use or operate any electronic telecommunication device during the academic school day" (Northington, 2007).

REFERENCES

Anderson, J. Q., & Rainie, L. (2008). *Future of the Internet III: How the experts see it. The Pew Internet & American Life Project.* Retrieved from http://74.125.47.132/search?q=cache:3u-nuWm5fCUJ:www.pewinternet.org/pdfs/PIP_FutureInternet3.pdf+The+Future+of+the+Internet+III&hl=en&ct=clnk&cd=2&gl=us&client=firefox-a (no longer accessible)

Anonymous. (2006, December 6). Study: Cancer risk not boosted by cell phone use. *CIO Technology Informer.* Retrieved from http://www.cio.com/article/27266/Study_Cancer_Risk_Not_Boosted_by_Cell_Phone_Use

Ayers, C. (2008). *Family of girl killed riding bike wants cell phone law.* Retrieved from http://www.myfoxcolorado.com/myfox/pages/News

/Detail?contentId=8007321&version=3&locale=EN
-US&layoutCode=TSTY&pageId=3.2.1

Barnett, S. (2008, January 16). *Which cell phone should you get for your kid? msnbc.com*. Retrieved from http://www.msnbc.msn.com/id/22674753/

Butt, R. (2005, November 30). Mobile phone firm launches handset for four-year-olds. *The Guardian*. Retrieved from http://www.guardian.co.uk/media/2005/nov/30/newmedia.gadgets

Camera phone counts infected blood cells. (2008, October, 1). *Ubergizmo*. Retrieved December 30, 2008, from http://www.ubergizmo.com/15/archives/2008/10/camera_phone_counts_infected_blood_cells.html

Campbell, M. A. (2005). Cyber bullying: An old problem in a new guise? *Australian Journal of Guidance & Counselling, 15*(1), 68-76.

Campbell, S. W. (2006). Perceptions of mobile phones in college classrooms: Ringing, cheating, and classroom policies. *Communication Education, 55*(3), 280-294.

Cancer doubt remains over mobiles. (2007, September 12). *BBC NEWS*. Retrieved May 7, 2009, from http://news.bbc.co.uk/go/pr/fr/-/1/hi/health/6990958.stm

Cell phones in the hospital. (2007, August 14). *WEAU.COM. Right Now*. Retrieved from http://www.weau.com/home/headlines/9160186.html#

Cell phone tops preschoolers wish lists this Christmas (2007, November 30). *Insanity's Oasis*. Retrieved January 10, 2009, from http://insanitys-oasis.com/?p=509

Childs, D. (2009, March 9). 7 surprising ways cell phones affect your health: Mobile devices can pose health risks—and not in the way you might think. *abcNEWS*. Retrieved from http://abcnews.go.com/print?id=7017768

Chmielewski, D. C. (2005, October 7). For some teenagers, cell phones become "an extension of me." *The Mercury News*. Retrieved from http://www.redorbit.com/news/technology/264475/for_some_teenagers_cell_phones_become_an_extension_of_me/index.html

City amends cell phones in school rule. (2006, November 9). *1010wins.com*. Retrieved May 7, 2009, from http://www.1010wins.com/pages/123048.php?contentType=4&contentId=238584

Clinch, L. (2009, May 6). *But, Dad, all the kids have cell phones! Are we there yet?* Retrieved from http://newstranscript.gmnews.com/news/2009/0506/editorials/067.html

Cyberbullying Research Center. (n.d.). Retrieved May 7, 200, from http://www.cyberbullying.us/

de Meglio, M. (2007, August 16). *Parents seek to trash cell-phone ban - They file suit in court to overturn Department of Education policy*. Retrieved from http://www.brooklyngraphic.com/site/printerFriendly.cfm?brd=2384&dept_id=552852&newsid=18716571

de Salles, A. A., G. Bulla, & Rodriguez, C. E. (2006). Electromagnetic absorption in the head of adults and children due to mobile phone operation close to the head. *Electromagnetic Biology and medicine, 25*(4), 349-60.

Dinkins, S. (2006, December 3). Cell phones: Good for emergencies, or just plain annoying? *The Courier Press*. Retrieved from http://www

.courierpress.com/news/2006/dec/03/cell-phones-good-for-emergencies
-or-just-plain/

Elgan, M. (2008, August 1). Is your cell phone trying to kill you? *Computer World*. Retrieved from http://www.computerworld.com/action/article .do?command=viewArticleBasic&articleId=9111373

Farby, J. (2006, August 2). *Research shows cell phones dirtier than toilet seats*. Retrieved from http://www.vitabeat.com/research-shows-cell-phones -dirtier-than-toilet-seats/v/3818/   or   http://www.howardforums.com/ showthread.php?referrerid=295219&t=1145457

Felton, A. (2008, September 5). *Cellphones and children: What age is appropriate?* Retrieved from http://www.parentdish.com/2008/09/05/cellphones -and-children-what-age-is-appropriate/

Freehling, A. (2006). *Cell phones aren't a health hazard—Still, it's best to turn them off at the hospital.* Retrieved from http://www.dailypress.com/features/lifestyle/dp-60535sy0nov01,1,1111921.story?coll=dp-features-healthylife&ctrack=1&cset=true (no longer accessible)

Gasser, U., & Palfrey, J. (2008). *Born digital: Understanding the first generation of digital natives.* New York, NY: Basic Books.

Goggin, G. (2006). *Cell phone culture: Mobile technology in everyday life.* New York, NY: Routledge.

Gray, T. (2007, October 22). *Device to keep kids with diabetes safe.* Retrieved from http://www.eveningnews24.co.uk/content/News/story.aspx?brand =ENOnline&category=News&tBrand=enonline&t Catgory=news&itemid =NOED22%20Oct%202007%2010%3A01%3A54%3A417

Haarala, C., Bergman, M., Laine, M., Revonsuo, A., Kovisto, M., & Hämäläinen, H. (2005). Electromagnetic field emitted by 902 MHz mobile phones shows no effects on children's cognitive function. *Bioelectromagnetics Supplement 7*, S144-50.

Hardell, L., Carlberg, M., Söderqvist F. & Mild, K. H., & Morgan, L. L. (2007). Long-term use of cellular phones and brain tumours: Increased risk associated with use for > or =10 years. *Journal of Occupational and Environmental Medicine, 64*(9), 626-32.

Heyboer, K. (2006, December 10). See Dick call. See Jane text. Why parents are giving in to younger children's requests for cell phones. *The Star Ledger*. Retrieved but no longer accessible from http://www.nj.com/news/ledger/ index.ssf?/base/news-10/1165729566320830.xml&coll=1#continue

Holleran, K. L. (2007, December 5). Cell phone users getting younger and younger. *Daily Mail*. Retrieved from http://www.dailymail.com/News/ 200712050240

Krause, C. M., Bjornberg, C. H., Pesonen, M., Hulten, A., Liesivuori, T., Koivisto, M., et al. (2006). Mobile phone effects on children's event-related oscillatory EEG during an auditory memory task. *International Journal of Radiation Biology, 2*(6), 443-50.

Kwan, M. (2006, August 2). Cell phones "crawling with potentially lethal bacteria." *Daily Mail*. Retrieved from http://www.mobilemag.com/content/100/340/ C8942/

Lean, G. (2008, March 30). *Mobile phones "more dangerous than smoking."* Retrieved from http://www.independent.co.uk/life-style/health-and-wellbeing /health-news/mobile-phones-more-dangerous-than-smoking-802602.html

Levine, D., McCright, J., Dobkin, L., Woodruff, A. J., & Klausner, J. D. (2008). SEXINFO: A sexual health text messaging service for San Francisco youth. *American Journal of Public Health, 98*(3). Retrieved from http://www.ajph.org/ cgi/doi/10.2105/AJPH.2007.110767

Levine, M. H., & Shuler, C. (2009, February 13). *Pockets of potential.* Retrieved from http://spotlight.macfound.org/main /entry/levine_shuler_pockets_potential/

Low, R. (2008, October 16). *Nickel cell phones can cause rash: Researchers.* Retrieved from http://www.ctvbc.ctv.ca/servlet/an/local/CTVNews/20081016 /BC_Rhonda_Nickel_081016/20081016/?hub=BritishColumbiaHome

Miller, V. (2008, October 10). *Children reported for nude cell-phone photos.* Retrieved from http://www.dailycamera.com/news/2008/oct/10/children-reported -for-nude-cell-phone-photos/

Nally, S. (2008, January 31). *Study says cell phones could interfere with sleep.* Retrieved from   http://media.www.cw.ua.edu/media/storage/paper959/news/2008/01/31/ News/Study.Says.Cell.Phones.Could.Interfere.With .Sleep-3178442.shtml

Neergaard, L. (2008, June 12). Nagging texts help teens remember to take meds. *USA TODAY.* Retrieved from http://www.usatoday.com/tech/news /techinnovations/2008-05-12-text-message-nagging_N.htm?loc =interstitialskip

Neisteadt, S. (2009, April 24). *Swabbing cell phones.* Retrieved from http://www.kelo- land.com/News/NewsDetail6373.cfm?Id=83725

Niccolai, J. (2005, August 31). Cell phones do not cause tumors, study finds. *Info- World.* Retrieved from http://www.infoworld.com/article /05/08/31/HNcelltumorstudy_1.html

Nine in ten ten-year-olds have cell phones (n.d.). Retrieved May 9, 2009, from http://www.aftenbladet.no/english/964664 /Nine_in_ten_ten-year-olds_have_cell_phones.html

Northington, A. (2007, December 19). *Caddo students can't use cell phones during school day.* Retrieved from http://www.shreveporttimes.com/apps/pbcs.dll /article?AID=/20071219/NEWS04/712190329

O'Brien, T. (2007, July 30). *Cell phones illuminate emergency surgery.* Retrieved from http://www.switched.com/2007/07/30/cell-phones-illuminate -emergency-surgery/

Parker-Pope, T. (2008). Experts revive debate over cellphones and cancer. *The New York Times,* June 3.

Phone mast allergy "in the mind." (n.d.). *BBC NEWS.* Retrieved December 15, 2007, from http://news.bbc.co.uk/1/hi/health/6914492.stm

Pogue, D. (2006, December 21). *Cellphones that track the kids.* Retrieved from http:// www.iht.com/articles/2006/12/21/technology/web.1221kids.php

Punamaki, R. L., Wallenius, M., Nygard, Ch., Saarni, L., & Rimpela, A. (2007). Use of information and communication technology (ICT) and perceived health in adolescence: The role of sleeping habits and waking-time tiredness.

Journal of Adolescence, 30(4), 569-585. Retrieved from http://www
.sciencedirect.com/science?_ob=ArticleURL&_udi
=B6WH0-4KXDWHY-
1&_user=10&_rdoc=1&_fmt=&_orig=search&_sort=d&view=c&_acct=C0
00050221&_version=1&_urlVersion=0&_userid=10&md5=6705011012a73
364d328666fc2f5dd23

Raskauskas, J. (2006, April 13). *Girls use cell phones to bully each other.* Retrieved
from http://www.textually.org/textually/archives/2006/04/012047.htm

Reardon, M. (2006, December 6). *Turning cell phones into lifelines.* Retrieved from
http://news.com.com/Turning+cell+phones+into+lifelines/2100
-1039_3-6140794.html

Richtel, M., & Stone, B. (2007, November 29). *For toddlers, toy of choice is tech device.*
Retrieved from http://www.nytimes.com/2007/11/29
/technology/29techtoys.html?_r=1&oref=slogin

Sarasohn-Kahn, J. (2008, July 29). *Cell phones and health: the yin-and-yang of wellness.* Retrieved from http://www.healthpopuli.com/2008/07/cell-phones
-and-health-yin-and-yang-of.html

Schehl, P. (2008, June 5). *Misuse of cell phones causing problems.* Retrieved from
http://www.mountvernonnews.com/local/08/06/05/cell_phones.html --

Shuler, C. (2009). *Pockets of potential: Using mobile technologies to promote children's
learning.* Retrieved from http://74.125.95
.132/search?q=cache:dz9aT0KO7vAJ:www.joanganzcooncycenter.org/pdf/
pockets_of_potential.pdf+%22Pockets+of+
Potential,%22&cd=1&hl=en&ct=clnk&gl=us&client=firefox-a

Singh, S. (2008, December 23). *Cell phones for health monitoring?* Retrieved from
http://blogs.livemint.com/blogs/labrats/archive/2008/12/23/cell-phones
-for-health-monitoring.aspx

Smithers, R. (2006, September 19). Most pupils in survey own mobiles by 12. *The
Guardian.* Retrieved from http://www.guardian.co.uk/technology/2006/sep/19/
news.newmedia

Soderqvist, F., Hardell, L., Carlberg, M., & Mild, K. H. (2007, June 13). Ownership and use of wireless telephones: A population-based study of Swedish
children aged 7-14 years. *BMC Public Health, 7*(147), 105

Spain treats child phone addicts. (2008, June 13). *BBC NEWS.* Retrieved May 9,
2009, from http://news.bbc.co.uk/2/hi/europe/7452463.stm

Stevens, T. (2007, July 16). *Cell phones causing skin infections.* Retrieved from http://
www.switched.com/2007/07/16/cell-phones-causing-skin-infections/

TechnologyExpert. (2007, December 21). Parents say safety is primary reason for
cell phones. *Propeller.* Retrieved December 23, 2007, from http://tech
.propeller.com/story/2007/12/21/parents-say-safety-is-primary-reason-for
-cell-phones-for-kids-kids-rofl

Thomson, I. (2004). Study looks at phone mast health risks. *VNUnet UK.*
Retrieved May 6, 2009, from http://nl2.vnunet.com/news/1159601

Timmer, J. (2008, July 30). Correlation found between cell phone use, childhood
problems. *Ars Technica.* Retrieved from http://arstechnica.com/news.ars/post/
20080730-correlation-found-between-cell-phone-use-childhood
-problems.html

United Press International. (2008, January 19). *Study: Cell phone use disrupts sleep.*
    Retrieved from http://www.upi.com/NewsTrack/Top_News/2008
    /01/19/study_cell_phone_use_disrupts_sleep/3591/
van den Bulck, J. (2003). Text messaging as a cause of sleep interruption in ado-
    lescents, evidence from a cross-sectional study. *Journal of Sleep Research, 12*(3),
    263-263.
Withers, K. (2006, October 22). Mobiles have "key role for young." *BBC NEWS.*
    Retrieved from http://news.bbc.co.uk/2/hi/technology/6070378.stm

CHAPTER 11

THE ONE LAPTOP PER CHILD PROJECT AND THE PROBLEMS OF TECHNOLOGY-LED EDUCATIONAL DEVELOPMENT

Marcus Leaning

This chapter critically examines the One Laptop Per Child (OLPC) and XO-1 or "Children's Machine" project currently being led by the founder of the Massachusetts Institute of Technology Media Lab, Nicholas Negroponte. The OLPC is a nonprofit organization that oversees the production of low-cost laptop computers that will be distributed to children in the developing world on a vast scale. The OLPC project's overt, stated mission is to "empower the children of developing countries to learn by providing one connected laptop to every school-age child" (One Laptop Per Child, 2008d). This aim will be achieved through the production and sale of a specially designed laptop computer suitable for children in developing countries. The current model of the computer is known as the XO-1, and it incorporates a number of key features that make it, as the designers argue, a "potent learning tool designed and built especially for children in developing countries, living in some of the most remote environments" (One Laptop Per Child, 2008a). These features include; built-

High-Tech Tots: Childhood in a Digital World, pp. 231–248

231

in wireless that allow mesh networking between computers, a dual-mode screen that can be read outdoors, low-power usage, and a tough casing. While these certainly differentiate the laptop from many commercial models, what really separates the XO-1 and the OLPC project as a whole is the intention to make the laptop available to the governments of developing countries at a very low price (initially $100, though this increased slightly).

In this chapter it will be argued that while the project is a distinct attempt to provide education for children in the developing world and is commendable for many reasons, the OLPC project raises a number of serious concerns. The chapter will be comprised of three sections. First, the chapter will provide a brief account of the history of the OLPC project. This will reference the ideas that led to the development of the project, the introduction of the project at the World Economic Summit in Davos in January 2005, its launch at the World Summit on the Information Society in Tunis in November 2005, and some of the recent developments. Second, the chapter will examine a number of critical issues in deploying technology on such a large scale. In doing so three key issues will be addressed. One, that the project is an example of technological determinism—a much-criticized model of technology dissemination in which the introduction of a particular technology is understood to lead directly and unarguably to discrete and discernable social benefits. Two, that the project seeks to impose the technology with little appreciation of local needs or conditions—moreover, some of the discourse surrounding the project verges on the "colonial" in tone. Three, that the program is concerned solely with providing the hardware and software of the computers while responsibility for the content, training, and support is to be the responsibility of the authorities of the countries in which the technology is used. Finally, the chapter will conclude by arguing that while commendable, the OLPC program should be rigorously evaluated, more attuned to local conditions, and far more wary and mindful of the needs and requirements of children. Media technology, if deployed and used indiscriminately without adequate attention being paid to the "soft" issues of critical understanding, can result in consequences far beyond those initially envisaged.

THE HISTORY OF THE PROJECT AND ITS CONSTRUCTIONIST ROOTS

While the OLPC project was made public by the former director of the Massachusetts Institute of Technology Nicholas Negoponte at the World Economic Summit in Davos, Switzerland in January 2005, many of the underlying ideas have an older history. Indeed, the official history of the

OLPC has been rewritten and amended to include reference to these earlier ideas (Vota, 2007a).

The project's own reported history attributes considerable importance to Seymore Papert's work on the development of constructionist pedagogy (One Laptop Per Child, 2008b). Papert, who initially trained as a mathematician and worked with Piaget in Geneva, joined MIT in 1963 and went on to found the *Epistemology and Learning Research Group* in the MIT Media Lab. Papert's work was a direct development of Piaget's theories of constructivist learning. The constructivist perspective is a broad socio-psychological vision of learning and pedagogic practice. Constructivists regard learning as an activity that is deeply linked to the specific context in which it takes place. Learning is not an abstract activity, and it cannot be separated from the context in which it occurs (Schunk, 2000). Furthermore, the act of learning is one of construction; of learners discovering or constructing knowledge through their own actions in particular situations (Nanjappa & Grant, 2003). The relationship of constructivism to constructionism is close, but there are differences. Papert contends:

> Constructionism ... shares constructivism's view of learning as "building knowledge structures" through progressive internalization of actions.... It then adds the idea that this happens especially felicitously in a context where the learner is consciously engaged in constructing a public entity, whether it's a sand castle on the beach or a theory of the universe. (Papert, 1980, p. 1)

Thus, from a constructionist perspective, learning best occurs when we are actually engaging in the act of producing something. Papert initially intended constructionism as a way of teaching in science and technology, but it soon became apparent that it could be applied in other academic fields. Furthermore, the gradual increase in the power of computing meant that the computer could be a tool via which children could engage in creative activity across other disciplines; in Papert's (and others') vision a computer was something that could be used to enhance learning (Papert, 1991). Indeed Papert's 1980 text *Mindstorms: Children, Computers and Powerful Ideas* is an explicit guide that advocates the use of computers in education.

In 1982 Papert and Negroponte engaged in a project with the French government to use computers in Senegalese Schools. While the official OLPC website time-line lauds the operation as a success (One Laptop Per Child, 2008b), a report in the May/June 1983 Massachusetts Institute of Technology magazine *Technology Review* notes that the project collapsed after a year, and both Papert and Negroponte had resigned from the project (Dray & Memosky, 1983).

In spite of this, Negroponte continued with Papert's idea of using computers in teaching, and he was involved with a number of other projects of a similar nature. Negroponte produced a visionary if populist statement of his views on how computing technology would change everyday life for the better in *Being Digital* (Negroponte, 1995). Many of the ideas that underpin the OLPC project were aired in *Being Digital* and the preceding (and constituent) columns in *Wired* magazine.

In 2002 Negroponte deployed 20 laptop computers in Reaksmey, a remote village in Cambodia. The school had been founded by Negroponte and his family in 1999, and they had previously installed a generator and a satellite receiver (Stahl, 2007). The intention was to facilitate the children's learning both in the classroom and at home, and the project has been widely reported as being successful.

At the Davos World Economic Forum in January 2005 Negroponte presented a mock up of the $100 laptop (Markoff, 2005). In November 2005 Negroponte and the then United Nations Secretary General Kofi Anan presented the *Green Machine*, a working prototype of the XO-1 at the World Summit on the Information Society in Tunis. This prototype, while still problematic, showcased to the general public many of the features of the final released model. In December 2005 OLPC announced that the laptops would be manufactured by Quanta Computer, the World's largest laptop ODM (Original Design Manufacturer).

Throughout 2006 the laptop continued to be developed; the dual-use screen was perfected; and the interface, *Sugar*, was launched in September. Sugar differed considerably from normal operating system shells (the user friendly front end) in that it did not make use of the office metaphor; rather, as one of the key designers put it, the interface was designed as a "tool for expression." Sugar contained applications that would allow children to creatively express themselves through textual, artistic and musical forms (Blizzard, 2006). In November the first laptops were being produced by Quanta. However, ensuring that the laptops were actually disseminated proved a harder task.

While many countries expressed interest in the computers, few orders were actually placed. In some instances Negroponte made claims of orders that eventually turned out to be no more than agreed trials (Vota, 2006a), and a number of key countries, India for example, announced that they would not be participating (Best, 2006). Furthermore, a number of rival projects were announced; India declared it would seek to develop its own even cheaper version of a laptop (Vota, 2006b), and Intel launched its *World Ahead Program* that resulted in the production of a direct rival to the XO, the *Classmate PC*. Indeed, it can be strongly argued that one distinct consequence of the OLPC has been the creation of a new market for laptops, the educational sector market in the developing world, and new technologies specifically for this market.

Testing and deployment continued throughout 2007 with setbacks and advancements seeming to come in equal measure. There were considerable delays in shipping large numbers (Shen, 2007) as well as difficulties of countries financing the purchase of the laptops (Vota, 2007b). Nevertheless, concrete orders began to accrue from countries such as Uruguay (Vota, 2007d) and Peru (Villanueava Manislla, 2007), though this was nowhere near what was predicted or required to make the project a success (Vota, 2007c). In a move to increase the numbers sold, a system of "Give One Get One" was launched for the U.S. market. In this scheme the XO-1 would be launched on the U.S. market at a $399 price. For each sale a second XO-1 would be given to a child in a developing country. Unfortunately, this sales scheme was very poorly managed, and after considerable problems in processing orders and extensive delays in delivering the computers to U.S. customers, the scheme was closed on December 31, 2007.

In 2008 a number of technical developments occurred, including the development of a dual boot facility to allow a version of Microsoft Windows to be run and the demonstration of the XO-2, the follow up to the XO-1 (Tweney, 2008). Sales continued, albeit at a far slower rate than hoped for, and a second "Give One Get One" scheme was run from November 2008. This proved far less successful than the preceding scheme (Vota, 2009) with sales of the OX-1 being only 7% of what they had been with the previous "Give One Get One" program (Brey, 2009). The global financial downturn also impacted the OLPC heavily, and at the start of 2009 Negroponte announced a number of changes to the organization and mission. Staff numbers were cut by 50% with pay reductions for those remaining. A number of subdivisions (including the Sugar interface) were made independent, and the focus was adjusted to the Middle East, Afghanistan, and North West Pakistan (Calore, 2009).

The future of the OLPC is uncertain. As of November 17, 2008 a total of 568,040 laptops had been deployed (Eliason, 2008). Regardless of whether the OLPC survives (though I hope most strongly it does), it presents a very interesting case of technology deployment for overt social and personal development. However, the dynamics of the deployment, the discourse used in describing and articulating the project, and the underpinning rationale all present an interesting instance of a well-meaning if problematic approach to using information and communication technology for educational purposes for children. In the remainder of this chapter I wish to address three aspects of this approach.

PROBLEMS WITH THE PROGRAM

While the project has been subject to considerable criticism from its outset here, I wish to examine three particular problems with the project. The issues raised here are not with the viability of the project or even its execution; rather here I wish to raise issues concerning the beliefs and ideals underpinning the project.

Technological Determinism

A number of commentators have noted that present within discourse surrounding the OLPC is a strong sense of *technological determinism*—the view that a specific instance of technology will result in a specific outcome (Cohen, 2009; Leinonen, 2009). Technological determinism is a relatively old model for examining how technology impacts upon individuals, communities, and societies (Winner, 1977). It has proven a strong and persistent strand of thought in understanding the role of technology within modern Western thought even though it seems rarely explicitly stated. Marx and Smith (1996) contend:

> A sense of technology's power as a crucial agent of change has a prominent place in the culture of modernity. It belongs to the body of widely shared tacit knowledge that is more likely to be acquired by direct experience than by the transmittal of explicit ideas. (p. ix)

Similarly, Bimber (1996) proposes: "Technological determinism seems to lurk in the shadows of many explanations of the role of technology" (p. 80). Technological determinism is the belief that technology is the prime determining factor in setting the pace and general direction of life; it is technology that causes social change. Furthermore, the introduction of technology will bring about change in a straightforward and linear manner—the deployment of technology will result in development. In this view science and technology orientate the direction of development, and there is an utter rejection of the "social" in accounts of technology's potency. Such a reading incorporates two claims: that "technological developments occur according to some given logic, which is not culturally or socially determined, and that these developments force social adaptation and change" (p. 84). Heilbroner (1996) summarizes the argument as follows: "Machines make history by changing the material conditions of human existence. It is largely machines ... that define what it is to live in a certain epoch" (p. 69).

Such an understanding may be criticized as being both simplistic and problematic for a number of reasons. First, the idea that technology is discreet, that it comes in small packages such as the XO-1, and that these are separate from larger cultural and material infrastructures is contentious. As will be argued below, technology is part of a larger "cultural framework"—it is developed within and articulates a specific perspective on the world. Technology is not "clean" and devoid of cultural meaning, rather it is like any other form of material or cultural production, and it carries a cultural "imprint" or cultural "baggage." In many developed countries specific programs of educational activity have been developed to equip students to deal with this baggage, to enable them to become critical users of the technology. As will be explored below the OLPC comes with no such protective measures.

Second, within the technological determinist vision the environment in which the technology is deployed and used is downplayed to a considerable degree, and this has attendant consequences. The OLPC is intended to be used worldwide, and the sheer heterogeneity of the situations in which it will be, and has been deployed, is vast. There is enormous differentiation between countries and regions in the developing world. This difference can be conceptualized in terms of hard tangible issues and "softer" less measurable issues. The hard, tangible and measurable concerns include topics such as the wealth of individuals and educational institutions, the educational levels of students, the infrastructures devoted to schooling and the diversity of bodies providing education in different countries (for example religious organizations play a huge part in some educational systems, and very little in others—furthermore in some instances these organizations are within the state educational system and in others they exist outside of the state). The soft and less measurable variables range from issues such as the value put upon education as a whole in different cultures to classroom gender dynamics. Even the very categories of student, teacher, and educational activity vary considerably in different countries (Phillips & Schweisfurth, 2007; Tickly, 2004), nor are these stable over time (Carnoy & Rhoten, 2002). To expect one piece of technology to impact upon such a range of different environments such as urban Uruguay and a rural Rwanda in a singular manner is highly optimistic, if not dangerously naive. The OLPC is in effect reducing difference, flattening disparities, and articulating a simplistic description of education in the developing world. More problematically it uses a default position that identifies a problem, a lack or shortcoming in the developing world to explain highly complex, historically differentiated situations. In this model, education in the developing world is at fault; it is a problem, and the solution is to provide laptop computers.

Third, the effects of the technology may be felt in more ways than planned. While the OLPC is intended to impact upon the recipients of the laptops and the community and wider society in a positive, progressive manner, technology has a history of operating in a different manner than anticipated (Postman, 1992).

For technological determinists, change occurs in a linear and often singular manner—a simple cause and effect relationship. However, technological change has a tendency to "bleed" into other areas of life—the introduction of a technology will cause changes beyond those intended. Postman (1992) argues that technological change should not be conceptualized in terms of its linear impact but upon its capacity to bring about totalizing change: "Technological change is neither additive nor subtractive. It is "ecological"... in the same sense used by environmental scientists.... A new technology does not add or subtract something. It changes everything" (p. 18). The widespread changes that occur with the introduction of technology cannot possibly be predicted, nor can they be considered singly "good" or "bad" as these are of course locally determined, value positions. However, we must recognize that technology will bring about change and that this change may not be all positive. The XO-1 may well provide a "means for learning, self-expression, and exploration" (One Laptop Per Child, 2008d) for many children. But it may also bring about changes in the subtle dynamics of cultural and historic classroom practice. Indeed, as Villanueva Mansilla notes (2005), this may actually be intended:

> We have the tool, now change everything else *to fit with the tool*. The few resources left will be used to adapt everything in the educational system to work with the tool, being software, adequate security measures or teacher training. And the original goals [of the education system] will be changed to fit the tool. (p. 2)

The laptops probably will cause change, and some of this will probably be for the better. The exact nature of the change, however, cannot be predicted. Moreover, as will be explored below the direction of the change may also be problematic.

Colonial Technology Dissemination

The OLPC is of course not the first attempt to use technology to alleviate poverty in the developing world. In spite of much of the rhetoric of originality that surrounded the OLPC (at least in its initial stages), there is a considerable history of the deployment of information and communications technology for social or community benefit. Indeed, the application of information and communications technology for development (ICTD) is a distinct field of academic inquiry that has been active for a considerable number of years. The concern of practitioners in the field of ICTD is that of deploying and making available new media, communicational, and computing technology with the prime intention of social development, and the discipline has gone through a number of changes since its inception (Heeks, 2008). Heeks identifies three strategies that have been used for deploying ICTD. First are *Pro-poor efforts*, approaches initiated from outside of the subject community but on their behalf. Here assistance is designed abroad and imported into the locality in question. Historically this approach has been the most used. Second are *Para-poor efforts*. These are development initiatives that work alongside the subject communities. Here the intention is to develop user-targeted assistance and for experts to work with local communities in developing solutions to locally identified issues and problems. Heeks notes the numerous problems of local political issues, of access and of the power of elite groups in such programs (Heeks, 2008). Third are *Per-poor efforts*. These are innovations and uses of ICT by communities themselves. These directly address local issues with minimum wastage. Many such innovations emerge out of the "Appropriate Technology" movement that seeks to identify new uses of technology and scale them to new localities (Heeks, 2008).

The OLPC project is an obvious, almost textbook example of pro-poor development. It is an external, 'one size fits all' approach to ICTD that seeks to use a single solution regardless of the specific requirements of the locality. While such an approach is problematic for financial reasons (i.e., the solution purchased by the state education departments may not fit the problems of the locality), there is an additional political or moral issue.

Most contemporary models of development advocate the strengthening of local or indigenous (and therefore more sustainable) solutions to problems (Malecki, 1997). Local solutions to educational and development issues are commonly more desired than externally developed solutions. A locally developed solution tends to be more suited to a situation than an externally developed one as in most instances it has evolved to fit the local problem. They do, however, have the counterproblem of not being scalable; their very localness means they may be ill-suited to application outside of their locality. They are also more ethically desirable as they foster the desired characteristics of empowerment and sustainability.

The OLPC is problematic as it is a top down system or "solution." As noted above it was developed from, makes explicit reference to, and articulates the values of a particular educational philosophy, that of the constructivist/constructionist framework. Such a solution may not be suitable for all situations in the developing world. Furthermore, much of the rhetoric surrounding the OLPC regards the system of education that resulted in the OLPC as inherently superior to any other system. The OLPC is the *best* way forward as it articulates the *best* way of educating children. Easterly (2006) describes such top-down systems of aid as a direct descendent of colonial regimes, imposing systems upon less developed countries. Indeed, Easterly goes as far to term the large aid programs "postmodern imperialism." While such statements are perhaps overly inflammatory, they do highlight a problem in top down approaches, that of the imposed 'one size fits all' nature of the solution.

Media Technology Only and the Need for Literacy

While the OLPC have dedicated considerable effort to developing and promoting the hardware, the operating system, and some of the applications of the XO-1, there has been far less attention paid to the content that will be made available via the XO-1. In addition to the shell and a programming debugging application, the XO-1 contains a number of applications developed from public domain, open source, or freeware software designed for educational purposes. These include: a web browser; a document viewing application; a chat client; a word processor; an RSS reader; an e-mail client; a voice over IP client; a journal program; a multimedia authoring and playback application; a music composition toolkit; a graphics application; and a number of games (One Laptop Per Child, 2008c). The software is generally considered to be of high quality and is thought to be of educational value (Lowes & Luhr, 2008), though more educational applications are required (Burnside, Klous, Mayton, & Plunkett, 2008).

It is important to note that the OLPC is concerned solely with providing the hardware and initial software of the computers. Responsibility for additional content, training, and support is to be the responsibility of the authorities of the countries in which the technology is used: "We are not providing the educational content. That is really done in the countries" (OLPCTalks, 2006, p. 1).

This divorcing of technology from content, training, and use is problematic for a number of reasons: First; it seemingly contradicts the promoted idea that the OLPC is "not a laptop project. It's an education project" (One Laptop Per Child, 2008d). Deploying technology as a solution to an educational problem is an extensively researched field (Abbott, 2000; Watson, 2001). A core principle in such activity is that technology can only ever be a component in a larger "blended" solution (Milrad, Spector, & Davidsen, 2003; Spector & Anderson, 2000). Technology on its own provides no real assistance; it is only when it is integrated into a coherent educational program that its benefits can be fully realized (Watson, 2001). As Villanueva Mansilla (2005) argues the technology has not been designed to fit into a particular syllabus, and it therefore necessitates that a syllabus to be developed around it. The OLPC provides no assistance in this task and actively distances itself from such activity. This disengaging from the task of assisting in the development of curricula to integrate the XO-1 into educational activities means that the OPLC is not fulfilling its claim to be an education project. It has the potential to be a *component* of one, but it still requires considerable additional investment in terms of time for training, learning material development, and curricula integration. Indeed, when compared to such large overheads, the actual technology is probably one of the least costly elements of such a project.

A second issue is that of information and media education and their consequence, information and media literacy. The XO-1 interface has been especially developed so as to enable a young, computer novice to make use of it (Pytlovany, 2007). However, more advanced skills, such as those of being able to recognize the need for information, find, evaluate and use information (the widely accepted definition of information literacy (Bawden, 2001), will need to be taught. In many developed countries there are extensive programs to develop information literacy. Unfortunately, however, such programs are far from universal.

There is also a further need for an additional form of literacy in child users. The inclusion of a web browser and the inherent networking capabilities of the XO-1 (providing it is used in an area in which a wireless connection to the Internet is possible) means that the XO-1 needs to be considered not solely as a laptop or, as Negroponte would have it, an educational device, but as a media technology that makes available almost limitless amounts of media content. As with information literacy, the need for media literacy is well recognized in many countries. However, while the history of media education dates back some 80 years in certain countries (Federov, 2009), the rationale for media education is far from constant either across time or between countries (Leaning, 2009b).

Three dominant positions tend to hold sway: In the first perspective children receive media education so as to protect them from harmful content. Media education in this model is understood as a form of protection against "harmful" or dangerous media, what critics and historians have identified as a notion of "inoculation" or protection against the disease of media (Buckingham, 2003, p. 7). This form of media education advocates a defensive approach to examining media texts. The media is considered alien and dangerous, and the role of media education is to instruct students in how to defend themselves against its pernicious effects. This version of media education is "education *against* the media" (Masterman, 2001, p. 20). It is important to note that such a model is very evident in many media literacy programs today. As Kubey (2003) notes, in the United States there is a strong emphasis upon "protecting" children and others from "harmful" media content. Drawing heavily upon the "effects theories," a considerable body of research is produced by members of the health, psychological, psychiatric, and education professions related to the detrimental effects of media upon children and adults (Vine, 1997). Much of this research identifies negative effects upon children following their exposure to too much media, the incorrect form of media, or inappropriate media. A further explanation for the popularity of this approach is the importance it places upon teachers. Masterman (2001) notes that teachers are accorded a position of considerable cultural significance within the model, and therefore the model receives extensive support from practitioners and media studies teachers.

The second approach draws upon developments in media and cultural studies which made use of advances in the fields of social theory, literary theory, linguistics, and semiotics. This approach has been heavily influenced by the critical theories of Marxism, feminism, post-colonial theory, and a strong dose of countercultural activism. At core is a concern that much mass-media content is in essence ideology and that the audience uncritically consume such content (Penman & Turnbull, 2007). The role of media education is to show the ideological premises behind media messages, to lay bare the political messages that were transmitted by the media. In identifying such messages the media would be "demystified" and shown to be a biased, ideological text.

The third approach is of recent genesis and arose out of the development of constructivist pedagogic practices; advances in how the act of media consumption is understood and the rise of digital media communications. Against the back drop of these three changes the 'participatory' model of literacy sees the role of media education as one of facilitating engagement with media through both critical and creative practice. As reports from Livingstone, van Couvering, and Thumim (2005) and Penman and Turnbull (2007) note, media literacy education is now often geared towards the development of skills to encourage the engagement with and production of media content. Media literacy from this perspective is concerned with allowing audiences to engage with and participate in media culture and not to be a victim of it.

All three of these rationales are still strong. In many developed countries the particular problems posed by the vastly increased and often unsanctioned flow of information and media content are regarded as of high importance (Penman & Turnbull, 2007), and considerable funds are directed towards developing programs of media literacy for children (Buckingham, 2005). These countries have considerable experience of a variety of forms of media, and they benefit from a relatively well educated and media literate population, enjoying widely disseminated information and communications technology. Even so, such countries constantly develop and refine programs of media education to deal with the perceived social problems associated with the advent of digital media and the flow of content it affords.

Developing countries—those that have comparatively little experience with such a form of mass distributed technology as the OLPC advocate—may be challenged by the sudden influx of technology and, to a large degree, unregulated media content. While the OLPC is a project that may provide large numbers of laptop computers to children in the developing world, it will simultaneously open a channel for considerable amounts of media content to be delivered to them. Developing media education to deal with such content is not something that should be considered separate from the introduction of the technology, but instead, central to the technologies successful deployment (Leaning, 2009a).

CONCLUSION AND RECOMMENDATIONS

The OLPC project is a vast and highly ambitious attempt to fast-track development for a huge number of people. It is global in scale and is perhaps a project that one would have thought (or wished) international intergovernmental entities, such as the agencies of the United Nations, to have attempted. That it is driven primarily by a small group of individuals led by Negroponte is impressive, and for such a small team (the paid employees of the OLPC never numbered more than 80 and are now about 35), the results have been truly impressive, even if they are not anywhere near what was initially hoped for.

However, as indicated above, the project articulates and is underpinned by a number of beliefs and values that can be considered problematic. While the project is global in scale, a number of its premises and values are firmly rooted in a particular Western (if not American) conceptual framework. Key among these beliefs is that one educational model is suitable for all educational environments and that the latest educational approach should displace historic, locally developed teaching approaches. Furthermore, it is thought that technology can and should replace other pedagogic activity and that an injection of technology alone is all that is needed. It is considered that the "softer" issues of content and information and media education are somehow external issues and beyond the remit of an "education project." Together these all indicate a particularly arrogant approach to education. For all its talk of empowerment, the OLPC seems more like an imposed solution. With these ideas in mind the following suggestions are made not so much in the belief that the current OLPC approach can be changed or improved but with the intention to stimulate debate concerning the possible shape of future projects of a similar nature.

First, it is argued that technology take a secondary role to the "soft," less measurable and human issues of education. Technology should not be the primary driver of educational activity; it should support it. Technology such as the XO-1 should only ever be considered as supportive of educational practice, never as core to it.

Second, an approach that is more sympathetic to local educational traditions and practices is advocated. Traditional and historical practices in education are important vehicles of cultural transference; they are sites of cultural activity and important in the reproduction of culture. Simply to label them as faulty is demonstrative of a naivety of the deep nature and function of educational mechanics. Furthermore, it indicates an arrogant sense of superiority and a "benign colonialist" attitude.

Third, projects of this nature should operate within the *per-poor* developmental framework described by Heeks (2008). Every effort should be made to develop a grassroots approach to the deployment and use of technology rather than the top-down approach of the OLPC.

Fourth, and perhaps most urgently, the dissemination of technology that makes available media content must be considered as only one aspect of a larger media technology deployment project. The dissemination of technology must be accompanied by media and information education programs. Media and information education programs are absolutely vital to a moral and ethically centered system of media technology dissemination. Furthermore, and in light of the above points, such programs must be home grown and considerate of the local cultural environment. Such programs are of course costly to develop, manage, and run. As such there is considerable overhead not factored in the initial pricing of the XO-1, but accompanying media education programs are a very real cost that must be considered.

I feel fair to conclude that the current difficulties faced by the OLPC will certainly not prevent similar projects from being attempted. Furthermore, such projects will undoubtedly encounter both similar problems and face new difficulties. However, I hope that they will be approached in a manner more mindful of local sensibilities and the intrinsic limitations of a project such as the OLPC.

REFERENCES

Abbott, C. (2000). *ICT: Changing education*. London: Routledge.

Bawden, D. (2001). Information and digital literacies: A review of concepts. *Journal of Documentation, 57*(2), 218-259.

Best, J. (2006, July 27). *India ditches "potentially harmful" $100 laptop plan.* Retrieved from http://hardware.silicon.com/desktops/0,39024645,39160928,00.htm

Bimber, B. (1996). Three faces of technological determinism. In M. Smith & L. Marx (Eds.), *Does technology drive history? The dilemma of technological determinism* (pp. 79-100). Cambridge, MA: Massachusetts Institute of Technology.

Blizzard, C. (2006, May 23). *Some more sugar notes.* Retrieved from http://www.0xdeadbeef.com/weblog/?p=200

Brey, H. (2009, January 9). *Fund loss staggers group giving laptops to poor children.* Retrieved from http://www.boston.com/business/technology/articles/2009/01/09/fund_loss_staggers_group_giving_laptops_to_poor_children/?page=full

Buckingham, D. (2003). *Media education: Literacy, learning and contemporary culture.* Cambridge, England: Polity Press.

Buckingham, D. (2005). *The media literacy of children and young people: A review of the research literature.* London: OFCOM.

Burnside, W., Klous, M., Mayton, B., & Plunkett, K. (2008). *CPXO: Classroom presenter for the OLPC XO-1 Laptop.* Seattle, WA: Department of Computer Science and Engineering University of Washington.

Calore, M. (2009, January 8). *OLPC cuts staff by half, drops sugar development.* Retrieved from http://blog.wired.com/business/2009/01/olpc-cuts-staff.html

Carnoy, M., & Rhoten, D. (2002). What does globalization mean for educational change? A comparative approach. *Comparative Education Review, 46*(1), 1-9.

Cohen, B. (2009, January 6). *The problems with the One Laptop Per Child.* Retrieved from http://scienceblogs.com/worldsfair/2009/01/the_problems_with_one_laptop_p.php

Dray, J., & Menosky, J. (1983, May/June). Computers and a new world order. *Technology Review, 86*(4), 12-16.

Easterly, W. (2006). *The white man's burden: Why the west's efforts to aid the rest have done so much ill and so little good.* New York, NY: The Penguin Press.

Eliason, E. (2008, November 17). *OLPC deployments, OLPC deployment statistics, by country.* Retrieved from http://maps.google.com/maps/ms?f=q&hl=cn&geocode=&time=&date=&ttype=&ie=UTF8&cd=1&om=1&msa=0&msid=107887635573341686661.00045a8f74844ef1681f8&ll=7.710992,11.25&spn=136.959067,316.40625&z=2

Federov, A. (2009). Media education in Russia: A brief history. In M. Leaning (Ed.), *Issues in information and media literacy: Criticism, history and policy* (pp. 173-194). San Jose, CA: Informing Science Institute Press.

Heeks, R. (2008, June). ICT4D 2.0: The next phase of applying ICT for international development. *Computer, 41*(6), 26-33.

Heilbroner, R. (1996). Technological determinism revisited. In M. Smith & L. Marx (Eds.), *Does technology drive history? The dilemma of technological determinism* (pp. 67-79). Cambridge, MA: Massachusetts Institute of Technology.

Kubey, R. (2003). Why U.S. media education lags behind the rest of the English speaking world. *Television & New Media, 4*(4), 351-370.

Leaning, M. (2009a). *The Internet, power and society: Rethinking the power of the Internet to change lives.* Oxford, England: Chandos.

Leaning, M. (2009b). Theories and models of media literacy. In *Issues in information and media literacy: Criticism, history and policy* (pp. 1-21). San Jose, CA: Informing Science Institute Press.

Leinonen, T. (2009, January 2009). *Thank you OLPC—Maybe now we may start to talk about education again.* Flosse Posse—Free, Libre and Open Source Software in Education. Retrieved from http://billkerr2.blogspot.com/2008/01/teemu-talks-nonsense-about-olpc.html

Livingstone, S., van Couvering, E., & Thumim, N. (2005). *Adult media literacy: A review of the research literature.* London: OFCOM.

Lowes, S., & Luhr, C. (2008). *Evaluation of the teaching matters one laptop per child (XO) Pilot at KAPPA IV.* New York, NY: Institute for Learning Technologies Teachers College/Columbia University.

Malecki, E. (1997). *Technology and economic development: The dynamics of local, regional and national competitiveness.* London: Addison Wesley Longman.

Markoff, J. (2005, January 31). *New economy; at Davos, the Johnny Appleseed of the digital era shares his ambition to propagate a $100 laptop in developing countries.* Retrieved from http://query.nytimes.com/gst/fullpage.html?res=9C04E1DA153BF932A05752C0A9639C8B63

Marx, L., & Smith, M. (1996). Introduction. In M. Smith, & L. Marx (Eds.), *Does technology drive history? The dilemma of technological determinism* (pp. xi-xv). Cambridge, MA: Massachusetts Institute of Technology.

Masterman, L. (2001). A rationale for media education. In R. Kubey (Ed.), *Media literacy in the information age: Current perspectives – Information and behaviour Volume 6* (pp. 15-67). Edison, NJ: Transaction.

Milrad, M., Spector, J. M., & Davidsen, P. I. (2003). Model facilitated learning. In S. Naidu (Ed.), *Learning & teaching with technology: Principles and practices* (pp. 13-28). London: Kogan Page.

Nanjappa, A., & Grant, M. M. (2003). *Constructing on constructivism: The role of technology.* Retrieved from http://ejite.isu.edu/Volume2No1/Nanjappa.htm

Negroponte, N. (1995). *Being Digital.* New York: Knopf.

OLPCTalks. (2006, February). *Nicholas Negroponte at TED - transcript.* Retrieved from http://www.olpctalks.com/nicholas_negroponte/negroponte_ted_speech.html

One Laptop Per Child. (2008a, November 1). *Laptop.* Retrieved from http://laptop.org/en/laptop/index.shtml

One Laptop Per Child. (2008b, November 10). *Project.* Retrieved from http://laptop.org/en/vision/project/index.shtml

One Laptop Per Child. (2008c, November 1). *Software Specs.* Retrieved from http://laptop.org/en/laptop/software/specs.shtml

One Laptop Per Child. (2008d, November 10). *Vision.* Retrieved from http://laptop.org/en/vision/index.shtml

Papert, S. (1980). *Mindstorms. Children, computers and powerful ideas.* New York, NY: Basic Books.

Papert, S. (1991). Situating constructionism. In I. Harel & S. Papert (Eds.), *Constructionism: Research reports and essays, 1985-1990* (pp. 1-11). Norwood, NJ: Ablex.

Penman, R., & Turnbull, S. (2007). *Media literacy – concepts, research and regulatory issues.* Belconnen: Australian Government, Australian Communications and Media Authority.

Phillips, D., & Schweisfurth, M. (2007). *Comparative and international education: An introduction to theory, method and practice.* London: Continuum.

Postman, N. (1992). *Technopoly: The surrender of culture to technology.* New York, NY: Alfred A. Knopf.

Pytlovany, B. (2007, December 18). *OLPC evaluation guide - first impressions.* Retrieved from http://billpstudios.blogspot.com/2007/12/olpc-evaluation-guide-first-impressions.html

Schunk, D. H. (2000). *Learning theories: An educational perspective.* Upper Saddle River, NJ: Prentice Hall.

Shen, S. (2007, April 20). *Quanta to delay OLPC notebook shipments to 4Q07.* Retrieved from http://www.digitimes.com/systems/a20070420PB202.html

Spector, J. M., & Anderson, T. (2000). *Integrated and holistic perspectives on learning, instruction and technology: Understanding complexity.* Dordrecht, The Netherlands: Kluwer.

Stahl, L. (2007, December 2). *What if every child had a laptop?* Retrieved from http://www.cbsnews.com/stories/2007/05/20/60minutes/main2830058.shtml

Tickly, L. (2004). Postcolonialism and comparative education. *International Review of Education, 45*(5-6), 603-621.

Tweney, D. (2008, May 20). *Negroponte shows second-generation OLPC: it's a book.* Retrieved from http://blog.wired.com/gadgets/2008/05/ncgroponte-show.html

Villanucava Manislla, E. (2007, October 14). *OLPC Peru's enigmatic 40,000 XO-1 laptop purchase.* Retrieved from http://www.olpcnews.com/countries/peru/olpc_peru_xo_laptop_purchase.html

Villanueava Mansilla, E. (2005, November 16). *One laptop per child: A sub-hundred dollar folly.* Retrieved from http://www.olpcnews.com/commentary/academia/sub_hundred_dollar_folly.html

Vine, I. (1997). The dangerous psycho-logic of media effects. In M. Barker & J. Petley (Eds.), *Ill effects: The media violence debate* (pp. 125-146). London: Routledge.

Vota, W. (2006a, August 22). *OLPCs ordered deployed tested in Thailand everywhere.* Retrieved from http://www.olpcnews.com/sales_talk/countries/olpcs_ordered_deploy.html

Vota, W. (2006b, September 26). *India to attempt $10 laptop per child.* Retrieved from http://www.olpcnews.com/countries/india/india_olpc_laptop_10.html

Vota, W. (2007a, April 7). *OLPC history lesson: An extension for the past.* Retrieved from http://www.olpcnews.com/commentary/olpc_news/olpc_history_lesson.html

Vota, W. (2007b, June 13). *Alternate one laptop per child financing options.* Retrieved from http://www.olpcnews.com/sales_talk/price/alternate_laptop_financing.html

Vota, W. (2007c, September 10). *Is "only government buyers" plan inhibiting XO Sales?* Retrieved from http://www.olpcnews.com/sales_talk/countries/sales_inhibiting_xo_distribution.html

Vota, W. (2007d, October 16). *Its official!! OLPC Uruguay is buying 100,000 xo laptops.* Retrieved from http://www.olpcnews.com/countries /uruguay/olpc_uruguay_buying_xo_laptops.html

Vota, W. (2009, January 9). *The real OLPC bust: G1G1 2008 XO laptop sales.* Retrieved from http://www.olpcnews.com/sales_talk /g1g1_2008/olpc_bust_g1g1_2008_sales.html

Watson, D. M. (2001). Pedagogy before technology: Re-thinking the relationship between ICT and teaching. *Education and Information Technologies, 6*(4), 251-266.

Winner, L. (1977). *Autonomous technology: Technics-out-of-control as a theme in political thought.* Cambridge, MA: The MIT Press.

CHAPTER 12

WEBKINZ AS CONSUMERIST DISCOURSE

A Critical Ideological Analysis

Charlie Dellinger-Pate and Rosemarie J. Conforti

The Ganz Corporation of Ontario, Canada introduced Webkinz in April, 2005. Webkinz are stuffed animals that come with an attached concealed secret code that allows children access to the Webkinz World website. Once in Webkinz World children own and interact with a virtual version of the plush pet. By September 2007 the site was reporting more than 6 million visitors per month (Navarro, 2007). In 2006 the company had stopped commenting on sales as its Webkinz toy sales approached the $1 million mark (Tedeschi, 2007). But it is easy to speculate on sales and revenue when Club Penguin, a similar online game site and social networking playground for children, was bought by The Walt Disney Company in 2006 in a deal worth $700 million dollars. That year, the annual revenue reported for Club Penguin was $50 million. The endgame is clear as children's entertainment companies aggressively construct virtual worlds that deliver quick financial growth while instilling brand loyalty in the youngest consumers (Barnes, 2007). Online sites such as those

High-Tech Tots: Childhood in a Digital World, pp. 249–269
Copyright © 2010 by Information Age Publishing
All rights of reproduction in any form reserved.

operated by Webkinz and Club Penguin are defined by the striking similarities in their focus on a consumerist worldview. The product-focused nature of these sites and others like them is examined by a variety of scholars (Montgomery, 2001; Strasburger, Wilson, & Jordan, 2009). The purchase of toys and brand loyalty to large corporations are identified as critical to the new trend of digital marketing to children and families.

This new phenomenon poses questions for parents who are trying to raise healthy children in the digital age. These questions are important because "families represent one of the fastest-growing segments of the population using the internet" (Montgomery, 2001, p. 637). In their quest for answers, parents can easily access discussions of the online educational and prosocial benefits to children concerning the educational and prosocial qualities of a virtual playground: learning how to manage money, caring for a pet, and forming online relationships. In addition, traditional media education and literacy efforts offer families insight that focuses on content, use, and information processing. Although these efforts are important, we examine the study of children's new media through a different theoretical lens. We approach media literacy from an ideological perspective, offering a critical understanding of the stories, rules and values that are generated through online practices and reinforce a particular worldview. In so doing, we propose that ideological literacy is crucial to a comprehensive media education agenda.

Our research focus—ideological literacy—positions Webkinz World as more than an aggressive capitalist enterprise or learning tool. It is also a social playground where the very nature of children's play sustains a particular ideological system that promotes a consumerist worldview. We explore the ideological constructions of Webkinz World as a confluence of stories, rules, and values that children engage in from the minute they enter the website. Here, relational and competitive strategies reinforce ideological meanings of consumption.

NEW MEDIA, NEW PERSPECTIVE

Traditional media research focuses on teaching children critical viewing skills, empowering parents to monitor online use, facilitating children's discussions of fantasy versus reality, guiding parental judgments of violent content, and addressing the pervasive presence of advertising (Buckingham, 2003; Montgomery, 2001; Potter, 1998; Singer, 2009; Strausburger, Wilson, & Jordan, 2009). As Singer notes, these are issues of concern with media content, specifically, "how children use and process the electronic sources of information and entertainment" (p. xvi). Yet researchers also call for a fresh, more interdisciplinary approach to the study of children and digital media as well as an awareness of the nature of new media which requires a new research focus (Donnerstein, 2009; Montgomery, 2001). Children's websites are often studied in relation to social problems. For example, some research critically explores aggressive advertising linked to childhood obesity. In their content analysis of children's websites and food marketing, Alvy and Calvert (2007) analyze the differences between food advertising on television-based websites for children (such as CartoonNetwork.com) and non-television-based websites (such as Neopets.com). The authors find that online food advertising mirrors television advertising for websites connected to television. However, they also argue that non-television-based websites reflect more of a "seamless transition from gaming to marketing." They summarize, "The seamless integration and marketing observed on Candystand.com and Neopets.com could make it very difficult for young children to separate entertainment and marketing on the sites" (p. 18). Moore's (2006) content analysis of the corporate food marketing sites that target children supports these findings. To this end, content analysis points to the importance of critically examining children's online entertainment but confines its scope to particular advertising practices and does not extend to the global nature of the consumer worldview. Similarly, in her description of Neopets.com, Seiter (2004) expresses some critical arguments regarding the website's aggressive marketing techniques and findings from an informal study of students. Her discussion centers on children's understanding of the creator of the website and not on ideological meanings. Donnerstein (2009) points to parents' concern over children's easy access to inappropriate material or possible contact with sexual predators online. Research here focuses on issues of privacy, policy, and government regulations. Although these are all valid areas of inquiry into new media, none offers a cultural perspective, which parents and educators need in order to make informed decisions about web usage.

New media research also lacks a perspective involving the critical exploration of ideological meanings of children's online playgrounds and their relation to larger cultural and social issues. Recent critical ideological inquiry ranges widely from studies of sports coverage in newspapers (Bishop, 2005) to gay magazines (Goltz, 2007) to video-game landscapes (Shoshana, 2006) to the national images of China constructed during the Olympics (Walkosz & Foss, 2007). Yet critical ideological inquiry has seldom been applied to a corporate medium capturing the hearts and minds of children.

For more general but critical work on the topic of marketing and children, we respond to the arguments of child and media-literacy advocates. Critics call attention to the aggressive marketing machine that now sees children's online entertainment as the quintessential capitalist device. As the editor in chief of Common Sense Media states, "Every interface is becoming an opportunity to sell children something, either brand awareness or real things. That's the end game" (Navarro, 2007, para. 15). From this perspective, new media is another, more aggressive form of targeting children and shaping consumerist values—a topic studied by psychologists and sociologists (Linn, 2004; Schor, 2004). For example, Linn argues,

> corporations are racing to stake their claim on the consumer group formerly known as children. What was once the purview of a few entertainment and toy companies has escalated into a gargantuan, multi-tentacled enterprise with a combined marketing budget at over $15 billion annually— about 2.5 times more than what was spent in 1992. (p. 1)

In addition, she questions how parents can compete with the culture of marketing that pervades every culture, rich or poor, and that competes with "parental values for children's hearts, minds and souls" (p. 32).

Within this scholarly discourse of varied motivations and concerns we pursue the critical ideological analysis of an extremely popular and profitable form of children's new media. From an ideological approach, Webkinz is not merely a mode of children's entertainment, a beloved stuffed toy, a profit-driven phenomenon, an educational tool, a source of family negotiation, an aggressive marketing device, a source of addiction, or a comment on cultural values. It is all of them.

THEORETICAL PERSPECTIVE

In the very first volume of the *Journal of Children and Media*, Livingstone (2007) outlines the polarized discussion of research into children's media created primarily between effects researchers and cultural theorists. She argues that the limitations of each theoretical perspective lend more confusion to families, educators, and policymakers trying to understand media's impact on children. Following her delineation of political and epistemological traps from both effects researchers and cultural critics, Livingstone says that the "field would benefit from better theory" for guiding research into the relationship between media and child development (p. 8). In calling for a "risk-based approach" to media studies and children, Livingstone says

> it seems wise to frame the question differently, eschewing the bald question— do the media have harmful effects or not, and instead insisting on a more complex formulation of the question, namely—in what way and to what extent do the media contribute, if at all, as one among several identifiable

factors that, in combination, account for the social phenomenon under consideration. (p. 9)

In the same volume, Ribak (2007) offers another problematic way that communication theorists conceptualize children's new media. Referring to Carey's (1989) work, she delineates the dueling "interpretations" of communication from the transmission view and the ritual view. "Where transmission deals with information, ritual is concerned with confirmation; and where transmission is designed to change attitudes, ritual presents an underlying order of things" (p. 68). She further argues that these perspectives offer important questions that we can continue to ask of new media, but in isolation they are "insufficient for capturing the scope of the relationships between children & media in the complicated contexts enabled by new communication technologies" (p. 69). Ribak is echoing Livingstone's point that new media is a unique phenomenon requiring different questions from those asked by past theoretical approaches, owing to changes of personal media ownership, diversification of media form, and the interactive element of children's entertainment. She concludes,

> it is notable that children engage with new media in ways that are socially and, significantly, materially new. And so, as we shift to mobile, private media, we need to consider the media of communication, beyond the traditional fascination with the effects (transmission) and the meanings (ritual) of the message: To study the medium of communication and the ways in which it is incorporated, as an object, into children's lives. (p. 69)

Our theoretical approach to the study of Webkinz World responds to Livingstone's call to change the question and focus on how this medium relates to a social phenomenon —particularly the cultural value of consumerism. Yet, in so doing, we also challenge a few assumptions that both Ribak and Livingstone make about new media. Our critical perspective positions Webkinz World within the corporate-constructed playground where children interact with the medium and thereby actively participate within an ideological world. We see that recognizing the "socially and, significantly, materially new" ways that children make media forms popular is important as long as we also recognize the "socially and, significantly, materially new" ways in which corporate media constructs and profits from these ideological practices.

In another departure from Ribak's (2007) argument, we revive Carey's ritual perspective of communication as a broad conceptual approach to the ideological study of Webkinz World. Because it asks critics to explore media as a cultural practice, we agree that "Carey's account does not provide a simple answer" to the study of media and children, as Ribak contends

(p. 68). However, for our study, the usefulness of the ritual approach allows for the critical pursuit of ideological meanings, making it an optimal lens for studying Webkinz World. Carey (2002) explains the ritual perspective as a focus on the shared beliefs of participants engaging with media. "The ritual view of communication," he explains, "is linked to terms such as sharing, participation, association, fellowship, and the possession of a common faith" (p. 39). Participation with media such as reading the newspaper, he maintains,

> creates an artificial though nonetheless real symbolic order which operates not to provide information but confirmation, not to alter attitudes or change minds but to represent an underlying order of things, not to perform functions but to manifest an ongoing fragile social process. (p. 39)

This "underlying order of things" and the social process of individuals engaging in media practices "together" relies on the notion that individuals respond to media, in part, by responding to the ideological meanings that media construct. Here, the ideological meanings of Webkinz World, as articulated through the stories, rules, and values constructed throughout the website, provide a "common faith" for its participating children on-line, and, in so doing, reinforce particular cultural values. The pursuit of this common faith encompasses other theoretical work in the critical study of ideology and communication rules.

We use Hall's (1986) definition of ideology as "the mental frameworks—the languages, the concepts, categories, imagery of thought, and the systems of representation—which different classes and social groups deploy in or to make sense of, define, figure out, and render intelligible the way society works" (p. 30). Foss (1996) argues "dominant ideology controls what participants see as natural or obvious by establishing the norm" (p. 295). Similarly, Grossberg (1991) argues that ideology works "not merely by producing a system of meanings which purport to represent the world but rather, by producing its own system of meanings as the real, natural (i.e., experienced) one" (p. 145). In our ideological analysis, we use these theoretical conceptions to explore the stories, rules, and values of Webkinz World as they both construct and reflect dominant cultural ideology. Moreover, we recognize that the ideological meanings of Webkinz World are "naturalized" to such an extent as to be mostly invisible to outside critical examination.

To understand ideology as a process by which individuals internalize and naturalize meanings, we turn to the work of family therapist and relational theorist Virginia Satir. Her work in family rules shows how children internalize belief structures in the home and these meanings become understood as "rules" of the world—what is good, bad, or unspeakable.

We see these rules as presenting an "underlying order of things" that children use to understand themselves and their worlds.

Satir (2000) argues that family rules are a "vital, dynamic, and extremely influential force in family life" because they implicitly teach family values and structure communication patterns. Her work shows that when most parents talk about their rules and critically examine them they find the rules are often "unfair" or "inappropriate." In other words, the rules children learn in families are often incongruent with the principles parents are trying to teach. Similarly, we find that critical studies often expose the contradictions and paradoxes between intended cultural values (the morals families strive to teach their children, such as "money isn't everything") and actual cultural practices (which reinforce a value of "win as much as you can.")

Satir (2000) is mostly concerned with the rules children learn in families concerning communication—who talks to whom about what. She argues that "rules are a very real part of the family's structure and functioning" and are crucial to child development because they teach children what is "good" and "bad" at the same time that children learn if they can be open in communication—free to ask all questions, without shame or regret—or restricted (p. 168). Here, children internalize meanings born out of parental logic about what is said, what is unsaid, and how things are said. Satir shows how parents inadvertently reinforce taboo topics through a myriad of responses, such as expressing disapproval, changing the subject, whispering, or asking children to leave the room. These responses not only designate taboo topics for children, but they also teach that the subjects causing this behavior are inherently "bad." Therefore, the complex issues that families should be discussing such as illnesses, addictions, sex, and anger are usually relegated to the world of the "unsaid" and internalized by children as "bad" things. Combine this rule structure with the communication rule "we don't talk about these things," and children learn that harmony (the "good" and the "said") is valued over honest and intimate communication (the "bad" and the "unsaid"). Much of Satir's work in family counseling pivoted around sexual problems or sexual deviancy. Her writing emphasizes the huge discrepancy between the values and intentions parents think they instill and the values and meanings they actually convey through implicit rules.

Like rules, family stories are also powerful forces in shaping a value and identity system for children. Stone's (2000) research shows that family stories are a vital, cohesive force in binding individuals to the collective and informing family members of what they should do for each other. Implicitly, stories offer families a vehicle for teaching values out of the experiences of the heroes, the deviants, the mischief-makers, and the saints. She concludes:

For good and for ill, they delineate the rules and the mores that govern family life, rules that succor and support as well as rules that chafe uncomfortably; rules that are out in the open as well as those that operate only by stealth. Indeed, family stories go a step further and define the family, saying not only what members should do, but who they are or should be. (p. 57)

From these perspectives, the ideological meanings of Webkinz include the said and the unsaid rules of the text. Here, the shared "confirmation" from the stories and practices become naturalized ideological constructions. Returning to the ritual perspective, the "underlying order of things" of Webkinz World must be studied as it confiscates children's experiences—the plethora of cognitions, emotions and moral obligations that children employ on a daily basis—and synthesizes them into a common faith. As we argue below, this faith, shared by millions of children everyday, solidifies a consumerist worldview and way of life. The overriding question guiding our analysis stems from Gitlin's (2002) critique of media research involving television. In his criticism of the dominant perspective as a theoretical paradigm, Gitlin explains how years of empirical studies regarding television fail to ask important questions regarding television's relationship to culture. Instead, he asks us to explore the way communication transforms culture without seeming to do so. Gitlin says the question analysts should ask is, "How has television transformed culture, then used itself to depict the change so normal as to make its very transformation invisible and natural?" (p. 25). When we apply the same question to Webkinz World, it becomes, "How has Webkinz transformed children's experience and possibly family dynamics, then used itself to depict the change in children's experience and family structure as normal and to make the very transformation invisible and natural?"

WEBKINZ WORLD: A WORLD OF CONSUMPTION

We begin our analytical journey of the website with a brief description of this particular playground and the argument that all activities within Webkinz World are articulated through the discourse of consumerism, naturalizing its ideological place. We then pose two strategies of Webkinz World's ideological power: relation and competition. These very different but equally important values work to sustain and promote consumption as a common faith for all participants.

Children enter the Webkinz World with the purchase of a plush animal toy from a local retailer for $10 to $14. Each toy comes with a code. Children log on to the site with the code and proceed to adopt and name their "pet." After a brief tutorial, children are free to play arcade games, decorate their pet's virtual room, and fill their virtual shopping carts with clothes, food and toys for their pet. To describe all of the features of Webkinz World is impossible in this analysis. However, an overview will serve to illustrate the extraordinary complexity of the site which offers a world worthy of critical examination from an ideological perspective.

The homepage greets children with a host of plush toys available for purchase. The site encourages children to "come in and play," and it lists a variety of locations to visit: the W Shop, the Curio Shop, the Trading Room, and the Wish Factory. Upon entering the site children see the front page of the Webkinz Newz, which features the conventions of sensationalistic headlines to reinforce the purchase of items with KinzCash, the currency of Webkinz World. The front page gives basic information for each player: an assessment of the child's acquisitions (held in the dock), the child's balance of KinzCash, numerous activities, and, always, changing advertisements for Webkinz. Because pets must be fed, watered, and loved, the pet's general condition is measured by a happiness, health, and hunger meter that is constantly displayed on the screen with smiley faces, hearts, and forks respectively. These indicators change for the better or worse with the child's activities within Webkinz World.

The site centers on playing games or working at jobs to acquire KinzCash necessary for purchasing items such as food and water as well as luxury items such as popcorn machines and wacky eucalyptus televisions for the pet. Children decorate their pet's room, choosing from items such as beds, wallpaper, rugs and lamps. In this virtual world pets can be dressed, which requires the purchase of clothing and accessories, from a fleece sweater and funky flowered pants to groovy swimsuits and tiaras. The lure of the site is to return each day to check on the well being of the pet and to continue the quest to acquire goods for its care. We have been visiting Webkinz World since November 2007, watching it evolve into a world of institutions for the pet, from hospitals to spas. For the child not interested in the care of a pet, Webkinz World currently offers nearly 50 games in its arcade and clubhouse, where the child can play and talk with others (restrictively and anonymously). The website also features an educational, or edutainment, component consisting of quizzes and online surveys. With the exception of some of the restricted socializing that takes place in the "clubhouse," children gain or lose KinzCash with their participation in all Webkinz World activities. Regardless of the KinzCash a child has at the end of one year, she or he must purchase a new pet off-line to continue participating in Webkinz World.

Get It While You Can! Child's Play and Consumer Discourse

The language of consumerism, ubiquitous in the adult world, facilitates children's attention throughout the website. The homepage entices children with a colorful and exciting world of information and choices all positioned within the discourse of consumption. The homepage of January 11, 2009 featured the headline news, "Catch a snowflake, win a prize!" The news article features a cartoon penguin in a winter landscape and describes the details of how children can play a snowflake game to win prizes for their pets. Over the headline are three boxes: What's New, Webkinz Pets & Stuff, and Wacky's Bingoz.

The "What's New" box reads, "Check out all the new and exciting things happening in Webkinz World." With a click, children see information on "Bulldog" the Webkinz pet of the month. Its description reads, "Be sure to adopt this loyal friend any time in January to get a Pet of the Month Loot Bag!" (Any Webkinz player knows that "adopt" here means to purchase the pet off-line and register it in Webkinz World). Two other important features of this "What's New" is information on "Winterfest," to take place on January 12 with all kinds of prizes to win. This is the exact same information that is the headline news advertising the snowflake game. The only "new" information on this page is the feature, "Trading–Better Than Ever."

When clicking on Webkinz Pets & Stuff, an even bigger advertisement for Bulldog appears and reads, "Loyal and true, this Bulldog is the perfect pet for you! Adopt Bulldog in January and you'll get a loot bag full of surprises and a Pet of the Month prize you can't get anywhere else!" At the bottom of the page are several buttons where children can access advertisements for all things Webkinz, from knapsacks and trading cards to lip gloss. Important "Store Locator" buttons appear throughout these pages so children know where these items can be purchased off line.

The third box over the headline features constantly changing announcements of children and their pets who are winning BINGOZ, one of the nearly 50 games in the arcade. On this day it reads, "Congratulations to Sop with Milkshake who has won this game of 1 Ball Bingoz." The first name, Sop, indicates the child's online name, and the second name, Milkshake, is the child's pet's name.

At the right of the headline news is a box of all the information one might need to navigate the website. To the right of that is a vertical stream of colorful boxes advertising the Webkinz e-store and Kinzville W Newz. Although seemingly new pieces of information, these boxes take children to the same stories and advertisements already featured on the homepage. Alongside the player's KinzCash balance and pet's health and happiness meters are tabs that read "Actions," "My Stuff," and "Things to Do."

The language of consumption used on the homepage ideologically frames children's activities in Webkinz World. "Get it now!" "Check out what's new!" "Find out faster!" "Don't miss this offer!," advertising slogans of the adult world, structure children's navigation in this playground. Two processes help naturalize its ideological power here: redundancy and real-world simulation. When children click on buttons offering "exciting" announcements, they find the same item or activity being featured elsewhere as with the example of Bulldog. This repetition reinforces the idea that Bulldog is important and therefore a "must have" item. A surface reading of this practice might conceptualize this as merely a promotion of a product in various forms, or a form of product placement. Yet, on an ideological level, the website sustains a deeper commitment to a consumerist worldview, for it creates opportunities for children's play that simulates practices they recognize in the "real world" and transforms these into the common practice of consumption. Specifically, the common cultural practice of reading a newspaper for information is transformed to reading a newspaper as participation in consumerism. Every day, the homepage features its "headlining" story in the language of advertising, but it poses as vital information for the children navigating the site. Children gather in this common space daily to learn of "special offers," "rare items," and "last chance" opportunities. This information prioritizes their activities within this website.

One of the most compelling aspects of the ideological nature of Webkinz World as an exercise in commodification is the Webkinz symbol for KinzCash—its own unique dollar sign. Here, a capital W with two horizontal lines running through its lower half serves as the equal counterpart to the dollar sign. The Webkinz W precedes a number to indicate the cost of a given product, activity, or service. A dollar figure and number permanently rests above the icon of the child's pet in the bottom of the screen, providing a constant KinzCash balance. This symbolic process is important to the understanding of Webkinz World and the ideology of consumerism in two important ways. First, every endeavor, from playing a game to buying food for the animal, is commodified through the Webkinz symbol. In all activities children know the KinCash value of what they are doing. For example, as a child is playing a game, the Webkinz money symbol and a number sit in the top right hand of the page. The number constantly increases as the child's game-playing skills improve.

The second way the KinzCash symbol holds ideological power is in the dual nature of the symbol itself. The symbol draws its meaning from the real world dollar sign, yet it is a unique symbol used only in Webkinz World. Here, commodification of material goods, a practice children are learning about in the real world, is naturally applied to the efforts in Webkinz World. Yet the unique construct in Webkinz World is a constant reminder that this is not "real money" but a virtual figure representing children's play. These different notions encompassed within the KinzCash symbol offer a cultural understanding that "everything is worth something" while simultaneously downplaying its economic emphasis because it is merely "child's play."

The KinzCash symbol is just one example of how Webkinz World constructs the consumerist world view by channeling games and pet care through major cultural institutions children recognize in their own lives. For example, when the pet attends Kinzville Academy and takes a training course or visits Dr. Quack for a physical then the child is participating in the educational and health institutions that mirror her or his own life. Yet Webkinz World also offers many less institutionalized but socially familiar cultural activities for the child and pet. Children can hire a pet tutor for special competition training in the Kinzville Academy, and they can send their pets on a spa weekend for much-needed mental relaxation. These activities, much like their real-world counterparts, come with a particularly high KinzCash price tag.

Just as in real life, children understand that to participate in these endeavors they must have a way to earn Kinzcash. The Kinzville Employment Office offers job opportunities for children. These tasks are actually games that test children's speed and memory as they build hamburgers or paint fences. Some jobs are almost impossible to master, but earn an incredible amount of KinzCash if the player is successful. The important part of this exercise is that once a child has failed or completed a job, she or he cannot come back to the employment office for eight hours. This cleverly builds children's pre-occupation with Webkinz World as they come back to try again the next day. There are countless other ways that children earn KinzCash as they participate in the many games and activities. Simply put, any participation with the website will earn small but incremental amounts of KinzCash that can then be applied to the pet's care.

So far, we have argued the "underlying order of things" of Webkinz confiscates children's experiences and synthesizes them into the discourse of consumerism. We conceptualize consumerism in Webkinz World—its language, symbols, and institutions—as more than an end result or skills children learn, but as the raison d'etre. This dramatically departs from reading Webkinz World as a virtual tutorial on the economic realities of our world. From this latter perspective, "If you want something, you must work for it" could be a rule that Webkinz might enforce. These types of rules resonate with parents as they mirror some cultural lessons as well. After all, our experiences within the real world are commodified. We must work for material possessions; pets need food and love to live; education and health care services are not free. However, the ritual perspective calls for more questions concerning the ideological meanings that unify our experiences within this world. In other words, it asks, "What is it about Webkinz World that provides a shared experience for all?" To answer this question, we provide two ideological processes at work in Webkinz World, relation and competition. The rules and values emerging from these practices emphasize individualism and competition over communal and cooperative concerns.

"You're Back! That Makes Me Smile!:" Pet and Child Relations

The relational aspect of Webkinz World is fundamental to this social playground, for the child enters only because of a relationship to a pet. Unlike other virtual games, the relationship between child and avatar is not simply virtual, for children buy their fuzzy creatures off-line, name them, and use that name in Webkinz World when the pet interacts with other pets. Iconically, the pet is the virtual representation of the "real" animal. In Webkinz World, the pet speaks directly to the child in a dialogue box over the animal, squared on the screen, when the child is attending to one of its three conditions (happiness, health, hunger). For example, if the pet has a low hunger score and it is fed only a pretzel, it will say, "That's an OK snack but I'd like something else." When it is then given a plate of cannelloni, the dialogue box then reads, "That was awesome! So tasty!" The hunger then moves up from a score of 41 to 92. Other ways the child is addressed in terms of her or his care for the animal is when accessing the cultural institutions described earlier. Dr. Quack says directly to the child things like, "You're taking very good care of your pet!" If the pet needs attention, Dr. Quack may say something like, "It could use a bit more sleep though. Sleep is very important to your pet's health!"

The relational messages are important as they validate a child's efforts to care for a virtual pet. The relational meanings here cannot be dismissed as "merely virtual" because they represent a connection between the child and the plush creature that lives with that child in the real world. Here, the cuddly animal in the bedroom comes to life, in a sense, in Webkinz World. The closer the child is with the animal off-line the more potential there is for a heightened emotional connection to online pet.

The "realness" of the on-line pet is largely due to the ideological impact of communication with the owner. Because the pet lives in Webkinz World, it can speak directly to the child who bought it—making requests and offering thanks. The most confirming aspect of this communication is the greeting pets give their owners when children log into Webkinz World each day, as the title of this section illustrates, creating the virtual illusion that they have been there waiting for them while they were away.

Authority figures borrowed from children's "real" cultural institutions also confirm the relationship between pet and child. Miss Birdie, the head teacher, and Dr. Quack address children, offering information and praise when children are playing in Webkinz World, trading and buying goods, enrolling their pets in school, and caring for their medical needs. These relational messages reward children for their Webkinz actions and cast them further into a care-giving role. From this perspective, the exact nature of the relationship of child to pet constitutes the former as accountable for all physical and emotional aspects of the latter. The child is responsible for trading or buying items or purchasing services when the animal is hungry, tired, sick, or bored. If a pet needs attention and the owner is low on KinzCash, the pet has to wait in its present condition for the child to earn money through the arcade or other activities.

Commodified intimacy. The relational meanings inherent in this conditioning process can be significant, as children respond to the affect of smiling or frowning faces, positive thoughts, requests for material goods, praise from authorities, or, in some cases of neglect, when they see their pets severely ill in the hospital.[1] The relationship between child and animal is paramount in exploring the consumer logic of Webkinz World. Because Webkinz World can be accessed only with the pet, and because the pet's health and survival in Webkinz World depend solely on the child's activities in Webkinz World, then the ideological nature of Webkinz World is primarily a relational one. Yet because all activities are commodified through KinzCash, the relationship between pet and child is ideologically reduced to that of pet and breadwinner. Nurturing qualities that arouse affect, drawing the child to Webkinz World, give way to the breadwinning role that actually sustains the pet's existence and well-being within that world. The ideological impact of Webkinz World transforms the relationship between child and pet into a commodified world of meaning, each action and source of validation conceptualized in terms of its KinzCash cost and benefit.

From our perspective, when all aspects of caring for and nurturing a pet in Webkinz World are translated into the language of economy, then the shared experience—the common faith of all its participants—becomes the economic process itself. This creates the understanding that "to care for another means buying, selling, and trading." Here, the potential rule, "Caring means spending money," raises questions of moral meanings constructed in Webkinz World. This rule also introduces its corollary, "Caring means getting money." This particular meaning is generated from competition, the second ideological dimension of Webkinz World.

"We Have a Winner!:" Competition in Webkinz World

Games of skill, games of chance, champions and their rewards are the news of the day, every day, in Webkinz World. There is very little to do in Webkinz World besides compete. The endgame is always to win KinzCash in order to preserve the pet's online existence. Without winning, all is literally lost.

A player's KinzCash balance is always displayed on the screen as a reminder of economic status. However, from an ideological perspective it also establishes the status of the Webkinz player. It answers the unspoken question of Webkinz World: Are you a winner? The only way to be a winner is to compete, win KinzCash, and win big. In a world where the rule is "Win as much as you can," you can never win enough. There are always more room dividers or football trophies to purchase, more quick cash to earn. Every hour offers more competitions, and the clock is always ticking. Both analog and digital clocks are featured alongside the player's KinzCash balance. Children watch the clock to see if enough time has elapsed since their last visit to the employment office so they can return for another job, one of the quickest ways to earn Kinzcash.

For a fee, pets can be entered into daily competitions in Webkinz Stadium. Popular competitions are beauty pageants and cooking contests. Winners are rewarded with applause, shouts from the crowd, confetti, and medals, and they stand on podiums much like Olympic winners. Beauty pageant winners receive gold, silver, and bronze virtual hairdryer trophies and the honor of seeing their pet's name listed as a winner or champion. More importantly, players pay for the opportunity for their pets to compete for celebrity status, to stand out from the crowd, and to win enormous amounts of KinzCash—sometimes as high as 20,000.

Informed and active citizens are seen as vital to the health of communities and nations. Newspaper stories of neighborhoods, cities, and states speak to the concerns of the larger population and serve as a location for information and discussion critical to educated individuals. Plumpy the Advice Hippo writes a column for the Webkinz Newz. A letter by "Crazy for KinzCash" titled "The BIG Challenge" explains how the player took a challenge to see how much KinzCash she or he could earn in five minutes of playing on Webkinz. A "Year in Review" piece discusses the stellar year experienced in Webkinz World with the addition of new games and new furniture and rugs for sale in the W Shop. The ideological concern is that the letters for advice are written and produced by a corporation that can direct the discourse to serve its profit-driven agenda. While the newspaper mimics a real-world institution, familiar to the child at home, what unifies the experience is the cultural value of consumerism. Problems are positioned as only economic issues and are centered on what to buy, how to win, how to win more, and how to win the most in the least amount of time. Here, reading the newspaper is not to obtain information about international or community concerns. Reading the newspaper is the location of consumer discourse and little else.

Childhood successes are essential to the well-being of any child. Achievements may come in the form of spelling bees, Little League sports, and even games invented by children themselves. Blue ribbons and trophies are celebrated by families and children alike. Webkinz World raises the bar on success as it refocuses the experience into one where only the cash prizes matter. The Cash Cow game allows players to accumulate points, and a truck bed fills with bottle caps to indicate the score. As points are earned, the pile grows and works its way up a subtle scoring device that reads, from bottom to top, Workin' Hard, Doing Well, Makin' Money, Raking It In, and, finally, Got the BIG Cash. The meaning reinforced is that success in the form of the website currency is what is important and should guide all behavior. Competitive activities that offer an economic reward are the ones worthy of attention or effort.

Some games are designed with the familiar trappings of television game show sets, complete with flashing lights, time clocks, scoreboards, a host, spotlights, and even applause. Ever present is the elusive gold cup for the champion. Alternatively, some games or areas within the site are designed like television news studios where a deep-voiced male announcer sits behind a desk and microphone and welcomes players to "coooooome ooooon in … where the best meet to compete." This has tremendous appeal in a world where the shared faith is individual competition enhanced by a Winner's Circle attitude. The newscast mirrors the setup of many popular nightly entertainment news programs. Just as celebrities vie for daily media exposure, Webkinz naturalizes competition for the momentary splash of confetti and sparkling lights coupled with a bit of KinzCash to fuel the competitive desire.

Individual triumph. The examples of contests, advice columns, and games offer the opportunity to identify some of the stories told, rules established, and the values understood that construct the on-line playground for children. The overarching story of competition in Webkinz World is that of the individual and the individual winner. There is no scenario where cooperation between players takes place. There is no true community in this playground. Although the site visuals offer the illusion of community (a village with shops and friendly, furry characters waving to each other, with open, green fields to run and play in), they are fleeting images and never experienced by the player. Activities such as helping an elderly neighbor to clean up her yard or cleaning the player's own bedroom exist in the world of the ideologically unsaid because these activities don't encourage competition or render cash rewards. Solitary players move through the site as robot-like characters on the hunt only for the next big cash win. The story of the traditional playground for children has been usurped by corporate consumer ideology and is now the story of the individual child moving as fast as she or he can from contest to contest in the pursuit of more cash with which to continue the virtual life. The high score of each game serves to motivate and in some ways goad the child into staying just a bit longer in the playground to see if perhaps today is the day her or his name will be featured in the story, displayed on the high score list or in the Winner's Circle, the envy of the other unseen, individual competitors. The story of the playground is refashioned into the story of the individual child working within a competitive orientation.

The rules of the playground are unlike those usually expected and experienced in the real world. Sharing, playing fair, cooperating with others, taking turns, and being helpful have no place in Webkinz World. Team camaraderie is nonexistent. Competitive endeavors in Webkinz World are guided instead by rules that address larger cultural and social issues and that support the consumer worldview and ignore the cooperative spirit usually encouraged at home and at school. Webkinz rules state "stand out from the others," "be the best," "accumulate the most Kinzcash as fast as you can," "buy the most stuff for your room." None of these rules are intended to build character or good citizens. Rules that are confirmed in Webkinz World are those that support only the individual and that individual's drive to win. This is not to say that competition is unhealthy or should not be encouraged in children. Our point is that the social playground of Webkinz confirms rules that state competition is good only as it applies to the winning of cash with the purpose of consuming goods.

"Caring is Winning": The Rules of Webkinz

In summary of this critical ideological perspective, the said stories and rules of Webkinz reinforce competition for the overall value of winning. However, ideologically, "winning" is constructed only as "winning cash." Webkinz transforms life into a game and rewards those players who understand and willingly take their place as participants in that game. Losers, such as those players unable to acquire the required number of tokens to gain access to the Webkinz Wish Machine, understand all too well that winning is everything, as it buys happiness as well as the exclusive gift promised only for winners. Losers may wander the virtual world, but without a full KinzCash till, their wishes will never be granted.

Although these are the explicit stories of Webkinz, just as prevalent are the meanings created through the unsaid. In this ideological realm, winning is partly conceptualized by what it is not: family pride, a cooperative spirit, love of country, or simply the "thrill of victory." Play is not valued for the sheer joy it can bring. Value is only in the success of play that results in a cash win because the pet's life depends on it.

The relational aspects that bring the child to Webkinz World are consumed within the ideology of competition. The relational connection between child and pet pales in comparison to the value of individualism promoted through the competitive efforts required to care for the pet. We see these confirming processes in Webkinz World sustaining individualism, a necessary component of a consumerist worldview.

Webkinz and a Culture of Consumption

Whybrow (2005) argues that we have fallen under the spell of a "new religion"—consumerism. This supports our argument that ideological literacy prompts us to ask not about effects or outcomes of this or that children's website, but to consider how excessive consumerism has become part of our everyday existence. He explains that material excess is tied to competition, a value we recognize in Webkinz World. He describes our "information saturated, turbo-charged mercantilism" as the Fast New World, which coincidentally sounds a great deal like the social playground of Webkinz (p. xviii). He points out that we are "reward-driven and self-absorbed" by instinct but that technology is now "in cahoots" with those instincts by removing the natural constraints that in the past have kept us from what he describes as an "orgy of self-indulgence" and unbridled mercantilism (p. xix). Our appetite for more is already making us sick--anxious, depressed, and obese, burdened by debt and caught in an "accelerated, competitive lifestyle" that is threatening our families, communities, and lives (pp. 3-4).

Shor (2004) details how this consumer culture undermines children's well-being. She found that "American children are deeply enmeshed in the culture of getting and spending, and they are getting more so" (p. 173). To summarize her survey, the more time children spend with media, the more they are involved in consumer culture (p. 169). "Involvement in consumer culture is a significant cause of depression, anxiety, low self-esteem, and psychosomatic complaints" (p. 167).

Linn (2004) underscores our argument that parents should be concerned with the messages of consumerism directed toward children. She reports that a

> survey of parents conducted by the Center for a New American Dream showed that 63% believed that their children define their self-worth in terms of what they own; 78% thought that marketing puts too much pressure on

children to buy things that are too expensive, unhealthy, or unnecessary; and 70% expressed the belief that commercialism has a negative effect on children's values and worldviews. (p. 8)

Linn's studies indicate that

people who value material goods (an orientation reinforced by consumer marketing) are likely to be more unhappy and have a lower quality of life than those who value more internal or non-material rewards such as creativity, competence, and contributing to the community. (p. 8)

Our analysis demonstrates how ideological literacy provides ways that families can read the stories, deconstruct the rules, and understand the values of the virtual world for what is unsaid, confirmed, and naturalized. The perspective we offer makes the implicit explicit. An ideological approach addresses how children can easily adopt not only the language but the logic of consumerism and respect its embedded stories, rules, and values. Webkinz World and other virtual playgrounds offer no alternative experiences or understandings of the world—online or off. The child's experience of play has been transformed by the virtual world into an act of consumption. As we have argued here, ideologies at work in Webkinz World depict the normal structure of things through competition and individual success. Yet ideological literacy offers a way for parents to see the incongruency between their own moral teachings and the often invisible rules of the social playground, confirming consumerism, acquisition, and the quest for cash.

We hope that through studies such as ours and through national media education efforts, critically informed families, when faced with the anonymous Webkinz voice that asks: "Are you REALLY sure you want to log out of Webkinz World?" will know the answer.

NOTE

1. A colleague illustrated the power of this relational connection on children when she told this story: She and her family were traveling for Christmas and unable to get to a computer easily when her son wanted to play on Webkinz. When her son was finally able to log on he became instantly panicked and cried uncontrollably over the fear that his pet was dying. He saw that his beloved avatar was very ill and in the hospital due to malnutrition. The mother knew the pet was, indeed, not going to die; the website makes that clear to parents in its introduction. Yet her son was distraught over having neglected his poor pet during the Christmas season. He vowed never to let that many days go by without caring for the animal's needs.

REFERENCES

Alvy, L., & Calvert, S. (2007, May). *Food marketing on popular children's websites: A content analysis.* Paper presented at the meeting of the International Communication Association, San Francisco, CA.

Barnes, B. (2007, December 31). Web playgrounds of the very young. *New York Times on the Web.* Retrieved from http://www.nytimes.com/2007/12/31/business/31/virtual.html

Bishop, R. (2005). The wayward child: An ideological analysis of sports contract holdout coverage. *Journalism Studies, 6,* 445-459.

Buckingham, D. (2003). *Media education: Literacy, learning and contemporary culture.* Cambridge, England: Polity Press.

Carey, J. W. (1989). *Communication as culture: Essays on media and society.* Boston, MA: Unwin Hyman.

Carey, J. W. (2002). A cultural approach to communication. In D. McQual (Ed.), *McQuail's reader in mass communication theory* (pp. 37-45). Thousand Oaks, CA: SAGE.

Donnerstein, E. (2009). Internet. In V. C. Strasburger, B. J. Wilson, & A. B. Jordon (Eds.), *Children, adolescents, and the media* (2nd ed., pp. 471-498). Los Angeles, CA: SAGE.

Foss, S. (1996). *Rhetorical criticism: Exploration & practice.* Prospect Heights, IL: Waveland Press.

Gitlin, T. (2002). Media sociology: The dominant paradigm. In D. McQual (Ed.), *McQuail's reader in mass communication theory* (pp. 25-35). Thousand Oaks, CA: SAGE.

Goltz, D. B. (2007). Laughing at absence: *Instinct* Magazine and hypermasculine gay future? *Western Journal of Communication, 71*(2), 93-113.

Grossberg, L. (1991) Strategies of Marxist cultural interpretation. In R. Avery & D. Eason (Eds.), *Critical perspectives on media and society* (pp. 126-162).

Hall, S. (1986). The problem of ideology: Marxism without guarantees. *Journal of Communication Inquiry, 10*(2), 28-44.

Linn, S. (2004). *Consuming kids: The hostile takeover of childhood.* New York, NY: The New Press.

Livingstone, S. (2007). Do the media harm children? Reflections on new approaches to an old problem. *Journal of Children and Media, 1,* 5-14.

Montgomery, K. C. (2001) Digital kids: The new on-line children's consumer culture. In D. G. Ginger & J. L. Singer (Eds.), *Handbook of children and the media* (pp. 635-650). Thousand Oaks, CA: SAGE.

Moore, E. S. (2006). *It's child's play: Advergaming and the online marketing of food to children.* The Kaiser Family Foundation. Retrieved from http://www.kff.org/entmedia/upload/7536.pdf

Navarro, M. (2007, October 28). Pay up, kid, or your igloo melts. *New York Times on the Web.* Retrieved from http://www.nytimes.com/2007/10/28/fashion/28virftual.html

Potter, W. J. (1998). *Media literacy.* Thousand Oaks, CA: SAGE.

Ribak, R. (2007). Children & new media: Some reflections on the ampersand. *Journal of Children and Media, 1,* 68-74.

Satir, V. (2000). The rules you live by. In K. M. Galvin & P. J. Cooper (Eds.), *Making connections: Readings in relational communication* (2nd cd., pp. 168-174). Los Angeles, CA: Roxbury.

Schor, J. B. (2004). *Born to buy: The commercialized child and the new consumer culture.* New York, NY: Scribner.

Seiter, E. (2004). The internet playground. In J. Goldstein, D. Buckingham, & G. Brougere (Eds.), *Toys, games and media* (pp. 93-108). Mahwah, NJ: Erlbaum.

Shoshana, M. (2006). Playing at colonization: Interpreting imaginary landscapes in the video game tropico. *Journal of Communication Inquiry, 30*(2), 142-162.

Singer, D. G. (2009). Introduction. In V. C. Strasburger, B. J. Wilson, & A. B. Jordon (Eds.), *Children, adolescents, and the media* (2nd ed., pp. xv-xvii). Los Angeles, CA: SAGE.

Stone, E. (2000) Family ground rules. In K. Galvin & P. Cooper (Eds.), *Making connections: Readings in relational communication* (2nd ed., pp. 49-57). Los Angeles, CA: Roxbury.

Strausburger, V. C., Wilson, J. B., & Jordan, A. B. (Eds.). (2009). *Children, adolescents, and the media* (2nd ed.). Los Angeles, CA: SAGE.

Tedeschi, B. (2007, March 26). Fuzzy critters with high prices offer lesson in new concepts. *New York Times on the Web.* Retrieved from http://www.nytimes.com/2007/02/26/technology/26econm.html.

Walkosz, B., & Foss, S. (2007, May). *China and the 2008 Olympics: The construction of a national image.* Paper presented at the meeting of the International Communication Association, San Francisco, CA.

Whybrow, P. C. (2005). *American mania: When more is not enough.* New York, NY: W. W. Norton.

ABOUT THE AUTHORS

Richard P. Beach, Dip.Teach., SSCP is an information security consultant at Inland Revenue (NZ) specializing in security awareness, education, and training. He has experience teaching young children and adolescents as a classroom teacher as well as an information and communication technology specialist. Richard has also contributed to education in a governance role, sitting on school boards and committees. He is an experienced public speaker, presenting to teachers, parents, and children in the area of cybersafety. Richard's current focus is on developing security awareness programs which demonstrate effective behavior change and a positive return on investment for large organizations.

Marina Umaschi Bers, PhD, is an associate professor at the Eliot-Pearson Department of Child Development and an adjunct associate professor in the Computer Science Department at Tufts University. Her research involves the design and study of innovative learning technologies to promote children's positive development. At Tufts, Prof. Bers heads the interdisciplinary Developmental Technologies research group. Prof. Bers received the 2005 Presidential Early Career Award for Scientists and Engineers, the highest honor given by the U.S. government to outstanding investigators at the early stages of their careers. She also received a National Science Foundation Young Investigator's Career Award and the American Educational Research Associations Jan Hawkins Award for Early Career Contributions to Humanistic Research and Scholarship in Learning Technologies. Over the past 14 years, Prof. Bers has conceived and designed diverse technological tools ranging from robotics to virtual worlds. She has conducted studies of after school programs, museums and hospitals, as well as schools in the U.S., Argentina, Colombia, Spain, Costa Rica, and Thailand. She also teaches seminars on learning technologies for educators and does consulting for toy companies and organizations on ways to use technology to promote positive youth development. Her book *Blocks to Robots: Learning with Technology in the Early Childhood Classroom* has been published by Teacher's College Press in 2008. Dr. Bers is from Argentina, where she did her undergraduate studies in social communication at Buenos Aires University. In 1994 she came to the U.S. where she received a master's degree in educational media and technology from Boston University and a master of science and PhD from the MIT Media Laboratory, working with Seymour Papert.

Ilene R. Berson, PhD, NCSP is an associate professor of early childhood education in the Department of Childhood Education and Literacy Studies at the University of South Florida. She has extensive experience working with children ages birth to eight, and she is a nationally certified and state licensed school psychologist. Her research focuses on prevention and intervention services for young children at imminent risk for socioemotional challenges associated with child maltreatment and other traumatic events. She leads collaborative reform initiatives, forging linkages between early childhood, child welfare, and health care systems, as well as international studies on the engagement of young children with digital technologies. Dr. Berson has extensively published books, chapters, and journal articles and has presented her research worldwide. Dr. Berson embodies the characteristics of an engaged scholar who works closely in reciprocal relationships with practitioners and policymakers to develop innovative solutions for emerging and long term issues to promote young children's well being.

Michael J. Berson, PhD, is a professor in the Secondary Education Department at the University of South Florida and a senior fellow in The Florida Joint Center for Citizenship. He instructs courses in social science methodology and is the coordinator of the doctoral program in social science education. His award-winning courses have been acknowledged for integrating emerging technologies into instruction and modeling dynamic and fluid pedagogy. Dr. Berson has disseminated his work worldwide through his books, chapters, journal articles, and presentations. His research on child advocacy and technology in social studies education has achieved global recognition.

Liz Butterfield MNZM is the managing director of Hector's World Limited (HWL), a New Zealand charitable venture that uses high quality animation to educate very young children and their families about digital citizenship. Prior to developing Hector's World, she managed NetSafe, New Zealand's online safety organization, from its inception in 1998 until 2006 when she became the Managing Director of its new subsidiary Hector's World Ltd. In 2003, Ms. Butterfield was made a member of the New Zealand Order of Merit (Queen's Birthday Honours) for her work in the field of Internet safety, and was also awarded the NZ NetGuide "Living Legend" Web Award for her contribution to the internet industry. In 2006, she was made the first female "Internet Fellow" by InternetNZ, the body that oversees the internet in New Zealand. She has been a frequent media commentator, presenter, and has written many articles on online safety issues. In the social and educational innovation of Hectors' World, Ms. Butterfield's commitment to international cross-sector collaboration on Internet issues has fused perfectly with her passion for creative and pragmatic education for children about the online environment.

Richard Chalfen, PhD, is senior scientist at the Center on Media and Child Health, Children's Hospital Boston. He was previously professor of anthropology at Temple University in Philadelphia, specializing in international studies of visual culture and continues to teach a summer session on Japanese visual culture in Tokyo at Temple University Japan. His primary research interests focus on comparative participatory media research, an academic interest that started with doctoral work on teenagers making their own films in the mid-1960s and extends to current applied work in medical research with adolescents making videotapes about living with a specific chronic illness. Other research has been in cross-cultural home media and, most recently, the problematic interface of cell phones, youth and health including sexting. Published books include *Snapshot Versions of Life* (1987), *Turning Leaves: The Photograph Collections of Two Japanese American Families* (1991), *Through Navajo Eyes--An Exploration in Film Communication and Anthropology* (coauthor, 1997). He is the author of over 120 publications, some of which have been translated into Italian, Hungarian, German and Russian.

Rosemarie J. Conforti, PhD, is an associate professor and the chairperson of the Department of Media Studies at Southern Connecticut State University. As a media ecologist, her teaching focuses on understanding media and media environments. Her research interests concentrate on the relationship between media technologies and their impact on society and culture. She speaks regularly to educators, parents, and young people about media education and media literacy. Recent keynote addresses and lectures include *Media, Ads and Branding: Behind the Scenes for Tweens and Teens, A Call for Media Education, Media Literacy and Education: Understanding and Application for Educational Leaders* and *Take Back the Media: Women's Voices and*

Media Policy Reform. She teaches courses in media criticism, media literacy and education, and media research and serves the national Popular Culture Association as Area Chair of Memory and Representation.

Jutta Croll, MA, is managing director of Stiftung Digitale Chancen/Digital Opportunities Foundation. The Digital Opportunities Foundation is a German NGO working on overcoming the Digital Divide, promoting E-Inclusion, and providing programs and tools to promote Digital Literacy for underserved groups. Jutta Croll has worked as a researcher in several projects concerning the use of media and digital literacy. She holds a university degree in political science, media science, and German literature and is member of several steering groups of European projects in the field of e-Inclusion and Digital Literacy. As an expert for youth protection and digital literacy, she works in close cooperation with the European Commission, the Council of Europe, and UNESCO.

Charlie Dellinger-Pate, PhD, is an associate professor in the Department of Media Studies at Southern Connecticut State University. Her courses emphasize a critical-cultural approach to the study of various media. She is particularly interested in media texts that construct popular meanings of gender, sexuality, race, and personal relationships. Her research interest also includes the study of television as it reinforces a consumerist worldview and offers areas of meaningful resistance from dominant ideology.

Lynn Hartle, PhD, is an associate professor in Early Childhood Education in the Department of Child, Family Community Sciences at the University of Central in Orlando, Florida. She began her career with 10 years as a Montessori Pre-Primary Directress, including 6 years at the Montessori Children's House that she founded. Her research interests focus on teachers' emerging understandings of how to differentiate practices for all children from culturally and linguistically diverse families. Her years of study and practical applications are synthesized in two published books, and she is currently completing the book *Transforming Young Minds in Creative Places: Arts Integration in Early Childhood Education.* She has been the principal investigator or subcontractor for several National grant-funded research projects and is a frequent speaker at national conferences. Dr. Hartle's research and practical application have been published in national peer-review journals. She also holds board positions for national, state, and local organizations.

Michael S. Horn, PhD, is an assistant professor of Learning Sciences and Computer Science at Northwestern University. His research involves the use of emerging human-computer interaction techniques in the design of technology-based learning experiences. He has extensive experience working with children in schools from kindergarten through eight grade, as well as in after school programs and museums. His projects include the design of tangible computer programming languages for children and the creation of interactive systems to explore concepts of biodiversity and evolution. Professor Horn earned a PhD in computer science from Tufts University where he was part of the Human-Computer Interaction Laboratory, and the Developmental Technologies research groups. His work can be seen at the Boston Museum of Science and the Harvard Museum of Natural History.

Candace Jaruszewicz, PhD, is associate professor at the College of Charleston in South Carolina. She is presently the director of the Miles Early Childhood Development Center, the on-campus laboratory and demonstration program for the School of Education, Health, and Human Performance. Her research and publications focus on the role of critical reflection in teacher development; her most recent work focuses on using emerging technologies to document children's thinking and teacher professional growth. Candace serves as a governing board member for the National Association of Early Childhood Teacher Educators and the South Carolina Association for the Education of Young Children.

Katharina Kunze is project manager for the Youth Protection Roundtable at Stiftung Digitale Chancen (SDC), Germany since 2007. She holds a university degree in educational science, with the main subject adult education and has worked in several pedagogical projects.

Dr Marcus Leaning is a senior lecturer and program leader for media studies in the School of Media and Film at the University of Winchester in the United Kingdom. His teaching and research interests focus upon the use of digital media for social and educational development. His work advocates a cautionary position regarding the benefits of new media, and he proposes that new media should be deployed in concert with local needs and conditions. He has spoken at conferences and events worldwide and has published numerous articles and book chapters on these and other topics related to new media. He was a visiting International Research Fellow at the University of Hokkaido, Japan in 2005. He is the author of *The Internet, Power and Society: Rethinking the Power of the Internet to Change Lives* (2009, Chandos: Oxford) and has edited two volumes on media and information literacy: *Issues in Information and Media Literacy: Criticism, History and Policy* (2009, Informing Science Press: Santa Rosa, CA.) and *Issues in Information and Media Literacy: Education, Practices and*

Pedagogy (2009, Informing Science Press: Santa Rosa, CA.). He lives in the United Kingdom with his wife and daughter.

Komalsingh Rambaree, PhD, is a senior lecturer in the Department of Social Studies at the University of Mauritius. He has worked for more than 15 years for the youth service within different national and international organizations before joining as lecturer. Komalsingh earned his doctorate in social policy and social work from the University of Manchester, United Kingdom. His PhD thesis is related to Internet and early adolescent sexuality. He also holds two master's degrees from the same University, a master's (Econs) in social policy and social development (2000) and a master's in research (MRes) in crime and criminal justice (2003). He is currently involved in several Internet, children and sexuality related research projects.

Dina Rosen, PhD, is an assistant professor at Kean University. A graduate from New York University (PhD in educational leadership, administration and technology) and Wagner College (MA in special education), she has made important contributions to the fields of teacher education, education and technology education. Applying her instructional experience at the middle school, elementary, and early childhood levels, she has directed and evaluated sponsored research projects. Dr. Rosen holds many important leadership positions that have allowed her to steward the Early Childhood field toward inclusion of technology. She has published many peer-reviewed articles, book chapters, and conducted more than 80 presentations at professional conferences. Dr. Rosen has provided keynote addresses in the United States as well as abroad for the Organization of American States (OAS). Her work has been published in important journals such as *Action in Teacher Education, Young Child, Journal of Early Childhood Teacher Education, Early Education and Development,* and *Computers in the Schools.* Her research on case-based multimedia instruction earned the honor of NAECTE Dissertation of the Year Award.

Andra Siibak, PhD, received a doctorate in media and communication (2009) from the Faculty of Social Sciences at the University of Tartu, Estonia, where she is a research fellow in media studies at the Institute of Journalism and Communication. Her research interests include online content creation practices of young people, visual and textual self presentation in social networking websites, and gender identity constructions in virtual environments. She is currently involved in the research project "Children and Young People in the Emerging Information and Consumer Society," financed by the Estonian Science Foundation and "Construction and normalization of gender online among young people in

Estonia and Sweden," financed by The Foundation for Baltic and East European Studies.

Kadri Ugur works as research fellow in the Institute of Journalism and Communication in Tartu University. She has extensive teaching experience at different education levels (secondary school, university, teacher in-service training). Her main interest of research is media literacy in the context of formal education, for example, media usage and media literacy of pupils and teachers. Kadri Ugur is involved in researching and developing Estonian national curricula. She is a supervisor and mentor.

X. Christine Wang, PhD, is an associate professor of early childhood education at the State University of New York (SUNY) at Buffalo. She is a native of China and completed her bachelors and master's degrees at Beijing Normal University. She obtained her PhD from the University of Illinois at Urbana-Champaign in 2003 and joined the SUNY-Buffalo faculty later that same year. Her primary research interests include young children's learning and collaboration in technology-rich environments, sociocultural research, and early childhood education in international contexts. She is also interested in qualitative research methods, especially in the use of video ethnography. Dr. Wang has published many peer-reviewed research articles and book chapters. Her work has been presented at national and international conferences and has appeared in research journals such as *Early Education and Development, Journal of Research in Childhood Education, Journal of Research on Technology in Education, Journal of Early Childhood Literacy, and Early Childhood Education Journal.* Her work also earned the honor of AERA 2007 Jan Hawkins Early Career Contributions to Humanistic Research and Scholarship in Learning Technologies Award.

Nicola Yelland, PhD, is a professor at the hong Kong Institute of Education. Over the last decade her research has been related to the use of ICT in school and community contexts. This has involved projects that have investigated the innovative learning of children as well as a broader consideration of the ways in which new technologies can impact on the pedagogies that teachers use and the curriculum in schools. Her multidisciplinary research focus has enabled her to work with early childhood, primary, and middle school teachers to enhance the ways in which ICT can be incorporated into learning contexts to make them more interesting and motivating for students, so that educational outcomes are improved. Her latest publications are *Rethinking learning in Early Childhood Education* (OUP) and *Rethinking Education with ICT: New directions for effective practices* (Sense Publishers). She is the author of *Shift to the Future:*

Rethinking learning with new technologies in education (Routledge, New York). She is also the author of *Early Mathematical Explorations* with Carmel Diezmann and Deborah Butler and has edited four books: *Gender in Early Childhood* (Routledge, United Kingdom), *Innovations in Practice* (NAEYC), *Ghosts in the Machine: Women's voices in Research with Technology* (Peter Lang) and *Critical Issues in Early Childhood* (OUP). Nicola has worked in Australia, the United States, United Kingdom, and Hong Kong. Her most recent edited collection is entitled *Contemporary Perspective on Early Childhood Education* and is to be published by OUP in early 2010.